THE WASHBURN MILLS.

TESTING FLOUR.

GRANULATING FLOOR.

PACKING FLOUR.

BRANDING

2

MISS PARLOA'S

NEW COOK BOOK.

BY

MARIA PARLOA,

PRINCIPAL OF THE SCHOOL OF COOKING IN BOSTON; AUTHOR OF "THE APPLEDORE COOK BOOK,"
"FIRST PRINCIPLES OF HOUSEHOLD MANAGEMENT AND COOKERY," "CAMP COOKERY,"
"MISS PARLOA'S NEW COOK BOOK," AND "MISS PARLOA'S
KITCHEN COMPANION."

MINNEAPOLIS:
WASHBURN, CROSBY CO.,
PUBLISHERS.

BOSTON

S. J. PARKHILL & Co., PRINTERS

PREFACE.

WHEN the author wrote the Appledore Cook Book, nine years ago, she had seen so many failures and so much consequent mortification and dissatisfaction as to determine her to give those minute directions which were so often wanting in cook books, and without which success in preparing dishes was for many a person unattainable. It seemed then unwise to leave much to the cook's judgment; and experience in lecturing and in teaching in her school since that time has satisfied the author that what was given in her first literary work was what was needed. In this book an endeavor has again been made to supply what is desired: to have the directions and descriptions clear, complete, and concise.

Of the hundreds of recipes in the volume only a few were not prepared especially for it, and nearly all of these were taken by the author from her other books. Many in the chapters on Preserving and Pickling were contributed by Mrs. E. C. Daniell, of Dedham, Mass., whose understanding of the lines of cookery mentioned is thorough. While each subject has received the attention it seemed to deserve, Soups, Salads, Entrées, and Dessert have been treated at unusual length, because with a good acquaintance with the first three, one can set a table more healthfully, economically, and elegantly than with meats or fish served in the common ways; and the light desserts could well take the place of the pies and heavy puddings of which many people are so fond. Many ladies will not undertake the making of a dish that requires hours for cooking, and often for the poor reason only that they do not so read a recipe as to see that the work will not be hard. If they would but forget cake and pastry long enough to learn something of food that is more satisfying!

After much consideration, it was decided to be right to call particular attention in different parts of the book to certain manufactured articles. Lest her motive should be misconstrued, or unfair criticisms be made, the author would state that there is not a word of praise which is not merited, and that every line of commendation appears utterly without the solicitation, suggestion, or *knowledge* of anybody likely to receive pecuniary benefit therefrom.

NOTE.

THE following is a table of measures and weights which will be found useful in connection with the recipes: —

One quart of flour	one pound.
Two cupfuls of butter	one pound.
One generous pint of liquid	one pound.
Two cupfuls of granulated sugar	one pound.
Two heaping cupfuls of powdered sugar	one pound.
One pint of finely chopped meat, packed solidly	one pound.

The cup used is the common kitchen cup, holding half a pint.

THE PUBLISHERS' COMPLIMENTS TO THE READER.

DEAR MADAM, — In the preparation of this book the author and publishers have expended much time and money, with the hope that it may lessen your cares, by enabling you to provide your household with appetizing and healthful food, at a reasonable outlay of expense and skill. Should they not be disappointed in this hope, and you find yourself made happier by the fond approval of those who enjoy the food which you set before them as a result of your use of this book, we trust you will recommend its purchase by your friends, to the end that they may also be benefited by it, and that both author and publisher may be recompensed for its preparation.

HOUSEKEEPERS, ATTENTION!

EVERY wife takes great pride in having on her table something extra nice in the way of bread. The following are the reasons why she should always use Washburn's Gold Medal Flour:

1st. Washburn's Gold Medal Flour is made in the most modern and perfectly equipped flour mills in the world.

2d. Washburn's Gold Medal Flour is made from selected hard wheat bought directly from the farmers of Minnesota and Dakota by elevators owned and operated by Washburn Crosby Co.

3d. Washburn's Gold Medal Flour will yield more bread to the barrel than flour made from winter wheat.

4th. Washburn's Gold Medal Flour will make more bread, whiter and better bread, than any other flour manufactured in America.

5th. Washburn's Gold Medal Flour makes the most delicious cakes and muffins.

6th. Washburn's Gold Medal Flour is guaranteed to give satisfaction.

7th. Washburn's Gold Medal Flour is sold by all first class grocers. If not in stock, they will obtain it for you, if you request them to do so. Be sure and ask for WASHBURN'S GOLD MEDAL FLOUR.

INSIST UPON HAVING IT,
AND TAKE NO OTHER.

THE THREE GREAT ANNUALS,

DEAR TO THE HEARTS OF ALL CHILDREN.

ALL STORIES AND PICTURES NEW, ORIGINAL, AND FASCINATING.

CHATTERBOX for 1891.

The authorized reprint from duplicates of the original English plates, containing a large amount of copyright American matter, which cannot be reprinted by any other firm.

The Genuine Chatterbox contains a great variety of original stories, sketches, and poems for the young, and every illustration which appears in it is expressly designed for this work by the most eminent English artists. It is the Largest, Brightest, Best Illustrated, and Cheapest Annual published. Over 200 full-page original illustrations. On this book our presses never rest, running from January to January, night and day.

1 vol., illuminated board covers, $1.25 ; cloth, black and gold stamps, $1.75.

OLIVER OPTIC'S ANNUAL.

A volume edited by OLIVER OPTIC appeals at once to the heart of every boy and girl, with all of whom his name is a synonyme for everything bright and entertaining in juvenile literature. This is the leading book of its kind of the year, and is an attractive collection of popular children's stories with original illustrations by the best-known American artists, engraved by ANDREW, and charmingly bound in a delicate and dainty cover, with two colored plates.

1 vol., 4to, illuminated board covers, colored frontispiece and colored plate, $1.50.

LITTLE ONES' ANNUAL. Vol. 10.

Illustrated Stories and Poems for the Little Ones. Edited by WILLIAM T. ADAMS (Oliver Optic). This beautiful volume, consists of original stories and poems by the very best writers of juvenile literature, carefully selected and edited. It is embellished with 370 entirely original illustrations, drawn expressly for the work by the most celebrated book illustrators in America, and engraved on wood in the highest style, under the superintendence of GEORGE T. ANDREW.

1 vol., 4to, illuminated board covers, $1.75 ; cloth and gilt, $2.25.

For sale by all booksellers, or sent, prepaid, on receipt of price, by

ESTES & LAURIAT, BOSTON.

MISS PARLOA'S NEW COOK BOOK.

SOUPS.

Remarks on Soup Stock.

THERE are a number of methods of making soup stocks, and no two will give exactly the same results. One of the simplest and most satisfactory is that of clear stock, or bouillon. By this the best flavor of the meat is obtained, for none passes off in steam, as when the meat is boiled rapidly. The second mode is in boiling the stock a great deal, to reduce it. This gives a very rich soup, with a marked difference in the flavor from that made with clear meat kept in water at the boiling point. The third way leaves a mixed stock, which will not be clear unless whites of eggs are used. In following the first method we buy clear beef specially for the stock, and know from the beginning just how much stock there will be when the work is completed. By the second method we are not sure, because more or less than we estimate may boil away. The third stock, being made from bones and pieces of meat left from roasts, and from the trimmings of raw meats, will always be changeable in color, quantity, and quality. This is, however, a very important stock, and it should always be kept on hand. No household, even where only a moderate amount of meat is used, should be without a stock pot. It can be kept on the back of the range or stove while cooking is going on. Two or three times a week it should be put on with the trimmings and bones left from cooked and uncooked meats. This practice will give a supply of stock at all times, which will be of the greatest value in making sauces, side dishes, and soups. Meat if only slightly tainted will spoil a stock; therefore great care must be taken that every particle is perfectly sweet.

Vegetables make a stock sour very quickly; so if you wish to keep a stock do not use them. Many rules advise putting vegetables into the stock pot with the meat and water, and cooking from the very beginning. When this is done they absorb the fine flavor of the meat and give the soup a rank taste. They should cook not more than an hour — the last hour — in the stock. A white stock is made with veal or poultry. The water in which a leg of mutton or fowl have been boiled makes a good stock for light soups and gravies. A soup stock must be cooled quickly or it will not keep well. In winter any kind of stock ought to keep good a week. That boiled down to a jelly will last the longest. In the warm months three days will be the average time stock will keep.

Stock for Clear Soups.

Five pounds of clear beef, cut from the lower part of the round; five quarts of cold water. Let come to a boil slowly; skim carefully, and set where it will keep just at the boiling point for eight or ten hours. Strain, and set away to cool. In the morning skim off all the fat and turn the soup into the kettle, being careful not to let the sediment pass in. Into the soup put an onion, one stalk of celery, two leaves of sage, two sprigs of parsley, two of thyme, two of summer savory, two bay leaves, twelve pepper-corns, and six whole cloves. Boil gently from ten to twenty minutes; salt and pepper to taste. Strain through an old napkin. This is now ready for serving as a simple clear soup, or for the foundation of all kinds of clear soups.

Mixed Stock.

Put the trimmings of your fresh meats and the bones and tough pieces left from roasts or broils into the soup pot with one quart of water to every two pounds of meat and bones. When it comes to a boil, skim and set back where it will simmer six hours; then add a bouquet of sweet herbs, one onion, six cloves, and twelve pepper-corns to each gallon of stock. Cook two hours longer; strain and set in a cool place. In the morning skim off the fat. Keep in a very cool place. This can be used for common soups, sauces, and where stock is used in made dishes. It should always be kept on hand, as it really costs nothing but the labor (which is very little), and enters so often into the preparation of simple yet toothsome dishes.

Consommé.

Eight pounds of a shin of veal, eight pounds of the lower part of the round of beef, half a cupful of butter, twelve quarts of cold water, half a small carrot, two large onions, half a head of celery, thirty pepper-corns, six whole cloves, a small piece each of mace and cinnamon, four sprigs each of parsley, sweet marjoram, summer savory, and thyme, four leaves of sage, four bay leaves, about one ounce of ham. Put half of the butter in the soup pot, and then put in the meat, which has been cut into very small pieces. Stir over a hot fire until the meat begins to brown; then add one quart of the water, and cook until there is a thick glaze on the bottom of the kettle (this will be about an hour). Add the remainder of the water, and let it come to a boil. Skim carefully, and set back where it will simmer for six hours. Fry the vegetables, which have been cut very small, in the remaining butter for half an hour, being careful not to burn them. When done, turn into the soup pot, and at the same time add the herbs and spice. Cook one hour longer; salt to taste, and strain. Set in a very cold place until morning, when skim off all the fat. Turn the soup into the pot, being careful not to turn in the sediment, and set on the fire. Beat the whites and shells of two eggs with one cup of cold water. Stir into the soup, and when it comes to a boil, set back where it will simmer for twenty minutes. Strain through a napkin, and, if not ready to use, put away in a cold place. This will keep a week in winter, but not more than three days in summer. It is a particularly nice-flavored soup, and is the foundation for any clear soup, the soup taking the name of the solid used with it, as *Consommé au Riz*, Consommé with Macaroni, etc

Bouillon.

Bouillon, for Germans and other parties, is made the same as the clear stock, using a pint of water to the pound of meat, and seasoning with salt and pepper, and with the spice, herbs, and vegetables or not, as you please. It should be remembered that the amount of seasoning in the recipe referred to is for one gallon of stock.

White Stock.

Six pounds of a shin of veal, one fowl, three table-spoonfuls of butter, four stalks of celery, two onions, one blade of mace, one stick of cinnamon, eight quarts of cold water, salt, pepper. Wash and cut the veal and fowl into small pieces. Put the butter in the bottom of the soup pot and then put in the meat. Cover, and cook gently (stirring often) half an hour, then add the water. Let it come to a boil, then skim and set back where it will boil gently for six hours. Add the vegetables and spice, and boil one hour longer. Strain and cool quickly. In the morning take off all the fat. Then turn the jelly gently into a deep dish, and with a knife scrape off the sediment which is on the bottom. Put the jelly into a stone pot and set in a cold place. This will keep a week in cold weather and three days in warm.

Consommé à la Royale.

Two eggs, two table-spoonfuls of milk, one fourth of a teaspoonful of salt. Beat eggs with a spoon, and add milk and salt. Turn into a buttered cup, and place in a pan of warm water. Cook in a slow oven until firm in the centre. Set away to cool. Cut into small and prettily shaped pieces; put into the tureen, and pour one quart of boiling consommé or clear stock on it.

Cheese Soup.

One and a half cupfuls of flour, one pint of rich cream, four table-spoonfuls of butter, four of grated Parmesan cheese, a speck of cayenne, two eggs, three quarts of clear soup stock. Mix flour, cream, butter, cheese, and pepper together. Place the basin in another of hot water, and stir until the mixture becomes a smooth, firm paste. Break into it the two eggs, and mix quickly and thoroughly. Cook two minutes longer, and set away to cool. When cold, roll into little balls about the size of an American walnut. When the balls are all formed drop them into boiling water and cook gently five minutes; then put them in the soup tureen and pour the boiling stock on them. Pass a plate of finely grated Parmesan cheese with the soup.

Thick Vegetable Soup.

One quart of the sediment which is left from the clear stock, one quart of water, one fourth of a cupful of pearl barley, one good-sized white turnip, one carrot, half a head of celery, two onions, about two pounds of cabbage, three potatoes, salt, and pepper. Wash the barley and put it on in the quart of water, and simmer gently for two hours. Then add all the vegetables (except the potatoes), cut very fine, and the quart of stock. Boil gently for one hour and a half, then add the potatoes and the salt and pepper. Cook thirty minutes longer. When there is no stock, take two pounds of beef and two quarts of water. Cook beef, barley, and water two hours, and add the vegetables as before. The meat can be served with the soup or as a separate dish.

Mulligatawney Soup.

One chicken or fowl weighing three pounds, three pounds of veal, two large onions, two large slices of carrot, four stalks of celery, three large table-spoonfuls of butter, one table-spoonful of curry powder, four of flour, salt, pepper, five quarts of water. Take two table-spoonfuls of the fat from the opening in the chicken and put in the soup pot. As soon as melted, put in the vegetables, which have been cut very fine. Let all cook together for twenty minutes, stirring frequently, that it may not burn; then add the veal, cut into small pieces. Cook fifteen minutes longer; then add the whole chicken and the water. Cover, and let it come to a boil. Skim, and set back where it will simmer for four hours (in the mean time taking out the chicken when it is tender). Now put the butter into a small frying-pan, and when hot add the dry flour. Stir until a rich brown; then take from the fire and add the curry powder. Stir this mixture into the soup, and let it cook half an hour longer; then strain through a sieve, rinse out the soup pot and return the strained soup to it. Add salt and pepper and the chicken (which has been freed from the bones and skin and cut into small pieces); simmer very gently thirty minutes. Skim off any fat that may rise to the top, and serve. This soup is served with plain boiled rice in a separate dish, or with small squares of fried or toasted bread. The rice can be served in the soup if you choose.

Mulligatawney Soup, No. 2.

Chicken or turkey left from a former dinner, bones and scraps from roast veal, lamb, or mutton, four quarts of water, four stalks of celery, four table-spoonfuls of butter, four of flour, one of curry, two onions, two slices of carrot, salt, pepper, half a small cupful of barley. Put on the bones of the poultry and meat with the water. Have the vegetables cut very fine, and cook gently twenty minutes in the butter; then skim them into the soup pot, being careful to press out all the butter. Into the butter remaining in the pan put the flour, and when that is brown add the curry powder, and stir all into the soup. Cook gently four hours; then season with salt and pepper, and strain. Return to the pot and add bits of chicken or turkey, as the case may be, and the barley, which has been simmering two hours and a half in clear water to cover. Simmer half an hour and serve.

Green Turtle Soup.

One can of green turtle, such as is put up by the "Merriam Packing Co." Separate the green fat from the other contents of the can, cut into dice, and set aside. Put one quart of water with the remainder of the turtle; add twelve pepper-corns, six whole cloves, two small sprigs each of parsley, summer savory, sweet marjoram and thyme, two bay leaves, two leaves of sage. Have the herbs tied together. Put one large onion, one slice of carrot, one of turnip, and a stalk of celery, cut fine, into a pan, with two large table-spoonfuls of butter. Fry fifteen minutes, being careful not to burn. Skim carefully from the butter and put into the soup. Now, into the butter in which the vegetables were fried put two table-spoonfuls of dry flour, and cook until brown. Stir into the soup; season with salt and pepper, and let simmer very gently one hour. Strain, skim off all the fat, and serve with thin slices of lemon, egg or force-meat balls, and the green fat. The lemon should have a very thin rind; should be put into the tureen and the soup poured over it. Cooking the lemon in this or any other soup often gives it a bitter taste. If the soup is wished quite thick, add a table-spoonful of butter to that in which the vegetables were cooked, and use three table-spoonfuls of flour instead of two. Many people use wine in this soup, but it is delicious without. In case you do use wine there should not be more than four table-spoonfuls to this quantity. If you desire the soup extremely rich, use a quart of rich soup stock. The green turtles are so very large that it is only in great establishments that they are available, and for this reason a rule for preparing the live turtle is not given. Few housekeepers would ever see one. The cans contain not what is commonly called turtle soup, but the meat of the turtle, boiled, and the proper proportions of lean meat, yellow and green fat put together. They cost fifty cents each, and a single can will make soup enough for six persons.

Black Bean Soup.

A pint of black beans, soaked over night in three quarts of water. In the morning pour off this water, and add three quarts of fresh. Boil gently six hours. When done, there should be one quart. Add a quart of stock, six whole cloves, six whole allspice, a small piece of mace, a small piece of cinnamon, a stalk of celery, a bouquet of sweet herbs, also one good-sized onion and one small slice each of turnip and carrot, all cut fine and fried in three table-spoonfuls of butter. Into the butter remaining in the pan put a spoonful of flour, and cook until brown. Add to soup, and simmer altogether one hour. Season with salt and pepper, and rub through a fine sieve. Serve with slices of lemon and egg balls, the lemon to be put in the tureen with the soup.

Scotch Broth.

Two pounds of the scraggy part of a neck of mutton. Cut the meat from the bones, and cut off all the fat. Then cut meat into small pieces and put into soup pot with one large slice of turnip, two of carrot, one onion, and a stalk of celery, all cut fine, half a cup of barley and three pints of cold water. Simmer gently two hours. On to the bones put one pint of water; simmer two hours, and strain upon the soup. Cook a table-spoonful of flour and one of butter together until perfectly smooth; stir into soup, and add a teaspoonful of chopped parsley. Season with salt and pepper.

Meg Merrilies Soup.

One hare, one grouse, four onions, one small carrot, four slices of turnip, a bouquet of sweet herbs, three table-spoonfuls of rice flour, four table-spoonfuls of butter, half a cupful of stale bread, half a cupful of milk, one egg, six quarts of water. Wash the grouse and hare and put to boil in the six quarts of cold water. When this comes to a boil, skim, and set back where it will simmer for one hour. Then take out the hare and grouse and cut all the meat from the bones. Return the bones to the soup and simmer two hours longer. Cut the meat into handsome pieces, roll in flour, and fry in the butter till a rich brown. Set aside for the present. Slice the onions, and fry in the butter in which the meat was fried; when brown, add to the soup. Make force-meat balls of the livers of the hare and grouse (which have been boiled one hour in the stock), the egg, bread and milk. Boil the bread and milk together until a smooth paste. Mash the livers with a strong spoon, then add bread and milk and the egg, unbeaten. Season well with pepper and salt, and, if you like, with a little lemon juice. Shape into small balls and fry in either chicken fat or butter. Put these into the soup twenty minutes before dishing. Have the turnip and carrot cut into small pieces and cooked one hour in clear water. When the bones and the onions have simmered two hours, strain and return to the soup pot. Add the fried meat and vegetables. Mix the rice flour with a cupful of cold water; add to the soup, season with salt and pepper, simmer ten minutes. Add force-meat balls and simmer twenty minutes longer.

Okra Soup.

One cold roast chicken, two quarts of stock (any kind), one of water, quarter of a pound of salt pork, one quart of green okra, an onion, salt, pepper, three table-spoonfuls of flour. Cut the okra pods into small pieces. Slice the pork and onion. Fry the pork, and then add the onion and okra. Cover closely, and fry half an hour. Cut all the meat from the chicken. Put the bones on with the water. Add the okra and onion, first being careful to press out all the pork fat possible. Into the fat remaining put the flour, and stir until it becomes a rich brown; add this to the other ingredients. Cover the pot, and simmer three hours; then rub through a sieve, and add the stock, salt and pepper, and the meat of the chicken, cut into small pieces. Simmer gently twenty minutes. Serve with a dish of boiled rice.

Okra Soup, No. 2.

One pint of green okra, one of green peas, one of green corn cut from the cob, half a pint of shell beans, two onions, four stalks of celery, two ripe tomatoes, one slice of carrot, one of turnip, two pounds of veal, quarter of a pound of fat ham or bacon, two table-spoonfuls of flour, four quarts of water, salt, pepper. Fry the ham or bacon, being careful not to burn. Cut the veal into dice; roll these in the flour and fry brown in the ham fat; then put them in the soup pot. Fry the onion, carrot, and turnip in the remaining fat. Add these to the veal, and then add the okra, cut into small pieces, the shell beans, celery, and water. Simmer two hours, and then add the tomatoes, corn, peas, and salt and pepper. Simmer half an hour longer and serve without straining. If dried okra be used for either soup, half the quantity given in the recipes is sufficient. Okra is often called Gumbo. The same kind of a soup is meant under both names.

Grouse Soup.

The bones of two roasted grouse and the breast of one, a quart of any kind of stock, or pieces and bones of cold roasts; three quarts of cold water, two slices of turnip, two of carrot, two large onions, two cloves, two stalks of celery, a bouquet of sweet herbs, three table-spoonfuls of butter, three of flour. Cook the grouse bones in three quarts of water four hours. The last hour add the vegetables and the cloves; then strain, and return to the fire with the quart of stock. Cook the butter and the flour together until a rich brown, and then turn into the stock. Cut the breast of the grouse into very sma... pieces and add to the soup. Season with salt and pepper and simmer gently half an hour. If there is any fat on the soup, skim it off. Serve with fried bread. When bones and meat are used instead of the stock, use one more quart of water, and cook them with the grouse bones.

Spring Soup.

Half a pint of green peas, half a pint of cauliflower, one pint of turnip, carrot, celery, and string beans (all the four vegetables being included in the pint), half a cupful of tomato, half a pint of asparagus heads, two quarts of soup stock — any kind will do; three table-spoonfuls of butter, three table-spoonfuls of flour, and salt and pepper. Cook all the vegetables, except the peas and tomato, in water to cover, one hour. Cook butter and dry flour together until smooth, but not brown; stir into the stock, which has been heated to the boiling point. Now add the tomato and simmer gently fifteen minutes; then strain. Add the peas and cooked vegetables to the strained soup, and simmer again for thirty minutes. Serve small slices of toasted bread in a separate dish.

Spring and Summer Soup without Stock.

Quarter of a pound of salt pork, or three large table-spoonfuls of butter; three large young onions, half a small head of cabbage, three potatoes, half a small carrot, half a small white turnip, three table-spoonfuls of flour, two quarts of water, six large slices of toasted bread, salt, pepper, one small parsnip. Cut the pork into thin slices; place these in the soup pot and let them fry out slowly. Have the vegetables (except the potatoes) cut quite fine, and when the pork is cooked put the vegetables into the pot with it. Cover tightly and let cook very gently, on the back of the stove, one hour. Stir frequently to prevent burning. Add the water, which should be boiling. Let simmer gently for one hour, and then add the potatoes, cut into slices, and the flour, which has been mixed with a little cold water. Season with salt and pepper, and simmer gently an hour longer. Have the toasted bread in the tureen. Turn the soup on it and serve. A pint of green peas, cooked in the soup the last half, is a great addition. When the butter is used, let it melt in the soup pot before adding the vegetables.

Giblet Soup.

The giblets from two or three fowls or chickens, any kind of stock, or if there are remains of roast chickens, use these; one large onion, two slices of carrot, one of turnip, two stalks of celery, two quarts of water, one of stock, two large table-spoonfuls of butter, two of flour, salt, pepper. Put the giblets on to boil in the two quarts of water, and boil gently until reduced to one quart (it will take about two hours); then take out the giblets. Cut all the hard, tough parts from the gizzards, and put hearts, livers, and gizzards together and chop rather coarse. Return them to the liquor in which they were boiled, and add the quart of stock. Have the vegetables cut fine, and fry them in the butter until they are very tender (about fifteen minutes), but be careful they do not burn; then add the dry flour to them and stir until the flour browns. Turn this mixture into the soup, and season with pepper and salt. Cook gently half an hour and serve with toasted bread. If the chicken bones are used, put them on to boil in three quarts of water, and boil the giblets with them. When you take out the giblets, strain the stock through a sieve and return to the pot; then proceed as before.

Potage à la Reine.

Boil a large fowl in three quarts of water until tender (the water should never more than bubble). Skim off the fat, and add a teacupful of rice, and also a slice of carrot, one of turnip, a small piece of celery, and an onion, which have been cooked slowly for fifteen minutes in two large table-spoonfuls of butter. Skim this butter carefully from the vegetables, and into the pan in which it is, stir a table-spoonful of flour. Cook until smooth, but not brown. Add this, as well as a small piece of cinnamon and of mace, and four whole cloves. Cook all together slowly for two hours. Chop and pound the breast of the fowl very fine. Rub the soup through a fine sieve; add the pounded breast and again rub the whole through the sieve. Put back on the fire and add one and a half table-spoonfuls of salt, a fourth of a teaspoonful of pepper, and a pint of cream, which has come just to a boil. Boil up once and serve. This is a delicious soup.

Tomato Soup.

One quart can of tomato, two heaping table-spoonfuls of flour, one of butter, one teaspoonful of salt, one of sugar, a pint of hot water. Let tomato and water come to a boil. Rub flour, butter, and a table-spoonful of tomato together. Stir into boiling mixture, add seasoning, boil all together fifteen minutes, rub through a sieve, and serve with toasted bread. This bread should first be cut in thin slices; should be buttered, cut into little squares, placed in a pan, buttered side up, and browned in a quick oven.

Mock Bisque Soup.

A quart can of tomato, three pints of milk, a large table-spoonful of flour, butter the size of an egg, pepper and salt to taste, a scant teaspoonful of soda. Put the tomato on to stew, and the milk in a double kettle to boil, reserving however half a cupful to mix with flour. Mix the flour smoothly with this cold milk, stir into the boiling milk, and cook ten minutes. To the tomato add the soda; stir well, and rub through a strainer that is fine enough to keep back the seeds. Add butter, salt, and pepper to the milk, and then the tomato. Serve immediately. If half the rule is made, stir the tomato well in the can before dividing, as the liquid portion is the more acid.

Onion Soup.

One quart of milk, six large onions, yolks of four eggs, three table-spoonfuls of butter, a large one of flour, one cupful of cream, salt, pepper. Put the butter in a frying-pan. Cut the onions into thin slices and drop in the butter. Stir until they begin to cook; then cover tight and set back where they will simmer, but not burn, for half an hour. Now put the milk on to boil, and then add the dry flour to the onions, and stir constantly for three minutes over the fire. Then turn the mixture into the milk and cook fifteen minutes. Rub the soup through a

strainer, return to the fire, season with salt and pepper. Beat the yolks of the eggs well; add the cream to them and stir into the soup. Cook three minutes, stirring constantly. If you have no cream, use milk, in which case add a table-spoonful of butter at the same time.

Potato Soup.

A quart of milk, six large potatoes, one stalk of celery, an onion, and a table-spoonful of butter. Put milk to boil with onion and celery. Pare potatoes and boil thirty minutes. Turn off the water, and mash fine and light. Add boiling milk and the butter, and pepper and salt to taste. Rub through a strainer and serve immediately. A cupful of whipped cream, added when in the tureen, is a great improvement. This soup must not be allowed to stand, not even if kept hot. Served as soon as ready, it is excellent.

Asparagus Soup.

Two bundles of asparagus, one quart of white stock or water, one pint of milk, and one of cream if stock is used, but if water use all cream; three table-spoonfuls of butter, three of flour, one onion, salt, and pepper. Cut the tops from one bunch of the asparagus and cook them twenty minutes in salted water to cover. The remainder of the asparagus cook twenty minutes in the quart of stock or water. Cut the onion into thin slices and fry in the butter ten minutes, being careful not to burn; then add the asparagus that has been boiled in the stock. Cook five minutes, stirring constantly; then add flour, and cook five minutes longer. Turn this mixture into the boiling stock and boil gently twenty minutes. Rub through a sieve, add the milk and cream, which has just come to a boil, and also the asparagus heads. Season with salt and pepper, and serve. Dropped eggs can be served with it if you choose, but they are rather heavy for such a delicate soup.

Green Pea Soup.

Cover a quart of green peas with hot water, and boil, with an onion, until they will mash easily. (The time will depend on the age of the peas, but will be from twenty to thirty minutes.) Mash, and add a pint of stock or water. Cook together two table-spoonfuls of butter, and one of flour until smooth, but not brown. Add to the peas, and then add a cupful of cream and one of milk. Season with salt and pepper, and let boil up once. Strain and serve. A cupful of whipped cream added the last moment is an improvement.

Pumpkin Soup.

Two pounds of pumpkin. Take out seeds and pare off the rind. Cut into small pieces, and put into a stewpan with half a pint of water. Simmer slowly an hour and a half, then rub through a sieve and put back on the fire with one and a half pints of boiling milk, butter the size of an egg, one teaspoonful of sugar, salt and pepper to taste, and three slices of stale bread, cut into small squares. Stir occasionally; and when it boils, serve.

Cream of Celery Soup.

A pint of milk, a table-spoonful of flour, one of butter, a head of celery, a large slice of onion, and a small piece of mace. Boil celery in a pint of water from thirty to forty-five minutes; boil mace, onion, and milk together. Mix flour with two table-spoonfuls of cold milk, and add to boiling milk. Cook ten minutes. Mash celery in the water in which it has been cooked, and stir into boiling milk. Add butter, and season with salt and pepper to taste. Strain and serve immediately. The flavor is improved by adding a cupful of whipped cream when the soup is in the tureen.

Tapioca Cream Soup.

One quart of white stock, one pint of cream or milk, one onion, two stalks of celery, one third of a cupful of tapioca, two cupfuls of cold water, one table-spoonful of butter, a small piece of mace, salt, pepper. Wash the tapioca, and soak over night in cold water. Cook it and the stock together, very gently, for one hour. Cut the onion and celery into small pieces, and put on to cook for twenty minutes with the milk and mace. Strain on the tapioca and stock. Season with salt and pepper, add butter, and serve.

Cream of Rice Soup.

Two quarts of chicken stock (the water in which fowl have been boiled will answer), one teacupful of rice, a quart of cream or milk, a small onion, a stalk of celery, and salt and pepper to taste. Wash rice carefully, and add to chicken stock, onion and celery. Cook slowly two hours (it should hardly bubble). Put through a sieve; add seasoning and the milk or cream, which has been allowed to come just to a boil. If milk, use also a table-spoonful of butter.

Cream of Barley Soup.

A teacupful of barley, well washed; three pints of chicken stock, an onion, and a small piece each of mace and cinnamon. Cook slowly together five hours; then rub through a sieve, and add one and a half pints of boiling cream or milk. If milk, add also two table-spoonfuls of butter. Salt and pepper to taste. The yolks of four eggs, beaten with four table-spoonfuls of milk, and cooked a minute in the boiling milk or cream, makes the soup very much richer.

Duchess Soup.

One quart of milk, two large onions, three eggs, two table-spoonfuls of butter, two of flour, salt, pepper, two table-spoonfuls of grated cheese. Put milk on to boil. Fry the butter and onions together for eight minutes; then add dry flour, and cook two minutes longer, being careful not to burn. Stir into the milk, and cook ten minutes. Rub through a strainer, and return to the fire. Now add the cheese. Beat the eggs, with a speck of pepper and half a teaspoonful of salt. Season the soup with salt and pepper. Hold the colander over the soup and pour the eggs through, upon the butter, and set back for three minutes where it will not boil. Then serve. The cheese may be omitted if it is not liked.

Yacht Oyster Soup.

A quart of milk, one of oysters, a head of celery, a small onion, half a cupful of butter, half a cupful of powdered cracker, one teaspoonful of Worcestershire sauce, a speck of cayenne, and salt and pepper to taste. Chop onion and celery fine. Put on to boil with milk for twenty minutes. Then strain, and add the butter, cracker, oyster liquor (which has been boiled and skimmed), and finally the seasoning and oysters. Cook three minutes longer, and serve.

Lobster Soup with Milk.

Meat of a small lobster, chopped fine; three crackers, rolled fine, butter size of an egg, salt and pepper to taste, and a speck of cayenne. Mix all in the same pan, and add, gradually, a pint of boiling milk, stirring all the while. Boil up once, and serve.

Lobster Soup with Stock.

One small lobster, three pints of water or stock, three large table-spoonfuls of butter and three of flour, a speck of cayenne, white pepper and salt to taste. Break up the body of the lobster, and cut off the scraggy parts of the meat. Pour over these and the body the water or stock. If there is "coral" in the lobster, pound it and use also. Boil twenty minutes. Cook the butter and flour until smooth, but not brown. Stir into the cooking mixture, and add the seasoning. Boil two minutes, and strain into a saucepan. Have the remainder of the lobster meat — that found in the tail and claws — cut up very fine, and add it to the soup. Boil up once, and serve.

Philadelphia Clam Soup.

Twenty-five small clams, one quart of milk, half a cupful of butter, one table-spoonful of chopped parsley, three potatoes, two large table-spoonfuls of flour, salt, pepper. The clams should be chopped fine and put into a colander to drain. Pare the potatoes, and chop rather fine. Put them on to boil with the milk, in a double kettle. Rub the butter and flour together until perfectly creamy, and when the milk and potatoes have been boiling fifteen minutes, stir this in, and cook eight minutes more. Add the parsley, pepper and salt, and cook three minutes longer. Now add the clams. Cook one minute longer, and serve. This gives a very delicate soup, as the liquor from the clams is not used.

Fish Chowder.

Five pounds of any kind of fish (the light salt-water fish is the best), half a pound of pork, two large onions, one quart of sliced potatoes, one quart of water, one pint of milk, two table-spoonfuls of flour, six crackers, salt, pepper. Skin the fish, and cut all the flesh from the bones. Put the bones on to cook in the quart of water, and simmer gently ten minutes. Fry the pork; then add the onions, cut into slices. Cover, and cook five minutes; then add the flour, and cook eight minutes longer, stirring often. Strain on this the water in which the fish bones were cooked, and boil gently for five minutes; then strain all on the potatoes and fish. Season with salt and pepper, and simmer fifteen minutes. Add the milk and the crackers, which were first soaked for three minutes in the milk. Let it boil up once, and serve. The milk may be omitted, and a pint of tomatoes used, if you like.

Corn Chowder.

Cut enough green corn from the cob to make a quart; pare and slice one quart of potatoes; pare and slice two onions. Cut half a pound of pork in slices, and fry until brown; then take up, and fry the onions in the fat. Put the potatoes and corn into the kettle in layers, sprinkling each layer with salt, pepper, and flour. Use half a teaspoonful of pepper, one and a half table-spoonfuls of salt, and three of flour. Place the gravy strainer on the vegetables, and turn the onions and pork fat into it, and with a spoon press the juice through; then slowly pour one and one fourth quarts of boiling water through the strainer, rubbing as much onion through as possible. Take out the strainer, cover the kettle, and boil gently for twenty minutes. Mix three table-spoonfuls of flour with a little milk, and when perfectly smooth add a pint and a half of rich milk. Stir this into the boiling chowder. Taste to see if seasoned enough, and if it is not, add more pepper and salt. Then add six crackers, split, and dipped for a minute in cold water. Put on the cover, boil up once, and serve.

Corn Soup.

One pint of grated green corn, one quart of milk, one pint of hot water, one heaping table-spoonful of flour, two table-spoonfuls of butter, one slice of onion, salt and pepper to taste. Cook the corn in the water thirty minutes. Let the milk and onion come to a boil. Have the flour and butter mixed together, and add a few table-spoonfuls of the boiling milk. When perfectly smooth stir into the milk, and cook eight minutes. Take out the onion and add the corn. Season to taste, and serve.

Glaze.

Boil four quarts of consommé rapidly until reduced to one quart. Turn into small jars, and cool quickly. This will keep for a month in a cool, dry place. It is used for soups and sauces and for glazing meats.

French Paste for Soups.

A preparation for flavoring and coloring soups and sauces comes in small tin boxes. In each box there are twelve little squares, which look very much like chocolate caramels. One of these will give two quarts of soup the most delicious flavor and a rich color. The paste shoul not be cooked with the soup, but put into the tureen, and the soup poure over it; and as the soup is served, stir with the ladle. If you let it boil with the clear soup the flavor will not be as fine and the soup not as clear. It may be used with any dark or clear soup, even when already seasoned. It is for sale in Boston by S. S. Pierce & Co. New York: Park, Tilford, & Co., retail; E. C. Hayward & Co., 192–194 Chamber Street, wholesale. Philadelphia: Githens & Rexsame's. Chicago: Rockwood Bros., 102 North Clark Street. St. Louis: David Nicholson. The paste costs only twenty-five cents per box.

Egg Balls.

Boil four eggs ten minutes. Drop into cold water, and when cool remove the yolks. Pound these in a mortar until reduced to a paste, and then beat them with a teaspoonful of salt, a speck of pepper, and the white of one raw egg. Form in balls about the size of a walnut. Roll in flour, and fry brown in butter or chicken fat, being careful not to burn.

Fried Bread for Soups.

Cut stale bread into dice, and fry in boiling fat until brown. It will take about half a minute. The fat must be smoking in the centre when the bread is put into it.

FISH.

A General Chapter on Fish.

It may seem as if a small number of recipes have been given, but the aim has been to present under the heads of Baking, Boiling, Broiling, Frying, and Stewing such general directions that one cannot be at a loss as to how to prepare any kind of fish. Once having mastered the five primary methods, and learned also how to make sauces, the variety of dishes within the cook's power is great. All that is required is confidence in the rules, which are perfectly reliable, and will always bring about a satisfactory result if followed carefully. Fish, to be eatable, should be perfectly fresh. Nothing else in the line of food deteriorates so rapidly, especially the white fish, — those that are nearly free of oil, like cod, cusk, etc. Most of the oil in this class centres in the liver. Salmon, mackerel, etc., have it distributed throughout the body, which gives a higher and richer flavor, and at the same time tends to preserve the fish. People who do not live near the seashore do not get that delicious flavor which fish just caught have. If the fish is kept on ice until used, it will retain much of its freshness; let it once get heated and nothing will bring back the delicate flavor. Fresh fish will be firm, and the skin and scales bright. When fish looks dim and limp, do not buy it. Fish should be washed quickly in only one (cold) water, and should not be allowed to stand in it. If it is cut up before cooking, wash while whole, else much of the flavor will be lost. For frying, the fat should be deep enough to cover the article, and yet have it float from the bottom. Unless one cooks great quantities of fish in this way it is not necessary to have a separate pot of fat for this kind of frying. The same pot, with proper care, will answer for chops, cutlets, muffins, potatoes, croquettes, etc. All the cold fish left from any mode of cooking can be utilized in making delicious salads, croquettes, and escallops.

Boiled Fish.

A general rule for boiling fish, which will hold good for all kinds, and thus save a great deal of time and space, is this :— Any fresh fish weighing between four and six pounds should be first washed in cold water and then put into boiling water enough to cover it, and containing one table-spoonful of salt. Simmer gently thirty minutes; then take up. A fish kettle is a great convenience, and it can be used also for boiling hams. When you do not have a fish kettle, keep a piece of strong white cotton cloth in which pin the fish before putting into the boiling water. This will hold it in shape. Hard boiling will break the fish, and, of course, there will be great waste, besides the dish's not looking so handsome and appetizing. There should be a gentle bubbling of the water, and nothing more, all the time the fish is in it. A fish weighing more than six pounds should cook five minutes longer for every additional *two* pounds. Boiled fish can be served with a great variety of sauces. After you have learned to make them (which is a simple matter), if you cannot get a variety of fish you will not miss it particularly, the sauce and mode of serving doing much to change the whole character of the dish. Many people put a table-spoonful of vinegar in the water in which the fish is boiled. The fish flakes a little more readily for it. Small fish, like trout, require from four to eight minutes to cook. They are, however, much better baked, broiled, or fried.

Court Bouillon.

This preparation gives boiled fish a better flavor than cooking in clear water does. Many cooks use wine in it, but there is no necessity for it. Four quarts of water, one onion, one slice of carrot, two cloves, two table-spoonfuls of salt, one teaspoonful of pepper, one table-spoonful of vinegar, the juice of half a lemon, and a bouquet of sweet herbs are used. Tie the onion, carrot, cloves, and herbs in a piece of muslin, and put in the water with the other ingredients. Cover, and boil slowly for one hour. Then put in the fish and cook as directed for plain boiling.

Boiled Cod with Lobster Sauce.

Boil the fish as directed [see Boiled Fish], and, when done, carefully remove the skin from one side ; then turn the fish over on to the dish on which it is to be served, skin side up. Remove the skin from this side. Wipe the dish with a damp cloth. Pour a few spoonfuls of the sauce over the fish, and the remainder around it; garnish with parsley, and serve. This is a handsome dish.

Boiled Haddock with Lobster Sauce.

The same as cod. In fact, all kinds of fish can be served in the same manner ; but the lighter are the better, as the sauce is so rich that it is not really the thing for salmon and bluefish. Many of the best cooks and caterers, however, use the lobster sauce with salmon, but salmon has too rich and delicate a flavor to be mixed with the lobster.

Cold Boiled Fish à la Vinaigrette.

If the fish is whole, take off the head and skin, and then place it in the centre of a dish. Have two cold hard-boiled eggs, and cut fine with a silver knife or spoon (steel turns the egg black). Sprinkle the fish with this, and garnish either with small lettuce leaves, water-cresses, or cold boiled potatoes and beets, cut in slices. Place tastefully around the dish, with here and there a sprig of parsley. Serve the vinaigrette sauce in a separate dish. Help to the garnish when the fish is served, and pour a spoonful of the sauce over the fish as you serve it. This makes a nice dish for tea in summer, and takes the place of a salad, as it is, in fact, a kind of salad.

If the fish is left from the dinner, and is broken, pick free from skin and bones, heap it lightly in the centre of the dish, sprinkle the sauce over it, and set away in a cool place until tea time. Then add the garnish, and serve as before. Many people prefer the latter method, as the fish is seasoned better and more easily served. The cold fish remaining from a bake or broil can be served in the same manner. This same dish can be served with a sauce piquante or Tartare sauce, for a change.

Baked Fish.

As for the boiled fish, a general rule that will cover all kinds of baked fish is herewith given : — A fish weighing about five pounds ; three large, or five small crackers, quarter of a pound of salt pork, two table-spoonfuls of salt, quarter of a teaspoonful of pepper, half a table-spoonful of chopped parsley, two table-spoonfuls of flour.

If the fish has not already been scraped free of scales, scrape, and wash clean ; then rub into it one table-spoonful of the salt. Roll the crackers very fine, and add to them the parsley, one table-spoonful of chopped pork, half the pepper, half a table-spoonful of salt, and cold water to moisten well. Put this into the body of the fish, and fasten together with a skewer. Butter a tin sheet and put it into a baking-pan. Cut gashes across the fish, about half an inch deep and two inches long. Cut the remainder of the pork into strips, and put these into the gashes. Now put the fish into the baking-pan, and dredge well with salt, pepper, and flour. Cover the bottom of the pan with hot water, and put into a rather hot oven. Bake one hour, basting often with the gravy in the pan, and dredging each time with salt, pepper, and flour. The water in the pan must often be renewed, as the bottom is simply to be covered with it each time. The fish should be basted every fifteen minutes. When it is cooked, lift from the pan on to the tin sheet, and slide it carefully into the centre of the dish on which it is to be served. Pour around it Hollandaise sauce, tomato sauce, or any kind you like. Garnish with parsley.

Broiled Fish.

Bluefish, young cod, mackerel, salmon, large trout, and all other fish, when they weigh between half a pound and four pounds, are nice for broiling. When smaller or larger they are not so good. Always use a double broiler, which, before putting the fish into it, rub with either butter or a piece of salt pork. This prevents sticking. The thickness of the fish will have to be the guide in broiling. A bluefish weighing four pounds will take from twenty minutes to half an hour to cook. Many cooks brown the fish handsomely over the coals and then put it into the oven to finish broiling. Where the fish is very thick, this is a good plan. If the fish is taken from the broiler to be put into the oven, it should be slipped on to a tin sheet, that it may slide easily into the platter at serving time ; for nothing so mars a dish of fish as to have it come to the table broken. In broiling, the inside should be exposed to

the fire first, and then the skin. Great care must be taken that the skin does not burn. Mackerel will broil in from twelve to twenty minutes, young cod (also called scrod) in from twenty to thirty minutes, bluefish in from twenty to thirty minutes, salmon in from twelve to twenty minutes, and whitefish, bass, mullet, etc., in about eighteen minutes. All kinds of broiled fish can be served with a seasoning of salt, pepper, and butter, or with any of the following sauces : *beurre noir*, *maître d'hôtel*, Tartare, sharp, tomato, and curry. Always, when possible, garnish with parsley or something else green.

Broiled Halibut.

Season the slices with salt and pepper, and lay them in melted butter for half an hour, having them well covered on both sides. Roll in flour, and broil for twelve minutes over a clear fire. Serve on a hot dish, garnishing with parsley and slices of lemon. The slices of halibut should be about an inch thick, and for every pound there should be three table-spoonfuls of butter.

Broiled Halibut with Maître d'Hôtel Butter.

Butter both sides of the broiler. Season the slices of halibut with salt and pepper, place them in the broiler and cook over clear coals for twelve minutes, turning frequently. Place on a hot dish, and spread on them the sauce, using one spoonful to each pound. Garnish with parsley.

Stewed Fish.

Six pounds of any kind of fish, large or small ; three large pints of water, quarter of a pound of pork, or half a cupful of butter ; two large onions, three table-spoonfuls of flour, salt and pepper to taste. Cut the heads from the fish, and cut out all the bones. Put the heads and bones on to boil in the three pints of water. Cook gently half an hour. In the mean while cut the pork in slices, and fry brown. Cut the onions in slices, and fry in the pork fat. Stir the dry flour into the onion and fat, and cook three minutes, stirring all the time. Now pour over this the water in which the bones have been cooking, and simmer ten minutes. Have the fish cut in pieces about three inches square. Season well with salt and pepper, and place in the stewpan. Season the sauce with salt and pepper, and strain on the fish. Cover tight, and simmer twenty minutes. A bouquet of sweet herbs, simmered with the bones, is an improvement. Taste to see if the sauce is seasoned enough, and dish on a large platter. Garnish with potato balls and parsley. The potato balls are cut from the raw potatoes with a vegetable scoop, and boiled ten minutes in salted water. Put them in little heaps around the dish.

Fried Fish.

All small fish, like brook trout, smelts, perch, etc., are best fried. They are often called pan-fish for this reason. They should be cleaned, washed, and drained, then well salted, and rolled in flour and Indian meal (half of each) which has been thoroughly mixed and salted. For every four pounds of fish have half a pound of salt pork, cut in thin slices, and fried a crisp brown. Take the pork from the pan and put the fish in, having only enough to cover the bottom. Fry brown on one side ; turn, and fry the other side. Serve on a hot dish, with the salt pork as a garnish. Great care must be taken that the pork or fat does not burn, and yet to have it hot enough to brown quickly. Cod, haddock, cusk, and halibut are all cut in handsome slices and fried in this manner ; or, the slices can be well seasoned with salt and pepper, dipped in beaten egg, rolled in bread or cracker crumbs, and fried in boiling fat enough to cover. This method gives the handsomer dish, but the first the more savory. Where Indian meal is not liked, all flour can be used. Serve very hot. Any kind of fried fish can be served with *beurre noir*, but this is particularly nice for that which is fried without pork. When the cooked fish is placed in the dish, pour the butter over it, garnish with parsley, and serve.

To Cook Salt Codfish.

The fish should be thoroughly washed, and soaked in cold water over night. In the morning change the water, and put on to cook. As soon as the water comes to the boiling point set back where it will keep *hot*, but will *not boil*. From four to six hours will cook a very dry, hard fish, and there are kinds which will cook in half an hour. The boneless codfish, put up at the Isles of Shoals by Brown & Seavey, will cook in from half an hour to an hour. Where a family uses only a small quantity of salt fish at a time, this is a convenient and economical way to buy it, as there is no waste with bone or skin. It comes in five-pound boxes, and costs sixty cents.

Dropped Fish Balls.

One pint bowlful of raw fish, two heaping bowlfuls of pared potatoes (let the potatoes be under medium size), two eggs, butter the size of an egg, and a little pepper. Pick the fish very fine, and measure it lightly in the bowl. Put the potatoes into the boiler, and the fish on top of them ; then cover with boiling water, and boil half an hour. Drain off all the water, and mash fish and potatoes together until fine and light. Then add the butter and pepper, and the egg, well beaten. Have a deep kettle of *boiling* fat. Dip a table-spoon in it, and then take up a spoonful of the mixture, having care to get it into as good shape as possible. Drop into the boiling fat, and cook until brown, which should be in two minutes. Be careful not to crowd the balls, and also that the fat is hot enough. The spoon should be dipped in the fat every time you take a spoonful of the mixture. These balls are delicious.

Common Fish Balls.

One pint of finely chopped cooked salt fish, six medium-sized potatoes, one egg, one heaping table-spoonful of butter, pepper, two table-spoonfuls of cream, or four of milk. Pare the potatoes, and put on in *boiling* water. Boil half an hour. Drain off all the water, turn the potatoes into the tray with the fish, and mash light and fine with a vegetable masher. Add the butter, pepper, milk, and eggs, and mix all very thoroughly. Taste to see if salt enough. Shape into smooth balls, the size of an egg, and fry brown in boiling fat enough to float them. They will cook in three minutes. If the potatoes are very mealy it will take more milk or cream to moisten them, about two spoonfuls more. If the fat is smoking in the centre, and the balls are made *very* smooth, they will not soak fat; but if the fat is not hot enough, they certainly will. Putting too many balls into the fat at one time cools it. Put in say four or five. Let the fat regain its first temperature, then add more.

Salt Fish with Dropped Eggs.

One pint of cooked salt fish, one pint of milk or cream, two table-spoonfuls of flour, one of butter, six eggs, pepper. Put milk on to boil, keeping half a cupful of it to mix the flour. When it boils, stir in the flour, which has been mixed smooth with the milk; then add the fish, which has been flaked. Season, and cook ten minutes. Have six slices of toasted bread on a platter. Drop six eggs into boiling water, being careful to keep the shape. Turn the fish and cream on to the toast. Lift the eggs carefully from the water, as soon as the whites are set, and place very gently on the fish. Garnish the dish with points of toast and parsley.

Salt Codfish in Purée of Potatoes.

Six large potatoes, one pint and one cupful of milk, two table-spoonfuls of butter, a small slice of onior (about the size of a silver quarter), one pint of cooked salt codfish, salt, pepper, one large table-spoonful of flour. Pare the potatoes and boil half an hour; then drain off the water, and mash them light and fine. Add the salt, pepper, one table-spoonful of butter, and the cupful of milk, which has been allowed to come to a boil. Beat very thoroughly, and spread a thin layer of the potatoes on the centre of a hot platter. Heap the remainder around the edge, making a wall to keep in the cream and fish, which should then be poured in. Garnish the border with parsley, and serve.

To prepare the fish. Put the pint of milk on to boil with the onion. Mix flour and butter together, and when well mixed, add two table-spoonfuls of the hot milk. Stir all into the boiling milk, skim out the onion, add the fish, and cook ten minutes. Season with pepper, and, if not salt enough, with salt. This is a nice dish for breakfast, lunch, or dinner.

Salt Fish Soufflé.

One pint of finely chopped cooked salt fish, eight good-sized potatoes, three fourths of a cupful of milk or cream, four eggs, salt, pepper, two generous table-spoonfuls of butter. Pare the potatoes and boil thirty minutes. Drain the water from them, and mash very fine; then mix thoroughly with the fish. Add butter, seasoning, and the hot milk. Have two of the eggs well beaten, which stir into the mixture, and heap this in the dish in which it is to be served. Place in the oven for ten minutes. Beat the whites of the two remaining eggs to a stiff froth, and add a quarter of a teaspoonful of salt; then add yolks. Spread this over the dish of fish; return to the oven to brown, and serve.

Cusk à la Crème.

A cusk, cod, or haddock, weighing five or six pounds; one quart of milk, two table-spoonfuls of flour, one of butter, one small slice of onion, two sprigs of parsley, salt, pepper. Put the fish on in boiling water enough to cover, and which contains one table-spoonful of salt. Cook gently twenty minutes; then lift out of the water, but let it remain on the tray. Now carefully remove all the skin and the head; then turn the fish over into the dish in which it is to be served (it should be stone china), and scrape off the skin from the other side. Pick out all the small bones. You will find them the whole length of the back, and a few in the lower part of the fish, near the tail. They are in rows like pins in a paper, and if you start all right it will take but a few minutes to remove them. Then take out the back-bone, starting at the head and working gently down toward the tail. Great care must be taken, that the fish may keep its shape. Cover with the cream, and bake about ten minutes, just to brown it a little. Garnish with parsley or little puff-paste cakes; or, you can cover it with the whites of three eggs, beaten to a stiff froth, and then slightly brown.

To prepare the cream. Put the milk, parsley, and onion on to boil, reserving half a cupful of milk to mix with the flour. When it boils, stir in the flour, which has been mixed smoothly with the cold milk. Cook eight minutes. Season highly with salt and pepper, add the butter, strain on the fish, and proceed as directed.

Escaloped Fish.

One pint of milk, one pint of cream, four table-spoonfuls of flour, one cupful of bread crumbs, and between four and five pounds of any kind of white fish, — cusk, cod, haddock, etc., — boiled twenty minutes in water to cover and two table-spoonfuls of salt. Put fish on to boil, then the cream and milk. Mix the flour with half a cupful of cold milk, and stir into boil-

ing cream and milk. Cook eight minutes and season highly with salt and pepper. Remove skin and bones from fish, and break it into flakes. Put a layer of sauce in a deep escalop dish, and then a layer of fish, which dredge well with salt (a table-spoonful) and pepper; then another layer of sauce, again fish, and then sauce. Cover with the bread crumbs, and bake half an hour. This quantity requires a dish holding a little over two quarts, or two smaller dishes will answer. If for the only solid dish for dinner, this will answer for six persons; but if it is in a course for a dinner party, it will serve twelve. Cold boiled fish can be used when you have it. Great care must be taken to remove every bone when fish is prepared with a sauce, (as when it is served *à la crème*, escaloped, etc.,) because one cannot look for bones then as when the sauce is served separately.

Turbot à la Crème.

Boil five or six pounds of haddock. Take out all bones, and shred the fish very fine. Let a quart of milk, a quarter of an onion, and a piece of parsley come to a boil; then stir in a scant cupful of flour, which has been mixed with a cupful of cold milk, and the yolks of two eggs. Season with half a teaspoonful of white pepper, the same quantity of thyme, half a cupful of butter, and well with salt. Butter a pan, and put in first a layer of sauce, then one of fish. Finish with sauce, and over it sprinkle cracker crumbs and a light grating of cheese. Bake for an hour in a moderate oven.

Matelote of Codfish.

Cut off the head of a codfish weighing five pounds. Remove bones from the fish, and fill it with a dressing made of half a pint of oysters, a scant pint of bread crumbs, a fourth of a teaspoonful of pepper, two tea-spoonfuls of salt, two table-spoonfuls of butter, half an onion, an egg, and half a table-spoonful of chopped parsley. Place five slices of pork both under and over the fish. Boil the bones in a pint of water, and pour this around the fish. Bake an hour, and baste often with gravy and butter. Have a bouquet in the corner of the baking-pan. Make a gravy, and pour around the fish. Then garnish with fried smelts.

Smelts a la Tartare.

Clean the smelts by drawing them between the finger and thumb, beginning at the tail. This will press out the insides at the opening at the gills. Wash them, and drain in the colander; salt well, and dip in beaten egg and bread or cracker crumbs (one egg and one cupful of crumbs to twelve smelts, unless these are very large). Dip first in the egg, and then roll in the crumbs. Fry in boiling fat deep enough to float them. They should be a handsome brown in two minutes and a half. Take them up, and place on a sheet of brown paper for a few moments to drain; then place on a hot dish. Garnish with parsley and a few slices of lemon, and serve with Tartare sauce in a separate dish; or they may be served without the sauce.

Smelts as a Garnish.

Smelts are often fried, as for *à la Tartare;* or, rolled in meal or flour, and then fried, they are used to garnish other kinds of fish. With baked fish they are arranged around the dish in any form that the taste of the cook may dictate; but in garnishing fish, or any other dish, the arrangement should always be simple, so as not to make the matter of serving any harder than if the dish were not garnished. Smelts are also seasoned well with salt and pepper, dipped in butter and afterwards in flour, and placed in a very hot oven for eight or ten minutes to get a handsome brown. They are then served as a garnish, or on slices of buttered toast. When smelts are used as a garnish, serve one on each plate with the other fish. If you wish to have the smelts in rings, for a garnish, fasten the tails in the opening at the gills, with little wooden toothpicks; then dip them in the beaten egg and in the crumbs, place in the frying-basket, and plunge into the boiling fat. When they are cooked, take out the skewers, and they will retain their shape.

Fish au Gratin.

Any kind of light fish, that is, cod, cusk, flounder, etc. Skin the fish by starting at the head and drawing down towards the tail; then take out the bones. Cut the fish into pieces about three inches square, and salt and pepper well. Butter such a dish as you would use for escaloped oysters. Put in one layer of fish, then moisten well with sauce; add more fish and sauce, and finally cover with fine bread crumbs. Bake half an hour. The dish should be rather shallow, allowing only two layers of fish.

Sauce for *au gratin*. One pint of stock, three table-spoonfuls of butter, two of flour, juice of half a lemon, half a table-spoonful of chopped parsley, a slice of onion the size of half a dollar and about as thick, chopped very fine (one table-spoonful of onion juice is better); one table-spoonful of vinegar, salt, pepper. Heat the butter in a small frying-pan, and when hot add the dry flour. Stir constantly until a rich brown; then add, gradually, the cold stock, stirring all the time. As soon as it boils, season well with salt and pepper, and then add the other seasoning. This quantity is enough for three pounds of fish, weighed after being skinned and boned, and will serve six persons if it is the only solid dish for dinner, or ten if served in a course.

Another way to serve fish *au gratin* is to skin it, cut off the head, and take out the back-bone; and there are then two large pieces of fish. Season the fish, and prepare the sauce as before. Butter a tin sheet that will fit loosely into a large baking-pan. Lay the fish on this, and

THE
GREATEST MILLING CENTER OF THE WORLD.

IN 1825 the United States Government erected on what is now the very heart of the milling district of Minneapolis, a small grist mill. The country at that time was but little more than a wilderness, and the mill was built in order to furnish food for a body of soldiers located a short distance down the river. From this insignificant beginning has arisen the mighty milling business of Minneapolis.

Various flour mills were erected on the Falls of St. Anthony in 1856–58–59–60 and 63. In 1871 the invention of the purifier marked a new era in the development of the milling business in Minneapolis, and from that time up to the year 1878, the mills of this city continued to grow in size and to send their product to foreign countries, as well as home markets, where it attained the high rank which it has ever since held, the favorite flour of the world.

In May, 1878, occurred an explosion which totally destroyed a large number of the best mills and damaged nearly all of them which were located on the west side of the river.

From the date of this explosion begins the history of the present group of modern mills which stands upon the Falls of St. Anthony. Every improvement which has been developed in the line of mill machinery has been promptly placed in the mills of Minneapolis. Her output of flour now reaches the enormous sum of 36,000 bbls. per day, and the product of her mills are shipped all over the earth.

Minneapolis has actually manufactured 7,000,000 bbls. of flour per annum, of which she has exported the enormous sum of 2,683,000 bbls. Foremost among the representative mills of this City are those of the C. C. WASHBURN FLOURING MILLS, operated by the WASHBURN CROSBY COMPANY, with a combined actual capacity of 10,000 bbls. per day.

The founder of this firm was Governor C. C. Washburn, illustrious as one of the most remarkable men in the North-West: a soldier, a law-maker, a statesman and a philanthropist, but with all a miller who was while he lived the leader of the development of the modern milling, the father of the present method of making flour — a method which is regarded as the very best and most approved in existence.

He it was who experimented at great expense in new process milling, who sent representatives all over Europe to learn all that was known there of making flour on rolls instead of stones, and who finally embodied all his experiments, discoveries and ideas, in magnificent mills, which he erected and has left as a lasting monument of his memory.

The mills operated by WASHBURN CROSBY COMPANY are therefore the most notable mills in the United States. Their history is the narrative of the most brilliant achievements in the manufacture of flour. The group of mills known as the Washburn Plant stands to-day at the head of American enterprise in this line. They are never suffered to deteriorate. From them is produced the very finest quality of flour, and their product has achieved a world-wide popularity.

By means of the facilities which the WASHBURN CROSBY Co. has at hand, it obtains the choicest qualities of the famous wheat of the North-West, and is enabled to manufacture its flour so as to produce the finest qualities at a minimum expense.

The WASHBURN MILLS, established in 1866, have now been in operation for more than a quarter of a century. Their brands are known the world over.

moisten well with the sauce. Cover thickly with bread crumbs, and cook twenty-five minutes in a rather quick oven. Then slip on a hot dish, and serve with tomato, Tartare, or Hollandaise sauce poured around the fish.

Eels à la Tartare.

Cut the eels into pieces about four inches long. Cover them with boiling water, in which let them stand five minutes, and then drain them. Now dip in beaten egg, which has been well salted and peppered, then in bread or cracker crumbs. Fry in boiling fat for five minutes. Have Tartare sauce spread in the centre of a cold dish. Place the fried eels in a circle on this, garnish with parsley, and serve.

Stewed Eels.

Cut two eels in pieces about four inches long. Put three large table-spoonfuls of butter into the stewpan with half a small onion. As soon as the onion begins to turn yellow, stir in two table-spoonfuls of flour, and stir until brown. Add one pint of stock, if you have it; if not, use water. Season well with pepper and salt; then put in the eels and two bay leaves. Cover, and simmer gently three quarters of an hour. Heap the eels in the centre of a hot dish, strain the sauce over them and garnish with toasted bread and parsley. If you wish, add a table-spoonful of vinegar or lemon juice to the stew.

OYSTERS.

On the Half-Shell.

Not until just before serving should they be opened. Marketmen often furnish some one to do this. Six large oysters are usually allowed each person. Left in half the shell, they are placed on a dinner plate, with a thin slice of lemon in the centre of the dish.

On a Block of Ice.

Having a perfectly clear and solid block of ice, weighing ten or fifteen pounds, a cavity is to be made in the top of it in either of two ways. The first is to carefully chip with an ice pick; the other, to melt with heated bricks. If the latter be chosen, the ice must be put into a tub or large pan, and one of the bricks held upon the centre of it until there is a slight depression, yet sufficient for the brick to rest in. When the first brick is cold remove it, tip the block on one side, to let off the water, and then use another brick. Continue the operation till the cavity will hold as many oysters as are to be served. These should be kept an hour previous in a cool place; should be drained in a colander, and seasoned with salt, pepper, and vinegar. After laying two folded napkins on a large platter, to prevent the block from slipping, cover the dish with parsley, so that only the ice is visible. Stick a number of pinks, or of any small, bright flowers that do not wilt rapidly, into the parsley. Pour oysters into the space in the top of the ice, and garnish with thin slices of lemon.

This gives an elegant dish, and does away with the unsightly shells in which raw oysters are usually served. It is not expensive, for the common oysters do as well as those of good size. Indeed, as many ladies dislike the large ones, here is an excellent substitute for serving in the shell, particularly as the oysters require no seasoning when once on the table. A quart is enough for a party of ten; but a block of the size given will hold two quarts.

Roasted Oysters on Toast.

Eighteen large oysters, or thirty small ones, one teaspoonful of flour, one table-spoonful of butter, salt, pepper, three slices of toast. Have the toast buttered and on a hot dish. Put the butter in a small sauce-pan, and when hot add the dry flour. Stir until smooth, but not brown; then add the cream, and let it boil up once. Put the oysters (in their own liquor) into a hot oven, for three minutes; then add them to the cream. Season, and pour over the toast. Garnish the dish with thin slices of lemon, and serve very hot. It is nice for lunch or tea.

Oysters Panned in their own Liquor.

Eighteen large, or thirty small oysters, one table-spoonful of butter, one of cracker crumbs, salt and pepper to taste, one teaspoonful of lemon juice, a speck of cayenne. Put the oysters on in their own liquor, and when they boil up add seasoning, butter, and crumbs. Cook one minute, and serve on toast.

Oysters Panned in the Shell.

Wash the shells and wipe dry. Place them in a pan with the round shell down. Set in a hot oven for three minutes; then take out and remove the upper shell. Put two or three oysters into one of the round shells, season with pepper and salt, add butter, the size of two peas, and cover with cracker or bread crumbs. Return to the oven and brown.

Oyster Sauté.

Two dozen large, or three dozen small oysters, two table-spoonfuls of butter, four of fine cracker crumbs, salt, pepper. Let the oysters drain in the colander. Then season with salt and pepper and roll in the crumbs. Have the butter very hot in a frying-pan, and put in enough of the oysters to cover the bottom of the pan. Fry crisp and brown, being careful not to burn. Serve on hot, crisp toast.

Oysters Roasted in the Shell.

Wash the shells clean, and wipe dry. Place in a baking-pan, and put in a hot oven for about twenty minutes. Serve on hot dishes the moment they are taken from the oven. Though this is not an elegant dish, many people enjoy it, as the first and best flavor of the oysters is retained in this manner of cooking. The oysters can, instead, be opened into a hot dish and seasoned with butter, salt, pepper, and lemon juice. They should be served immediately.

Little Pigs in Blankets.

Season large oysters with salt and pepper. Cut fat English bacon in very thin slices, wrap an oyster in each slice, and fasten with a little wooden skewer (toothpicks are the best things). Heat a frying-pan and put in the "little pigs." Cook just long enough to crisp the bacon,—about two minutes. Place on slices of toast that have been cut into small pieces, and serve immediately. Do not remove the skewers. This is a nice relish for lunch or tea; and, garnished with parsley, is a pretty one. The pan must be very hot before the "pigs" are put in, and then great care must be taken that they do not burn.

Fricasseed Oysters.

One hundred oysters (about two quarts), four large table-spoonfuls of butter, one teaspoonful of chopped parsley, one table-spoonful of flour, a speck of cayenne, salt, yolks of three eggs. Brown two table-spoonfuls of the butter, and add to it the parsley, cayenne, and salt, and the oysters well drained. Mix together the flour and the remainder of the butter, and stir into the oysters when they begin to curl. Then add yolks, well beaten, and take immediately from the fire. Serve on a hot dish with a garnish of fried bread and parsley.

Creamed Oysters.

A pint of cream, one quart of oysters, a small piece of onion, a very small piece of mace, a table-spoonful of flour, and salt and pepper to taste. Let the cream, with the onion and mace, come to a boil. Mix flour with a little cold milk or cream, and stir into the boiling cream. Let the oysters come to a boil in their own liquor, and skim carefully. Drain off all the liquor, and turn the oysters into the cream. Skim out the mace and onions, and serve.

Croustade of Oysters.

Have a loaf of bread baked in a round two-quart basin. When two or three days old, with a sharp knife cut out the heart of the bread, being careful not to break the crust. Break up the crumbs very fine, and dry them slowly in an oven; then quickly fry three cupfuls of them in two table-spoonfuls of butter. As soon as they begin to look golden and are crisp, they are done. It takes about two minutes over a hot fire, stirring all the time. Put one quart of cream to boil, and when it boils, stir in three table-spoonfuls of flour, which has been mixed with half a cupful of cold milk. Cook eight minutes. Season well with salt and pepper. Put a layer of the sauce into the *croustade*, then a layer of oysters, which dredge well with salt and pepper; then another layer of sauce and one of fried crumbs. Continue this until the *croustade* is nearly full, having the last layer a thick one of crumbs. It takes three pints of oysters for this dish, and about three teaspoonfuls of salt and half a teaspoonful of pepper. Bake slowly half an hour. Serve with a garnish of parsley around the dish.

Escaloped Oysters.

Two quarts of oysters, half a cupful of butter, half a cupful of cream or milk, four teaspoonfuls of salt, half a teaspoonful of pepper, two quarts of stale bread crumbs, and spice, if you choose. Butter the escalop dishes, and put in a layer of crumbs and then one of oysters. Dredge with the salt and pepper, and put small pieces of butter here and there in the dish. Now have another layer of oysters, seasoning as before; then add the milk, and, finally, a thick layer of crumbs, which dot with butter. Bake twenty minutes in a rather quick oven. The crumbs must be light and flaky. The quantity given above is enough to fill two dishes.

Escaloped Oysters, No. 2.

Put a layer of rolled crackers in an oval dish, and then a layer of oysters, and lay on small pieces of butter. Dredge with salt and pepper, and moisten well with milk (or equal parts of milk and water). Add another layer of cracker and of oysters, and butter, dredge and moisten as before. Continue these alternate layers until the dish is nearly full; then cover with a thin layer of cracker and pieces of butter. If the dish be a large one, holding about two quarts, it will require an hour and a half or two hours to bake.

Oysters served in Escalop Shells.

The shells may be tin, granite ware, or silver-plated, or the natural oyster or escalop shells. The ingredients are: one quart of oysters, half a pint of cream or milk, one pint of bread crumbs, one table-spoonful of butter if cream is used, or three if milk, salt and pepper, a grating of nutmeg, and two table-spoonfuls of flour. Drain all the liquor from the oysters into a stewpan. Let it come to a boil, and skim; then add the cream or milk, with which the flour should first be mixed. Let this boil two minutes, and add the butter, salt, pepper, and nutmeg, and then the oysters. Take from the fire immediately. Taste to see if seasoned enough. Have the shells buttered, and sprinkled lightly with crumbs. Nearly fill them with the prepared oysters; then cover thickly with crumbs. Put the shells in a baking-pan, and bake fifteen minutes. Serve very hot, on a large platter, which garnish with parsley. The quantity given above will fill twelve common-sized shells.

Oyster Chartreuse.

One quart of oysters, one pint of cream, one small slice of onion, half a cupful of milk, whites of four eggs, two table-spoonfuls of butter, salt, pepper, two table-spoonfuls of flour, one cupful of fine, dry bread crumbs, six potatoes. Pare and boil the potatoes. Mash fine and light, and add the milk, salt, pepper, one spoonful of butter, and then the whites of the eggs, beaten to a stiff froth. Have a two-quart charlotte-russe mould well buttered, and sprinkle the bottom and sides with the bread crumbs (there must be butter enough to hold the crumbs). Line the mould with the potato, and let stand for a few minutes. Put the cream and onion on to boil. Mix the flour with a little cold milk or cream — about one fourth of a cupful — and stir into the boiling cream. Season well with salt and pepper, and cook eight minutes. Let the oysters come to a boil in their own liquor. Skim them, and drain off all the juice. Take the piece of onion from the sauce, and add the oysters. Taste to see if seasoned enough, and turn gently into the mould. Cover with the remainder of the potato, being careful not to put on too much at once, as in that case the sauce would be forced to the top. When covered, bake half an hour in a hot oven. Take from the oven ten minutes before dishing time, and let it stand on the table. Place a large platter over the mould and turn both dish and mould at the same time. Remove the mould very gently. Garnish the dish with parsley, and serve. A word of caution: every part of the mould must have a thick coating of the mashed potato, and when the covering of potato is put on, no opening must be left for sauce to escape.

To Pickle Oysters.

Two hundred large oysters, half a pint of vinegar, half a pint of white wine, four spoonfuls of salt, six spoonfuls of whole black pepper, and a little mace. Strain the liquor, and add the above-named ingredients. Let boil up once, and pour, while boiling hot, over the oysters. After these have stood ten minutes, pour off the liquor, which, as well as the oysters, should then be allowed to get cold. Put into a jar and cover tight. The oysters will keep some time.

LOBSTER.

Lobster, to be eatable, should be perfectly fresh. One of the tests of freshness is to draw back the tail, for if it springs into position again, it is safe to think the fish good. The time of boiling varies with the size of the lobster and in different localities. In Boston, Rockport, and other places on the Massachusetts coast, the time is fifteen or twenty minutes for large lobsters and ten for small. The usual way is to plunge them into boiling water enough to cover, and to continue boiling them until they are done. Some people advocate putting the lobsters into cold water, and letting this come to a boil gradually. They claim that the lobsters do not suffer so much. This may be so, but it seems as if death must instantly follow the plunge into boiling water. Cooking a lobster too long makes it tough and dry. When, on opening a lobster, you find the meat clinging to the shell, and very much shrunken, you may be sure the time of boiling was too long. There are very few modes of cooking lobster in which it should be more than thoroughly heated, as much cooking toughens it and destroys the fine, delicate flavor of the meat.

To Open a Lobster.

Separate the tail from the body, and shake out the tom-alley, and also the "coral," if there is any, upon a plate. Then, by drawing the body from the shell with the thumb, and pressing the part near the head against the shell with the first and second finger, you will free it from the stomach or "lady." Now split the lobster through the centre, and, with a fork, pick the meat from the joints. Cut the under side of the tail shell open and take out the meat without breaking. On the upper part of that end of this meat which joined the body is a small piece of flesh, which should be lifted; and a strip of meat attached to it should be turned back to the extreme end of the tail. This will uncover a little vein, running the entire length, which must be removed. Sometimes this vein is dark, and sometimes as light as the meat itself. It and the stomach are the only parts not eatable. The piece that covered the vein should be turned again into place. Hold the claws on edge on a thick board, and strike hard with a hammer until the shell cracks. Draw apart, and take out the meat. If you have the claws lying flat on the board when you strike, you not only break the shell, but mash the meat, and thus spoil a fine dish. Remember that the stomach of the lobster is found near the head, and is a small, hard sack containing poisonous matter; and that the intestinal vein is found in the tail. These should always be carefully removed. When lobster is opened in the manner explained, it may be arranged handsomely on a dish, and each person can season it at the table to suit himself.

Lobster Broiled in the Shell.

Divide the tail into two parts, cutting lengthwise. Break the large claws in two parts, and free the body from the small claws and stomach. Replace the body in the shell. Put the meat from the claws in half of the shells it came from, and put the other half of the shells where they will get hot. Put the lobster into the double broiler, and cook, with the meat side exposed to the fire, for eight minutes; then turn, and cook ten minutes longer. Place on a hot dish, and season slightly with salt and cayenne, and then well with maître d'hôtel butter. Cover the claws with the hot shells. Garnish the dish with parsley, and serve.

Broiled Lobster.

Split the meat of the tail and claws, and season well with salt and pepper. Cover with soft butter and dredge with flour. Place in the broiler, and cook over a bright fire until a delicate brown. Arrange on a hot dish, pour Bechamel sauce around, and serve.

Breaded Lobster.

Split the meat of the tail and claws, and season well with salt and pepper. Dip in beaten egg and then in bread crumbs, which let dry on the meat; and then repeat the operation. Place in a frying-basket, and plunge into boiling fat. Cook till a golden brown — about two minutes. Serve with Tartare sauce.

Stewed Lobster.

The meat of a two and a half pound lobster, cut into dice; two table-spoonfuls of butter, two of flour, one pint of stock or water, a speck of cayenne, salt and pepper to taste. Let the butter get hot, and add the dry flour. Stir until perfectly smooth, when add the water, gradually, stirring all the while. Season to taste. Add the lobster; heat thoroughly, and serve.

Curry of Lobster.

The meat of a lobster weighing between two and three pounds, one very small onion, three table-spoonfuls of butter, two of flour, a scant one of curry powder, a speck of cayenne, salt, a scant pint of water or stock. Let the butter get hot; and then add the onion, cut fine, and fry brown. When the onion is cooked add the flour and curry powder, and stir all together for two minutes. Add stock; cook two minutes, and strain. Add the meat of lobster, cut into dice, and simmer five minutes. Serve with a border of boiled rice around the dish.

Devilled Lobster in the Shell.

Two lobsters, each weighing about two and a half pounds; one pint of cream, two table-spoonfuls of butter, two of flour, one of mustard, a speck of cayenne, salt, pepper, a scant pint of bread crumbs. Open the lobster, and with a sharp knife cut the meat rather fine. Be careful, in opening, not to break the body or tail shells. Wash these shells and wipe dry; join them in the form of a boat, that they may hold the prepared meat. Put the cream on to boil. Mix the butter, flour, mustard, and pepper together, and add three spoonfuls of the boiling cream. Stir all into the remaining cream, and cook two minutes. Add the lobster, salt and pepper, and boil one minute. Fill the shells with the mixture, and place in a pan, with something to keep them in position (a few small stones answer very well). Cover with the bread crumbs, and brown for twenty minutes in a hot oven. Serve on a long, narrow dish; the body in the centre, the tails at either end. Garnish with parsley. If for a large company, it would be best to have a broad dish, and have four lobsters, instead of two. This is a very handsome dish, and is really not hard to cook. There is always a little more of the prepared lobster than will go into the shells without crowding, and this is nice warmed and served on slices of crisp toast.

Escaloped Lobster.

Prepare the lobster as for devilling, omitting, however, the mustard. Turn into a buttered escalop dish, and cover thickly with crumbs. Brown in a hot oven, and serve.

White stock may be used instead of the cream. Many people, who cannot eat lobster when prepared with cream or milk, find it palatable when prepared with stock or water.

Lobster Cutlets.

A lobster weighing between two and a half and three pounds, three table-spoonfuls of butter, half a cupful of stock or cream, one heaping table-spoonful of flour, a speck of cayenne, salt, two eggs, about a pint of bread crumbs, twelve sprigs of parsley. Cut the meat of the lobster into fine dice, and season with salt and pepper. Put the butter on heat. Add the flour, and when smooth, add the stock and one well beaten egg. Season. Boil up once, add the lobster, and take from the fire immediately. Now add a table-spoonful of lemon juice. Butter a platter, and pour the mixture upon it, to the thickness of about an inch. Make perfectly smooth with a knife, and set away to cool. When cool, cut into chops, to resemble cutlets. Dip in beaten egg and then in bread crumbs, being sure to have every part covered. Place in the frying-basket and plunge into boiling fat. Cook till a rich brown. It will take about two minutes. Drain for a moment in the basket; then arrange on a hot dish, and put part of a small claw in each one, to represent the bone in a cutlet. Put the parsley in the basket, and plunge for a moment into the boiling fat. Garnish with this, or pour a white or Bechamel sauce around the dish, and garnish with fresh parsley. The quantity given will make six or seven cutlets.

Canned Lobster.

Canned lobster can be used for cutlets, stews, curries, and patties, can be escaloped, or served on toast.

OTHER SHELL-FISH.

Stewed Terrapins.

Put them into boiling water, and boil rapidly for ten or fifteen minutes, or until the nails will come out and the black skin rub off, — the time depending upon the size of the fish. After this, put into fresh boiling water, and boil until the under shell cracks, which will be about three quarters of an hour. Remove the under shell, throw away the sand and gall bags, take out intestines, and put the terrapins to boil again in the same water for an hour. Pick liver and meat from upper shell. Cut the intestines in small pieces, and add to this meat. Pour over all a quantity of the liquor in which the intestines were boiled, sufficient to make very moist. Put away until the next day. For each terrapin, if of good size, a gill of cream and of wine, half a cupful of butter, yolks of two hard-boiled eggs, rubbed smooth, salt, pepper, and cayenne are needed. Pour over the terrapin, let it come to a boil, and serve. — [Mrs. Furness, of Philadelphia.

Soft-Shell Crabs.

Lift the shell at both sides and remove the spongy substance found on the back. Then pull off the "apron," which will be found on the under side, and to which is attached a substance like that removed from the back. Now wipe the crabs, and dip them in beaten egg, and then in fine bread or cracker crumbs. Fry in boiling fat from eight to ten minutes, the time depending upon the size of the crabs. Serve with Tartare sauce. Or, the egg and bread crumbs may be omitted. Season with salt and cayenne, and fry as before.

When broiled, crabs are cleaned, and seasoned with salt and cayenne; are then dropped into boiling water for one minute, taken up, and broiled over a hot fire for eight minutes. They are served with *maître d'hôtel* butter or Tartare sauce.

MEATS.

BOILING.

All pieces, unless very salt, should be plunged into boiling water, and boiled rapidly for fifteen minutes, to harden the albumen that is on the outside, and thus keep in the juices. The kettle should then be put back where it will just simmer, for meat that is boiled rapidly becomes hard and stringy, while that which is kept just at the boiling point (where the water hardly bubbles) will cut tender and juicy, provided there is any juiciness in it at the beginning. White meats, like mutton and poultry, are improved in appearance by having rice boiled with them; or, a still better way is to thickly flour a piece of coarse cotton cloth, pin the meat in it, and place in the boiling water. Meat cooked in this way will be extremely juicy.

Leg of Mutton.

Cook, as directed, in boiling water to cover. A leg that weighs eight or nine pounds will cook in one hour and a quarter if it is wanted done rare. Allow five minutes for every additional pound. Save the water for soups.

Lamb.

Cook the same as mutton. Serve with drawn butter.

Boiled Ham.

Wash the ham very clean, and put on with cold water to cover. Simmer gently five hours, and set the kettle aside for one or two hours. When nearly cold, take out the ham and draw off the skin. Cover with cracker crumbs and about three table-spoonfuls of sugar. Place in the oven, in a baking-pan, for thirty or forty minutes. Many people stick cloves into the fat part of the ham, and use only a few crumbs. The time given is for a ham weighing about twelve pounds; every pound over that will require fifteen minutes more. The fish kettle comes next to a regular ham kettle, and answers quite as well as both. If you have neither kettle, and no pot large enough to hold all the meat, cut off the knuckle, which will cook in about two hours. But this rather hurts the flavor and appearance of the dish.

Salt Tongue.

Soak over night, and cook from five to six hours. Throw into cold water and peel off the skin.

Fresh Tongue.

Put into boiling water to cover, with two table-spoonfuls of salt. Cook from five to six hours. Skin the same as salt tongue.

Corned Beef.

Wash, and put into cold water, if very salt; but such a piece as one finds in town and city shops, and which the butchers corn themselves, put into boiling water. Cook very slowly for six hours. This time is for a piece weighing eight or ten pounds. When it is to be served cold, let it stand for one or two hours in the water in which it was boiled. If the beef is to be pressed, get either a piece of the brisket, flank, or rattleran. Take out the bones, place in a flat dish or platter, put a tin sheet on top, and lay on it two or three bricks. If you have a corned beef press, use that, of course.

ROASTING.

There are two modes of roasting: one is to use a tin kitchen before an open fire, and the other and more common way is to use a very hot oven. The former gives the more delicious flavor, but the second is not by any means a poor way, if the meat is put on a rack, and basted constantly when in the oven. A large piece is best for roasting, this being especially true of beef. When meat is cooked in a tin kitchen it requires more time, because the heat is not equally distributed, as it is in the oven.

To prepare for roasting. Wipe the meat with a wet towel. Dredge on all sides with salt, pepper, and flour; and if the kitchen is used, dredge the flour into that. Run the spit through the centre of the meat, and place very near the fire at first, turning as it browns. When the flour in the kitchen is browned, add a pint of hot water, and baste frequently with it, dredging with salt and flour after each basting. Roast a piece of beef weighing eight pounds fifty minutes, if to be rare, but if to be medium, roast one hour and a quarter, and ten minutes for each additional pound.

Roasting in the Oven.

Prepare the meat as before. Have a rack that will fit loosely into the baking-pan. Cover the bottom of the pan rather lightly with flour, put in rack, and then meat. Place in a very hot oven for a few minutes, to brown the flour in the pan, and then add hot water enough to cover the bottom of the pan. Close the oven, and in about ten minutes open and baste the meat with the gravy. Dredge with salt, pepper, and flour. Do this every fifteen minutes; and as soon as one side of the meat is brown, turn, and brown the other. Make gravy as before. Allow a quarter of an hour less in the oven than in the tin kitchen. The heat for roasting must be very great at first, to harden the albumen, and thus keep in the juices. After the meat is crusted over it is not necessary to keep up so great a heat, but for rare meats the heat must, of course, be greater than for those that are to be well done. The kitchen can be drawn back a little distance from the fire and the drafts closed. Putting salt on fresh meat draws out the juices, but by using flour a paste is formed, which keeps in all the juices and also enriches and browns the piece. *Never* roast meat without having a rack in the pan. If meat is put into the water in the pan it becomes soggy and looses its flavor. A meat-rack costs not more than thirty or forty cents, and the improvement in the looks and flavor of a piece of meat is enough to pay for it in one roasting.

The time given for roasting a piece of beef is for rib roasts and sirloin. The same weight in the face or the back of the rump will require twenty minutes longer, as the meat on these cuts is in a very compact form.

If a saddle or loin of mutton is to be roasted, cook the same time as beef if the weight is the same; but if a leg is to be roasted, one hour and a quarter is the time. Lamb should be cooked an hour and a half; veal, two hours and three quarters; pork three hours and a quarter. Ten minutes before dishing the dinner turn the gravy into a saucepan, skim off all the fat, and set on the stove. Let it come to a boil; then stir in one table-spoonful of flour, mixed with half a cupful of cold water. Season with salt and pepper, and cook two minutes. Serve the meat on a hot dish and the gravy in a hot tureen.

Rolled Rib Roast.

Either have the butcher remove the bones, or do it yourself by slipping a sharp knife between the flesh and bones, — a simple matter with almost any kind of meat. Roll up the piece and tie with strong twine. Treat the same as plain roast beef, giving the same time as if it were a piece of rump (one hour and a half for eight pounds), as the form it is now in does not readily admit the heat to all parts. This piece of beef can be larded before roasting, or it can be larded and braised. Serve with tomato or horseradish sauce.

Roast Beef, with Yorkshire Pudding.

A rib or sirloin roast should be prepared as directed for roasting. When within three quarters of an hour of being done, have the pudding made. Butter a pan like that in which the meat is being cooked, and pour in the batter. Put the rack *across* the pan, not *in* it. Place the meat on the rack, return to the oven, and cook forty-five minutes. If you have only one pan, take up the meat, pour off the gravy and put in the pudding. Cut in squares, and garnish the beef with these. Another method is to have a pan that has squares stamped in it. This gives even squares and crust on all the edges, which baking in the flat pan does not. When the meat is roasted in the tin-kitchen, let the pudding bake in the oven for half an hour, and then place it under the meat to catch the drippings.

For the Yorkshire pudding, one pint of milk, two thirds of a cupful of flour, three eggs, and one scant teaspoonful of salt will be needed. Beat the eggs very light. Add salt and milk, and then pour about half a cupful of the mixture upon the flour; and when perfectly smooth, add the remainder. This makes a small pudding, — about enough for six persons. Serve it hot.

Fillet of Veal, Roasted.

About eight or ten pounds of the fillet, ham force-meat (see rule for force-meat), half a cupful of butter, half a teaspoonful of pepper, two table-spoonfuls of salt, two lemons, half a pound of salt pork. Rub the salt and pepper into the veal; then fill the cavity, from which the bone was taken, with the force-meat. Skewer and tie the fillet into a round shape. Cut the pork in thin slices, and put half of these on a tin sheet that will fit into the dripping-pan; place this in the pan, and the fillet on it. Cover the veal with the remainder of the pork. Put hot water enough in the pan to just cover the bottom, and place in the oven. Bake slowly for four hours, basting frequently with the gravy in the pan, and with salt, pepper, and flour. As the water in the pan cooks away, it must be renewed, remembering to have only enough to keep the meat and pan from burning. After it has been cooking three hours, take the pork from the top of the fillet, spread the top thickly with butter, and dredge with flour. Repeat this after thirty minutes, and then brown handsomely. Put the remainder of the butter, which should be about three table-spoonfuls, in a saucepan, and, when hot, add two heaping table-spoonfuls of flour, and stir until dark brown. Add to it half a pint of stock or water; stir a minute, and set back where it will keep warm, but not cook. Now take up the fillet, and skim all the fat off of the gravy; add water enough to make half a pint of gravy, also the sauce just made. Let this boil up, and add the juice of half a lemon, and more salt and pepper if needed. Strain, and pour around the fillet. Garnish the dish with potato puffs and slices of lemon.

Roast Ham.

Prepare the ham as for boiling, and if it is of good size (say ten pounds), boil three hours. Remove the skin, and put the ham in a baking-pan. Let it cook two hours in a moderate oven. Serve with champagne sauce.

BROILING.

THE fire for broiling must be clear, and for meats it must be hotter and brighter than for fish. Coals from hard wood or charcoal are best, but in all large towns and cities hard coal is nearly always used, except in hotels and restaurants, where there is usually a special place for broiling with charcoal. The double broiler is the very best thing in the market for broiling meats and fish. When the meat is placed in it, and the slide is slipped over the handles, all there is to do is to hold the broiler over the fire, or, if you have an open range, before the fire. A fork or knife need not go near the meat until it is on the dish. A great amount of the juice is saved. With the old-fashioned gridirons it is absolutely necessary to stick a fork into the meat to turn it, and although there are little grooves for the gravy to run into, what is saved in this way does not compare with what is actually kept within the meat where the double broiler is used. Professional cooks can turn a steak without running a fork into the meat, but not one in a hundred common cooks can do it.

Mutton Chops.

Sprinkle the chops with salt, pepper, and flour. Put them in the double broiler. Broil over or before the fire for eight minutes. Serve on a *hot* dish with butter, salt, and pepper for tomato sauce. The fire for chops should not be as hot as for steak. Chops can be seasoned with salt and pepper, wrapped in buttered paper, and broiled ten minutes over a hot fire.

Beef Steak.

Have it cut thick. It will never be good, rich, and juicy if only from one fourth to one half an inch thick. It ought to be at least three quarters of an inch thick. Trim off any suet that may be left on it, and dredge with salt, pepper, and flour. Cook in the double broiler, over or before clear coals, for ten minutes, if to be rare; twelve, if to be rather well done. Turn the meat constantly. Serve on a hot dish with butter and salt, or with mushroom sauce, *maître d'hôtel* butter, or tomato sauce. Do not stick a knife or fork into the meat to try it. This is the way many people spoil it. Pounding is another bad habit: much of the juice of the meat is lost. When, as it sometimes happens, there is no convenience for broiling, heat the frying-pan very hot, then sprinkle with salt, and lay in the steak. Turn frequently.

MISCELLANEOUS MODES.
Braised Beef.

TAKE six or eight pounds of the round or the face of the rump, and lard with quarter of a pound of salt pork. Put six slices of pork in the bottom of the braising-pan, and as soon as it begins to fry, add two onions, half a small carrot, and half a small turnip, all cut fine. Cook these until they begin to brown; then draw them to one side of the pan and put in the beef, which has been well dredged with salt, pepper, and flour. Brown on all sides, and then add one quart of boiling water and a bouquet of sweet herbs; cover, and cook *slowly* in the oven for four hours, basting every twenty minutes. Take up, and finish the gravy as for braised tongue. Or, add to the gravy half a can of tomatoes, and cook for ten minutes. Strain, pour around the beef, and serve.

Fricandeau of Veal.

Have a piece of veal, weighing about eight pounds, cut from that part of the leg called the cushion. Wet the vegetable masher, and beat the veal smooth; then lard one side thickly. Put eight slices of pork in the bottom of the braising-pan; place the veal on this, larded side up. Add two small onions, half a small turnip, two slices of carrot, one clove, and a bouquet of sweet herbs, — these to be at the sides of the meat, not on top, — and one quart of white stock or water. Dredge with salt, pepper, and flour. Cover, and place in a rather moderate oven. Cook three hours, basting every fifteen minutes. If cooked rapidly the meat will be dry and stringy, but if slowly, it will be tender and juicy. When done, lift carefully from the pan. Melt four table-spoonfuls of glaze, and spread on the meat with a brush. Place in the open oven for five minutes. Add one cupful of hot water to the contents of the braising-pan. Skim off all the fat, and then add one heaping teaspoonful of corn starch, which has been mixed with a little cold water. Let it boil one minute; then strain, and return to the fire. Add two table-spoonfuls of glaze, and when this is melted pour the sauce around the fricandeau, and serve. Potato balls, boiled for twelve minutes in stock, and then slightly browned in the oven, make a pretty garnish for this dish. It is also served on a bed of finely chopped spinach or mashed potatoes.

Leg of Lamb à la Française.

Put a leg of lamb, weighing about eight pounds, in as small a kettle as will hold it. Put in a muslin bag one onion, one small white turnip, a few green celery leaves, three sprigs each of sweet marjoram and summer savory, four cloves, and twelve allspice. Tie the bag and place it in the kettle with the lamb; then pour on two quarts of boiling water. Let this come to a boil, and then skim carefully. Now add four heaping table-spoonfuls of flour, which has been mixed with one cupful of cold water, two table-spoonfuls of salt, and a speck of cayenne. Cover tight, and set back where it will just simmer for four hours. In the mean time make a pint and a half of veal or mutton force-meat, which make into little balls and fry brown. Boil six eggs hard. At the end of four hours take up the lamb. Skim all the fat off of the gravy, and take out the bag of seasoning. Now put the kettle where the contents will boil rapidly for ten minutes. Put three table-spoonfuls of butter in the frying-pan, and when hot stir in two of flour; cook until a dark brown, but not burned, and stir into the gravy. Taste to see if seasoned enough. Have the whites and yolks of the hard-boiled eggs chopped separately. Pour the gravy over the lamb; then garnish with the chopped eggs, making a hill of the whites, and capping it with part of the yolks. Sprinkle the remainder of the yolks over the lamb. Place the meat balls in groups around the dish. Garnish with parsley, and serve.

Braised Breast of Lamb.

With a sharp knife, remove the bones from a breast of lamb; then season it well with salt and pepper, and roll up and tie firmly with twine. Put two table-spoonfuls of butter in the braising-pan, and, when melted, add one onion, one slice of carrot, and one of turnip, all cut fine. Stir for five minutes, and then put in the lamb, with a thick dredging of flour. Cover, and set back where it will not cook rapidly, for half an hour; then add one quart of stock or boiling water, and place in the oven, where it will cook *slowly*, for one hour. Baste often. Take up the meat, skim all the fat off of the gravy, and then put it where it will boil rapidly for five minutes. Take the string from the meat. Strain the gravy, and pour over the dish. Serve very hot. Or serve with tomato or Bechamel sauce. The bones should be put in the pan with the meat, to improve the gravy.

Beef Stew.

Two pounds of beef, the round, flank, or any cheap part (if there is bone in it, two and a half pounds will be required), one onion, two slices of carrot, two of turnip, two potatoes, three table-spoonfuls of flour, salt, pepper, and a generous quart of water. Cut all the fat from the meat, and put it in a stewpan; fry gently for ten or fifteen minutes. In the mean time cut the meat in small pieces, and season well with salt and pepper, and then sprinkle over it two table-spoonfuls of flour. Cut the vegetables in very small pieces, and put in the pot with the fat. Fry them five minutes, stirring well, to prevent burning. Now put in the meat, and move it about in the pot until it begins to brown; then add the quart of boiling water. Cover; let it boil up once, skim, and set back, where it will just bubble, for two and a half hours. Add the potatoes, cut in thin slices, and one table-spoonful of flour, which mix smooth with half a cupful of cold water, pouring about one third of the water on the flour at first, and adding the rest when perfectly smooth. Taste to see if the stew is seasoned enough, and if it is not, add more salt and pepper. Let the stew come to a boil again, and cook ten minutes; then add dumplings. Cover tightly, and boil rapidly ten minutes longer.

Mutton, lamb, or veal can be cooked in this manner. When veal is used, fry out two slices of pork, as there will not be much fat on the meat. Lamb and mutton must have some of the fat put aside, as there is so much on these meats that they are otherwise very gross.

Irish Stew.

About two pounds of the neck of mutton, four onions, six large potatoes, salt, pepper, three pints of water, and two table-spoonfuls of flour. Cut the mutton in handsome pieces. Put about half the fat in the stewpan, with the onions, and stir for eight or ten minutes over a hot fire; then put in the meat, which sprinkle with the flour, salt and pepper. Stir ten minutes, and add the water, boiling. Set for one hour where it will simmer; then add the potatoes, peeled, and cut in quarters. Simmer an hour longer, and serve. You can cook dumplings with this dish, if you choose. They are a great addition to all kinds of stews and ragouts.

Toad in the Hole.

This is an English dish, and a good one, despite the unpleasant name. One pound of round steak, one pint of milk, one cupful of flour, one egg, and salt and pepper. Cut the steak into dice. Beat the egg very light; add milk to it, and then half a teaspoonful of salt. Pour upon the flour, gradually, beating very light and smooth. Butter a two-quart dish, and in it put the meat. Season well, and pour over it the batter. Bake an hour in a moderate oven. Serve hot. This dish can be made with mutton and lamb in place of steak.

Scotch Roll.

Remove the tough skin from about five pounds of the flank of beef. A portion of the meat will be found thicker than the rest. With a sharp knife, cut a thin layer from the thick part, and lay upon the thin. Mix together three table-spoonfuls of salt, one of sugar, half a teaspoonful of pepper, one eighth of a teaspoonful of clove, and one teaspoonful of summer savory. Sprinkle this over the meat, and then sprinkle with three table-spoonfuls of vinegar. Roll up, and tie with twine. Put away in a cold place for twelve hours. When it has stood this time, place in a stewpan, with boiling water to cover, and simmer gently for three hours and a half. Mix four heaping table-spoonfuls of flour with half a cupful of cold water, and stir into the gravy. Season to taste with salt and pepper. Simmer half an hour longer. This dish is good hot or cold.

POULTRY AND GAME.

To Clean and Truss Poultry.

First singe, by holding the bird over a blazing paper. It is best to do this over the open stove, when all the particles of burnt paper will fall into the fire. Next open the vent and draw out the internal organs, if this has not been done at the butcher's. Be careful not to break the gall bladder. Wash quickly in one water. If there are large black pin-feathers, take out what you can with the point of a knife (it is impossible to get out all). Cut the oil bag from the tail. Be sure that you have taken out every part of the windpipe, the lights, and crop. Turn the skin back, and cut the neck quite short. Fill the crop with dressing, and put some in the body also. With a short skewer, fasten the legs together at the joint where the feet were cut off. [Be careful, in cutting off the feet of game or poultry, to cut in the joint. If you cut above, the ligaments that hold the flesh and bones together will be severed, and, in cooking, the meat will shrink, leaving a bare, unsightly bone. Besides, you will have nothing to hold the skewer if the ligaments are cut off.] Run the skewer into the bone of the tail, and tie firmly with a long piece of twine. Now take a longer skewer, and run through the two wings, fastening them firmly to the sides of the bird. With another short skewer, fasten the skin of the neck on to the back-bone. Place the bird on its breast, and draw the strings, with which the legs were tied, around the skewers in the wings and neck; pass them across the back three times, and tie very tightly. By following these directions, you will have the bird in good shape, and all the strings on the back, so that you will avoid breaking the handsome crust that always forms on properly basted and roasted poultry. When cooked, first cut the strings, then draw out the skewers. The fat that comes from the vent and the gizzard of chickens should be tried out immediately, and put away for shortening and frying. That of geese, turkeys, and ducks is of too strong a flavor to be nice in cookery.

To clean the giblets: Cut the gall bag from the lobe of the liver, cutting a little of the liver with it, so as not to cut into the bag. Press the heart between the finger and thumb, to extract all the blood. With a sharp knife, cut lightly around the gizzard, and draw off the outer coat, leaving the lining coat whole. If you cannot do that (and it does require practice), cut in two, and, after removing the filling, take out the lining. When the poultry is to be boiled, and is stuffed, the vent must be sewed with mending cotton or soft twine. Unless the bird is full of dressing, this will not be necessary in roasting.

Fowl and Pork.

Clean and truss, pin in the floured cloth, and put into water in which one pound of rather lean pork has been boiling three hours. The time of cooking depends upon the age of the fowl. If they are not more than a year old an hour and a half will be enough, but if very old they may need three hours. The quantity of pork given is for only a pair of fowl, and more must be used if a large number of birds be cooked. Serve with egg sauce. The liquor should be saved for soups.

Boiled Fowl with Macaroni.

Break twelve sticks of macaroni in pieces about two inches long; throw them into one quart of boiling water, add a table-spoonful of salt and half a table-spoonful of pepper. Boil rapidly for twelve minutes; then take up, and drain off all the water. Season with one table-spoonful of butter and one teaspoonful of salt. After the fowl have been singed and cleaned, stuff with the macaroni. Truss them, and then pin in a floured cloth and plunge into enough boiling water to cover them. Boil rapidly for fifteen minutes; then set back where they will just simmer for from one and a half to two and a half hours. The time of cooking depends upon the age of the birds. Serve with an egg or Bechamel sauce. The quantity of macaroni given is for two fowl. Plain boiled macaroni should be served with this dish.

Boiled Turkey with Celery.

Chop half a head of celery very fine. Mix with it one quart of bread crumbs, two scant table-spoonfuls of salt, half a teaspoonful of pepper, two heaping table-spoonfuls of butter, and two eggs. Stuff the turkey with this; sew up and truss. Wring a large square of white cotten cloth out of cold water, and dredge it thickly with flour. Pin the turkey in this, and plunge into boiling water. Let it boil rapidly for fifteen minutes; then set back where it will simmer. Allow three hours for a turkey weighing nine pounds, and twelve minutes for every additional pound. Serve with celery sauce. The stuffing may be made the same as above, only substitute oysters for celery, and serve with oyster sauce.

Boiled Turkey.

Clean and truss the same as for roasting. Rub into it two spoonfuls of salt, and put into boiling water to cover. Simmer gently three hours, if it weighs nine or ten pounds, and is tender. If old and tough it will take longer. Serve with oyster, celery, or egg sauce. Pour some of the sauce over the turkey, and serve the rest in a gravy boat.

Roast Turkey.

Proceed the same with a turkey as with a chicken, allowing one hour and three quarters for a turkey weighing eight pounds, and ten minutes for every additional pound.

Roast Turkey with Chestnut Stuffing and Sauce.

Clean the turkey and lard the breast. Throw fifty large chestnuts into boiling water for a few minutes; then take them up, and rub off the thin, dark skin. Cover them with boiling water, and simmer for one hour; take them up, and mash fine. Chop one pound of veal and half a pound of salt pork very fine. Add half of the chestnuts to this, and add, also, half a teaspoonful of pepper, two table-spoonfuls of salt, and one cupful of stock or water. Stuff the turkey with this. Truss and roast as already directed. Serve with a chestnut sauce. The remaining half of the chestnuts are for this sauce.

Boned Turkey.

Get a turkey that has not been frozen (freezing makes it tear easily). See that every part is whole; one with a little break in the skin will not do. Cut off the legs, in the joints, and the tips of the wings. Do not draw the bird. Place it on its breast, and with a small, sharp boning knife, cut in a straight line through to the bone, from the neck down to that part of the bird where there is but little flesh, where it is all skin and fat. Begin at the neck, and run the knife between the flesh and the bones until you come to the wing. Then cut the ligaments that hold the bones together and the tendons that hold the flesh to the bones. With the thumb and forefinger, *press* the flesh from the smooth bone. When you come to the joint, carefully separate the ligaments and remove the bone. Do not try to take the bone from the next joint, as that is not in the way when carving, and it gives a more natural shape to the bird. Now begin at the wish-bone, and when that is free from the flesh, run the knife between the sides and the flesh, always using the fingers to press the meat from the smooth bones, as, for instance, the breast-bone and lower part of the sides. Work around the legs the same as you did around the wings, always using great care at the joints not to cut the skin. Drawing out the leg-bones turns that part of the bird inside out. Turn the bird over, and proceed in the same manner with the other side. When all is detached, carefully draw the skin from the breast-bone; then run the knife between the fat and bone at the rump, leaving the small bone in the extreme end, as it holds the skewers. Carefully remove the flesh from the skeleton, and turn it right side out again. Rub into it two table-spoonfuls of salt and a little pepper, and fill with dressing. Sew up the back and neck, and then the vent. Truss the same as if not boned. Take a strong piece of cotton cloth and pin the bird firmly in it, drawing very tight at the legs, as this is the broadest place, and the shape will not be good unless this precaution be taken. Steam three hours, and then place on a buttered tin sheet, which put in a baking-pan. Baste well with butter, pepper, salt, and flour. Roast one hour, basting every ten minutes, and twice with stock. When cold, remove the skewers and strings, and garnish with aspic jelly, cooked beets, and parsley. To carve: first cut off the wings, then about two thick slices from the neck, where it will be quite fat, and then cut in thin slices. Serve jelly with each plate.

Filling for a turkey weighing eight pounds: The flesh of one chicken weighing four pounds, one pound of clear veal, half a pound of clear salt pork, one small cupful of cracker crumbs, two eggs, one cupful of broth, two and a half table-spoonfuls of salt, half a teaspoonful of pepper, one teaspoonful of summer savory, one of sweet marjoram, one of thyme, half a spoonful of sage, and, if you like, one table-spoonful of capers, one quart of oysters, and two table-spoonfuls of onion juice. Have the meat uncooked and free from any tough pieces. Chop *very* fine. Add seasoning, crackers, etc., mix thoroughly, and use. If oysters are used, half a pound of the veal must be omitted. Where one cannot eat veal, use chicken instead. Veal is recommended for its cheapness. Why people choose boned turkey, instead of a plain roast turkey or chicken, is not plain, for the flavor is not so good; but at the times and places where boned birds are used, it is a very appropriate dish. That is, at suppers, lunches, and parties, where the guests are served standing, it is impracticable to provide anything that cannot be broken with a fork or spoon;

therefore, the advantage of a boned turkey, chicken, or bird is apparent. One turkey weighing eight pounds before being boned will serve thirty persons at a party, if there are, also, say oysters, rolls, coffee, ices, cake, and cream. If the supper is very elaborate, the turkey will answer for one of the dishes for a hundred or more persons. If nothing more were gained in the boning of a bird, the knowledge of the anatomy, and the help this will give in carving, pay to bone two or three chickens. It is advisable to bone at least two fowls before trying a turkey, for if you spoil them there is nothing lost, as they make a stew or soup.

Aspic jelly: One and a half pints of clear stock,—beef if for amber jelly, and chicken or veal if for white; half a box of gelatine, the white of one egg, half a cupful of cold water, two cloves, one large slice of onion, twelve pepper-corns, one stalk of celery, salt. Soak gelatine two hours in the cold water. Then put on with other ingredients, the white of the egg being beaten with one spoonful of the cold stock. Let come to a boil, and set back where it will just simmer for twenty minutes. Strain through a napkin, turn into a mould or shallow dish, and put away to harden. The jelly can be made with the bones of the turkey and chicken, by washing them, covering with cold water, and boiling down to about three pints; by then straining and setting away to cool, and in the morning skimming off all the fat and turning off the clear stock. The bones may, instead, be used for a soup.

Roast Goose.

Stuff the goose with a potato dressing made in the following manner: Six potatoes, boiled, pared, and mashed fine and light; one table-spoonful of salt, one teaspoonful of pepper, one spoonful of sage, two table-spoonfuls of onion juice, two of butter. Truss, and dredge well with salt, pepper, and flour. Roast before the fire (if weighing eight pounds) one hour and a half; in the oven, one hour and a quarter. Make gravy the same as for turkey. No butter is required for goose, it is so fat. Serve with apple sauce. Many people boil the goose half an hour before roasting, to take away the strong flavor. Why not have something else if you do not like the real flavor of the goose?

Roast Duck.

Ducks, to be good, must be cooked rare: for this reason it is best not to stuff. If, however, you do stuff them, use the goose dressing, and have it very hot. The better way is to cut an onion in two, and put into the body of the bird; then truss, and dredge with salt, pepper, and flour, and roast, if before the fire, forty minutes, and if in the oven, thirty minutes. The fire must be very hot if the duck be roasted in the kitchen, and if in the oven, this must be a quick one. Serve with currant jelly and a sauce made the same as for turkey.

Roast Chicken.

Clean the chicken, and stuff the breast and part of the body with dressing made as follows: For a pair of chickens weighing between seven and eight pounds, take one quart of stale bread (being sure not to have any hard pieces) and break up in very fine crumbs. Add a table-spoonful of salt, a scant teaspoonful of pepper, a teaspoonful of chopped parsley, half a teaspoonful of powdered sage, one of summer savory, and a scant half-cupful of butter. Mix well together. This gives a rich dressing that will separate like rice when served. Now truss the chickens, and dredge well with salt. Take soft butter in the hand, and rub thickly over the chicken; then dredge rather thickly with flour. Place on the side, on the meat rack, and put into a hot oven for a few moments, that the flour in the bottom of the pan may brown. When it is browned, put in water enough to cover the pan. Baste every fifteen minutes with the gravy in the pan, and dredge with salt, pepper, and flour. When one side is browned, turn, and brown the other. The last position in which the chicken should bake is on its back, that the breast may be nicely frothed and browned. The last basting is on the breast, and should be done with soft butter, and the breast should be dredged with flour. Putting the butter on the chicken at first, and then covering with flour, makes a paste, which keeps the juices in the chicken, and also supplies a certain amount of rich basting that is absorbed into the meat. It really does not take as much butter to baste poultry or game in this manner as by the old method of putting it on with a spoon after the bird began to cook. The water in the pan must often be renewed; and always be careful not to get in too much at a time. It will take an hour and a quarter to cook a pair of chickens, each weighing between three and a half and four pounds; anything larger, an hour and a half. A sure sign that they are done is the readiness of joints to separate from the body. If the chickens are roasted in the tin-kitchen, before the fire, it will take a quarter of an hour longer than in the oven.

Gravy for chickens: Wash the hearts, livers, gizzards, and necks, and put on to boil in three pints of water; boil down to one pint. Take them all up. Put the liver on a plate, and mash fine with the back of the spoon; return it to the water in which it was boiled. Mix two table-spoonfuls of flour with half a cupful of cold water. Stir into the gravy, season well with salt and pepper, and set back where it will simmer, for twenty minutes. Take up the chickens, and take the meat rack out of the pan. Then tip the pan to one side, to bring all the gravy together. Skim off the fat. Place the pan on top of the stove and turn into it one cupful of water. Let this boil up, in the mean time scraping everything from the sides and bottom of the pan. Turn this into the made gravy, and let it all boil together while you are removing the skewers and strings from the chickens.

Chicken à la Matelote.

Cut up an uncooked chicken. Rub in butter and flour, and brown in an oven. Fry in four table-spoonfuls of chicken fat, or butter, for about twenty minutes, a small carrot, onion, and parsnip, all cut into dice. When the chicken is browned, put it in a stewpan with the cooked vegetables and one quart of white stock. Then into the fat in which the vegetables were fried put two table-spoonfuls of flour, and cook until brown. Stir this in with the chicken. Add the liver, mashed fine, one table-spoonful of capers, and salt and pepper to taste. Cook very gently three quarters of an hour; then add one fourth of a pound of mushrooms, cut in small pieces. Cook fifteen minutes longer. Serve with a border of boiled macaroni, mashed potatoes, or rice.

Chicken à la Reine.

Clean, stuff, and truss a pair of chickens, as for roasting. Dredge well with salt, pepper, and flour. Cut a quarter of a pound of pork in slices, and put part on the bottom of a deep stewpan with two slices of carrot and one large onion, cut fine. Stir over the fire until they begin to color; then put in the chickens, and lay the remainder of the pork over them. Place the stewpan in a hot oven for twenty minutes; then add white stock to half cover the chicken (about two quarts), and a bouquet of sweet herbs. Dredge well with flour. Cover the pan and return to the oven. Baste about every fifteen minutes, and after cooking one hour, turn over the chickens. Cook, in all, two hours. Serve with Hollandaise sauce or with the sauce in which the chickens were cooked, it being strained over them.

Chicken à la Tartare.

Singe the chicken, and split down the back. Wipe thoroughly with a damp cloth. Dredge well with salt and pepper, cover thickly with softened butter, and dredge thickly on both sides with fine, dry bread crumbs. Place in a baking-pan, the inside down, and cook in a very hot oven thirty minutes, taking care not to burn. Serve with Tartare sauce.

Broiled Chicken.

Singe the chicken, and split down the back, if not already prepared; and wipe with a damp cloth. Never wash it. Season well with salt and pepper. Take some soft butter in the right hand and rub over the bird, letting the greater part go on the breast and legs. Dredge with flour. Put in the double broiler, and broil over a moderate fire, having the breast turned to the heat at first. When the chicken is a nice brown, which will be in about fifteen minutes, place in a pan and put into a moderate oven for twelve minutes. Place on a hot dish, season with salt, pepper, and butter, and serve immediately. This rule is for a chicken weighing about two and a half pounds. The chicken is improved by serving with *maître d'hôtel* butter or Tartare sauce.

Chicken Stew with Dumplings.

One chicken or fowl, weighing about three pounds; one table-spoonful of butter, three of flour, one large onion, three slices of carrot, three of turnip, three pints of boiling water, and salt and pepper. Cut the chicken in slices suitable for serving. Wash, and put in a deep stewpan, add the water, and set on to boil. Put the carrot, turnip, and onion, cut fine, in a saucepan, with the butter, and cook slowly half an hour, stirring often; then take up the vegetables in a strainer, place the strainer in the stewpan with the chicken, and dip some of the water into it. Mash the vegetables with the back of a spoon, and rub as much as possible through the strainer. Now skim two spoonfuls of chicken fat from the water, and put in the pan in which the vegetables were cooked. When boiling hot, add the three table-spoonfuls of flour. Stir over the fire until a dark brown; then stir it in with the chicken, and simmer until tender. Season well with pepper and salt. The stew should only simmer all the while it is cooking. It must not boil hard. About two hours will be needed to cook a year old chicken. Twelve minutes before serving draw the stewpan forward, and boil up; then put in the dumplings, and cook *ten* minutes. Take them up, and keep in the heater while you are dishing the chicken into the centre of the platter. Afterwards, place the dumplings around the edge. This is a very nice and economical dish, if pains be taken in preparing. One stewed chicken will go farther than two roasted.

Larded Grouse.

Clean and wash the grouse. Lard the breast and legs. Run a small skewer into the legs and through the tail. Tie firmly with twine. Dredge with salt, and rub the breast with soft butter; then dredge thickly with flour. Put into a quick oven. If to be very rare, cook twenty minutes; if wished better done, thirty minutes. The former time, as a general thing, suits gentlemen better, but thirty minutes is preferred by ladies. If the birds are cooked in a tin-kitchen, it should be for thirty or thirty-five minutes. When done, place on a hot dish, on which has been spread bread sauce. Sprinkle fried crumbs over both grouse and sauce. Garnish with parsley. The grouse may, instead, be served on a hot dish, with the parsley garnish, and the sauce and crumbs served in separate dishes. The first method is the better, however, as you get in the sauce all the gravy that comes from the birds.

Larded Partridges.

Partridges are cooked and served the same as grouse.

Larded Quail.

The directions for cooking and serving are the same as those for grouse, only that quails cook in fifteen minutes. All dry-meated birds are cooked in this way. The question is sometimes asked, Should ducks be larded? Larding is to give richness to a dry meat that does not have fat enough of its own; therefore, meats like goose, duck, and mutton are *not* improved by larding.

Broiled Quail.

Split the quail down the back. Wipe with a damp towel. Season with salt and pepper, rub thickly with soft butter, and dredge with flour. Broil ten minutes over clear coals. Serve on hot buttered toast, garnishing with parsley.

Broiled Pigeons.

Prepare, cook, and serve the same as quail. They should be young for broiling, squabs being the best.

Broiled Small Birds.

All small birds can be broiled according to the directions for quail, remembering that for extremely small ones it takes a very bright fire. As the birds should be only browned, the time required is very brief.

Small Birds, Roasted.

Clean, by washing quickly in one water after they have been drawn. Season with salt and pepper. Cut slices of salt pork *very* thin, and with small skewers fasten a slice around each bird. Run a long skewer through the necks of six or eight, and rest it on a shallow baking-pan. When all the birds are arranged, put into a *hot* oven for twelve minutes, or before a hot fire for a quarter of an hour. Serve on toast.

Potted Pigeons.

Clean and wash one dozen pigeons. Stand them on their necks in a deep earthen or porcelain pot, and turn on them a pint of vinegar. Cut three large onions in twelve pieces, and place a piece on each pigeon. Cover the pot, and let it stand all night. In the morning take out the pigeons, and throw away the onions and vinegar. Fry, in a deep stew-pan, six slices of fat pork, and when browned take them up, and in the fat put six onions, sliced fine. On these put the pigeons, having first trussed them, and dredge well with salt, pepper, and flour. Cover, and cook slowly for forty-five minutes, stirring occasionally; then add two quarts of boiling water, and simmer gently two hours. Mix four heaping table-spoonfuls of flour with a cupful of cold water, and stir in with the pigeons. Taste to see if there is enough seasoning, and if there is not, add more. Cook half an hour longer. Serve with a garnish of rice or riced potatoes. More or less onion can be used; and, if you like it so, spice the gravy slightly.

Pigeons in Jelly.

Wash and truss one dozen pigeons. Put them in a kettle with four pounds of the shank of veal, six cloves, twenty-five pepper-corns, an onion that has been fried in one spoonful of butter, one stalk of celery, a bouquet of sweet herbs, and four and a half quarts of water. Have the veal shank broken in small pieces. As soon as the contents of the kettle come to a boil, skim carefully, and set for three hours where they will just simmer. After they have been cooking one hour, add two table-spoonfuls of salt. When the pigeons are done, take them up, being careful not to break them, and remove the strings. Draw the kettle forward, where it will boil rapidly, and keep there for forty minutes; then strain the liquor through a napkin, and taste to see if seasoned enough. The water should have boiled down to two and a half quarts. Have two moulds that will each hold six pigeons. Put a thin layer of the jelly in these, and set on ice to harden. When hard, arrange the pigeons in them, and cover with the jelly, which must be cold, but liquid. Place in the ice chest for six, or, better still, twelve hours. There should be only one layer of the pigeons in the mould.

To serve: Dip the mould in a basin of warm water for one minute, and turn on a cold dish. Garnish with pickled beets and parsley. A Tartare sauce can be served with this dish.

If squabs are used, two hours will cook them. All small birds, as well as partridge, grouse, etc., can be prepared in the same manner. Remember that the birds must be cooked tender, and that the liquor must be so reduced that it will become jellied.

Roast Rabbit.

First make a stuffing of a pound of veal and a quarter of a pound of pork, simmered two hours in water to cover; four crackers, rolled fine; a table-spoonful of salt, a scant teaspoonful of pepper, a teaspoonful of summer savory, a large table-spoonful of butter, and one and a quarter cupfuls of the broth in which the veal and pork were cooked. Chop the meat fine, add the other ingredients, and put on the fire to heat. Cut off the rabbit's head, open the vent, and draw. Wash clean, and season with salt and pepper. Stuff while the dressing is hot, and sew up the opening. Put the rabbit on its knees, and skewer in that position. Rub thickly with butter, dredge with flour, and put in the baking-pan, the bottom of which should be covered with hot water. Bake half an hour in a quick oven, basting frequently. Serve with a border of mashed potatoes, and pour the gravy over the rabbit.

Curry of Rabbit.

Cut the rabbit in small pieces. Wash, and cook the same as chicken curry.

Saddle of Venison.

Carefully scrape off the hair, and wipe with a damp towel. Season well with salt and pepper, and roll up and skewer together. Rub thickly with soft butter and dredge thickly with flour. Roast for an hour before a clear fire or in a *hot* oven, basting frequently. When half done, if you choose, baste with a few spoonfuls of claret. Or, you can have one row of larding on each side of the back-bone. This gives a particularly nice flavor.

To make the gravy: Pour off all the fat from the baking-pan, and put in the pan a cupful of boiling water. Stir from the sides and bottom, and set back where it will keep hot. In a small frying-pan put one table-spoonful of butter, a small slice of onion, six pepper-corns, and four whole cloves. Cook until the onion is browned, and then add a generous teaspoonful of flour. Stir until this is browned; then, gradually, add the gravy in the pan. Boil one minute. Strain, and add half a teaspoonful of lemon juice and three table-spoonfuls of currant jelly. Serve both venison and gravy very hot. The time given is for a saddle weighing between ten and twelve pounds. All the dishes and plates for serving must be hot. Venison is cooked in almost the same manner as beef, always remembering that it must be served *rare* and *hot*.

Roast Leg of Venison.

Draw the dry skin from the meat, and wipe with a damp towel. Make a paste with one quart of flour and a generous pint of cold water. Cover the venison with this, and place before a hot fire, if to be roasted in the tin-kitchen, or else in a very hot oven. As the paste browns, baste it frequently with the gravy in the pan. When it has been cooking one hour and a half, take off the paste, cover with butter, and dredge thickly with flour. Cook one hour longer, basting frequently with butter, salt, and flour. Make the gravy the same as for a saddle of venison, or serve with game sauce. The time given is for a leg weighing about fifteen pounds.

ENTRÉES.

Fillet of Beef, Larded.

THE true fillet is the tenderloin, although sometimes one will see a rib roast, boned and rolled, called a fillet. A short fillet, weighing from two and a half to three pounds (the average weight from a very large rump), will suffice for ten persons at a dinner where this is served as one course; and if a larger quantity is wanted a great saving will still be made if two short fillets are used. They cost about two dollars, while a large one, weighing the same amount, would cost five dollars. Fillet of beef is one of the simplest, safest, and most satisfactory dishes that a lady can prepare for either her own family or guests. After a single trial she will think no more of it than of broiling a beefsteak. First, remove from the fillet, with a sharp knife, every shred of muscle, ligament, and thin, tough skin. If it is not then of a good round shape, skewer it into shape. Draw a line through the centre, and lard with two rows of pork, having them meet at this line. Dredge with salt, pepper, and flour, and put, without water, in a very small pan. Place in a hot oven for thirty minutes. Let it be in the lower part of the oven the first ten minutes, then place on the upper grate. Serve with mushroom, Hollandaise, or tomato sauce, or with potato balls. If with sauce, this should be poured around the fillet. The time given cooks a fillet of any size, the shape being such that it will take half an hour for either two or six pounds. Save the fat trimmed from the fillet for frying, and the lean part for soup stock.

Fillet of Beef à la Hollandaise.

Trim and cut the short fillet into slices about half an inch thick. Season these well with salt, and then lay in a pan with six table-spoonfuls of butter, just warm enough to be oily. Squeeze the juice of a quarter of a lemon over them. Let them stand one hour; then dip lightly in flour, place in the double broiler, and cook for six minutes over a very bright fire. Have a mound of mashed potatoes in the centre of a hot dish, and rest the slices against this. Pour a Hollandaise sauce around. Garnish with parsley.

Fillet of Beef à l'Allemand.

Trim the fillet and skewer it into a good shape. Season well with pepper and salt. Have one egg and half a teaspoonful of sugar well beaten together; roll the fillet in this and then in bread crumbs. Bake in the oven for thirty minutes. Serve with Allemand sauce poured around it.

Fillet of Beef in Jelly.

Trim a short fillet, and cut a deep incision in the side, being careful not to go through to the other side or the ends. Fill this with one cupful of veal, prepared as for quenelles, and the whites of three hard-boiled eggs, cut into rings. Sew up the openings, and bind the fillet into good shape with broad bands of cotton cloth. Put in a deep stewpan two slices of ham and two of pork, and place the fillet on them; then put in two calf's feet, two stalks of celery, and two quarts of clear stock. Simmer gently two hours and a half. Take up the fillet, and set away to cool. Strain the stock, and set away to harden. When hard, scrape off every particle of fat, and put on the fire in a clean saucepan, with half a slice of onion and the whites of two eggs, beaten with four table-spoonfuls of cold water. When this boils, season well with salt, and set back where it will just simmer for half an hour; then strain through a napkin. Pour a little of the jelly into a two-quart charlotte-russe mould (half an inch deep), and set on the ice to harden. As soon as it is hard, decorate with the egg rings. Add about three spoonfuls of the liquid jelly, to set the eggs. When hard, add enough jelly to cover the eggs, and when this is also hard, trim the ends of the fillet, and draw out the thread. Place in the centre of the mould, and cover with the remainder of the jelly. If the fillet floats, place a slight weight on it. Set in the ice chest to harden. When ready to serve, place the mould in a pan of warm water for half a minute, and then turn out the fillet gently upon a dish. Garnish with a circle of egg rings, each of which has a stoned olive in the centre. Put here and there a sprig of parsley.

Alamode Beef.

Six pounds of the upper part, or of the vein, of the round of beef, half a pound of fat salt pork, three table-spoonfuls of butter, two onions, half a carrot, half a turnip, two table-spoonfuls of vinegar, one of lemon juice, one heaping table-spoonful of salt, half a teaspoonful of pepper, two cloves, six allspice, a small piece of stick cinnamon, a bouquet of sweet herbs, two scant quarts of boiling water, and four table-spoonfuls of flour. Cut the pork in thick strips, as long as the meat is thick, and, with a large larding needle (which comes for this purpose), draw these through the meat. If you do not have the large needle, make the holes with the boning knife or the carving steel, and press the pork through with the fingers. Put the butter in a six-quart stewpan, and when it melts add the vegetables, cut fine. Let them cook five minutes, stirring all the while. Put in the meat, which has been well dredged with the flour; brown on one side, and then turn, and brown the other. Add one quart of the water; stir well, and then add the other, with the spice, herbs, vinegar, salt, and pepper. Cover tightly, and *simmer gently* four hours. Add the lemon juice. Taste the gravy, and, if necessary, add more salt and pepper. Let it cook twenty minutes longer. Take up the meat, and draw the stewpan forward, where it will boil rapidly, for ten or fifteen minutes, having first skimmed off all the fat. Strain the gravy on the beef, and serve. This dish may be garnished with potato balls or button onions.

Macaronied Beef.

Six pounds of beef from the upper part of the round, or the vein, a quarter of a pound of macaroni (twelve sticks), half a cupful of butter, four large onions, one quart of peeled and sliced tomatoes, or a quart can of the vegetable : two heaping table-spoonfuls of flour, salt, pepper, and two cloves. Make holes in the beef with the large larding needle or the steel, and press the macaroni into them. Season with salt and pepper. Put the butter and the onions, which have been peeled and cut fine, in a six-quart stewpan, and stir over the fire until a golden brown ; then put in the meat, first drawing the onions aside. Dredge with the flour, and spread the top of the meat with the fried onions. Put in the spice and one quart of boiling water. Cover tightly, and simmer *slowly* for three hours ; then add the tomato, and cook one hour longer. Take up the meat, and strain the gravy over it. Serve hot. The tomato may be omitted if one pint more of water and an extra table-spoonful of flour are used instead. Always serve macaroni with this dish.

Cannelon of Beef.

One thin slice of the upper part of the round of beef. Cut off all the fat, and so trim as to give the piece a regular shape. Put the trimmings in the chopping tray, with a quarter of a pound of boiled salt pork and one pound of lean cooked ham. Chop very fine ; then add a speck of cayenne, one teaspoonful of mixed mustard, one of onion juice, one table-spoonful of lemon juice and three eggs. Season the beef with salt and pepper. Spread the mixture over it, and roll up. Tie with twine, being careful not to draw too tightly. Have six slices of fat pork fried in the braising-pan. Cut two onions, two slices of carrot, and two of turnip into this, and stir for two minutes over the fire. Roll the cannelon in a plate of flour, and put it in the braising-pan with the pork and vegetables. Brown slightly on all sides ; then add one quart of boiling water, and place in the oven. Cook three hours, basting every fifteen minutes. When it has been cooking two hours, add half a cupful of canned tomatoes or two fresh ones. Taste to see if the gravy is seasoned enough ; if it is not, add seasoning. The constant dredging with flour will thicken the gravy sufficiently. Slide the cake turner under the beef, and lift carefully on to a hot dish. Cut the string in three or four places with a *sharp* knife, and gently draw it away from the meat. Skim off all the fat. Strain the gravy through a fine sieve on to the meat. Garnish with a border of toast or riced potatoes. Cut in thin slices with a sharp knife.

Cannelon of Beef, No. 2.

Two pounds of the round of beef, the rind of half a lemon, three sprigs of parsley, one teaspoonful of salt, barely one fourth of a teaspoonful of pepper, a quarter of a nutmeg, two table-spoonfuls of melted butter, one raw egg, and half a teaspoonful of onion juice. Chop meat, parsley, and lemon rind *very* fine. Add other ingredients, and mix thoroughly. Shape into a roll, about three inches in diameter and six in length. Roll in buttered paper, and bake thirty minutes, basting with butter and water.

When cooked, place on a hot dish, gently unroll from the paper, and serve with Flemish sauce poured over it. You may serve tomato or mushroom sauce if you prefer either.

Beef Roulette.

Have two pounds of the upper part of the round, cut very thin. Mix together one cupful of finely chopped ham, two eggs, one teaspoonful of mixed mustard, a speck of cayenne, and three table-spoonfuls of stock or water. Spread upon the beef, which roll up firmly and tie with soft twine, being careful not to draw too tightly, for that would cut the meat as soon as it began to cook. Cover the roll with flour, and fry brown in four table-spoonfuls of ham or pork fat. Put it in as small a saucepan as will hold it. Into the fat remaining in the pan put two finely chopped onions, and cook until a pale yellow ; then add two table-spoonfuls of flour, and stir three minutes longer. Pour upon this one pint and a half of boiling water. Boil up once, and pour over the roulette ; then add two cloves, one fourth of a teaspoonful of pepper, and one heaping teaspoonful of salt. Cover the saucepan, and set where it will simmer slowly for three hours. After the first hour and a half, turn the roulette over. Serve hot, with the gravy strained over it. It is also nice to serve cold for lunch or supper. Ham force-meat balls and parsley make a pretty garnish.

Beef Olives.

One and a half pounds of beef, cut very thin. Trim off the edges and fat ; then cut in strips three inches wide and four long ; season well with salt and pepper. Chop fine the trimmings and the fat. Add three table-spoonfuls of powdered cracker, one teaspoonful of sage and savory mixed, one fourth of a teaspoonful of pepper, and two teaspoonfuls of salt. Mix very thoroughly and spread on the strips of beef. Roll them up, and tie with twine. When all are done, roll in flour. Fry brown a quarter of a pound of pork. Take it out of the pan, and put the olives in. Fry brown, and put in a small saucepan that can be tightly covered. In the fat remaining in the pan put one table-spoonful of flour, and stir until perfectly smooth and brown ; then pour in, gradually, nearly a pint and a half of boiling water. Stir for two or three minutes, season to taste with salt and pepper, and pour over the olives. Cover the saucepan, and let simmer two hours. Take up at the end of this time and cut the strings with a sharp knife. Place the olives in a row on a dish, and pour the gravy over them.

Veal Olives.

These are made in the same manner, except that a dressing, like chicken dressing, is made for them. For one and a half pounds of veal take three crackers, half a table-spoonful of butter, half a teaspoonful of savory, one fourth of a teaspoonful of sage, a teaspoonful of salt, a very little pepper, and an eighth of a cupful of water. Spread the strips with this, and proceed as for beef olives.

Fricandelles of Veal.

Two pounds of clear veal, half a cupful of finely chopped cooked ham, one cupful of milk, one cupful of bread crumbs, the juice of half a lemon, one table-spoonful of salt, half a teaspoonful of pepper, one cupful of butter, a pint and a half of stock, three table-spoonfuls of flour. Chop the veal fine. Cook the bread crumbs and milk until a smooth paste, being careful not to burn. Add to the chopped veal and ham, and when well mixed, add the seasoning and four table-spoonfuls of the butter. Mix thoroughly, and form into balls about the size of an egg. Have the yolks of three eggs well beaten, and use to cover the balls. Fry these, till a light brown, in the remainder of the butter, being *very* careful not to burn. Stir the three table-spoonfuls of flour into the butter that remains after the balls are fried. Stir until dark brown, and then gradually stir the stock into it. Boil for two minutes. Taste to see if seasoned enough ; then add the balls, and cook *very slowly* for one hour. Serve with a garnish of toast and lemon.

Fricandelles can be made with chicken, mutton, lamb, and beef, the only change in the above directions being to omit the ham.

Braised Tongue.

Wash a fresh beef tongue, and, with a trussing needle, run a strong twine through the roots and end of it, drawing tightly enough to have the end meet the roots ; then tie firmly. Cover with boiling water, and boil gently for two hours ; then take up and drain. Put six table-spoonfuls of butter in the braising-pan, and when hot put in half a small carrot, half a small turnip, and two onions, all cut fine. Cook five minutes, stirring all the time, and then draw to one side. Roll the tongue in flour, and put in the pan. As soon as browned on one side, turn, and brown the other. Add one quart of the water in which it was boiled, a bouquet of sweet herbs, one clove, a small piece of cinnamon, and salt and pepper. Cover, and cook two hours in a slow oven, basting often with the gravy in the pan, and salt, pepper, and flour. When it has been cooking an hour and a half, add the juice of half a lemon to the gravy. When done, take up. Melt two table-spoonfuls of glaze, and pour over the tongue. Place in the heater until the gravy is made. Mix one table-spoonful of corn-starch with a little cold water, and stir into the boiling gravy, of which there should be one pint. Boil one minute ; then strain, and pour around the tongue. Garnish with parsley, and serve.

Fillets of Tongue.

Cut cold boiled tongue in pieces about four inches long, two wide, and half an inch thick. Dip in melted butter and in flour. For eight fillets put two table-spoonfuls of butter in the frying-pan, and when hot put in the tongue. Brown on both sides, being careful not to burn. Take up, and put one more spoonful of butter in the pan, and then one heaping teaspoonful of flour. Stir until dark brown; then add one cupful of stock, half a teaspoonful of parsley, and one table-spoonful of lemon juice, or one teaspoonful of vinegar. Let this boil up once, and then pour it around the tongue, which has been dished on thin strips of toast. Garnish with parsley, and serve. For a change, a table-spoonful of chopped pickles, or of capers, can be stirred into the sauce the last moment.

Escaloped Tongue.

Chop some cold tongue, not too fine, and have for each pint one table-spoonful of onion juice, one teaspoonful of chopped parsley, one heaping teaspoonful of salt, one teaspoonful of capers, one cupful of bread crumbs, half a cupful of stock, and three table-spoonfuls of butter. Butter the escalop dish, and cover the bottom with bread crumbs. Put in the tongue, which has been mixed with the parsley, salt, pepper, and capers, and add the stock, in which has been mixed the onion juice. Put part of the butter on the dish with the remainder of the bread crumbs, and then bits of butter here and there. Bake twenty minutes, and serve hot.

Tongue in Jelly.

Boil and skin either a fresh or salt tongue. When cold, trim off the roots. Have one and a fourth quarts of aspic jelly in the liquid state. Cover the bottom of a two-quart mould about an inch deep with it, and let it harden. With a fancy vegetable cutter, cut out leaves from cooked beets, and garnish the bottom of the mould with them. Gently pour in three table-spoonfuls of jelly, to set the vegetables. When this is hard, add jelly enough to cover the vegetables, and let the whole get very hard. Then put in the tongue, and about half a cupful of jelly, which should be allowed to harden, and so keep the meat in place when the remainder is added. Pour in the remainder of the jelly and set away to harden. To serve: Dip the mould for a few moments in a pan of warm water, and then gently turn on to a dish. Garnish with pickles and parsley. Pickled beet is especially nice.

Lambs' Tongues in Jelly.

Lambs' tongues are prepared the same as beef tongues. Three or four moulds, each holding a little less than a pint, will make enough for a small company, one tongue being put in each mould. The tongues can all be put on the same dish, or on two, if the table is long.

Lambs' Tongues, Stewed.

Six tongues, three heaping table-spoonfuls of butter, one large onion, two slices of carrot, three slices of white turnip, three table-spoonfuls of flour, one of salt, a little pepper, one quart of stock or water, and a bouquet of sweet herbs. Boil the tongues one hour and a half in clear water; then take up, cover with cold water, and draw off the skins. Put the butter, onion, turnip, and carrot in the stewpan, and cook slowly for fifteen minutes; then add the flour, and cook until brown, stirring all the while. Stir the stock into this, and when it boils up add the tongue, salt, pepper, and herbs. Simmer gently for two hours. Cut the carrots, turnips, and potatoes into cubes. Boil the potatoes in salted water ten minutes, and the carrots and turnips one hour. Place the tongues in the centre of a hot dish. Arrange the vegetables around them, strain the gravy, and pour over all. Garnish with parsley, and serve.

Stewed Ox Tails.

Two ox tails, three table-spoonfuls of butter, two of flour, one large onion, half a small carrot, three slices of turnip, two stalks of celery, two cloves, a pint and a half of stock or water, salt and pepper to taste. Divide the tails in pieces about four inches long. Cut the vegetables in small pieces. Let the butter get hot in the stewpan; then add the vegetables, and when they begin to brown, add the flour. Stir for two minutes. Put in the tails, and add the seasoning and stock. Simmer gently three hours. Serve on a hot dish with gravy strained over them.

Ox Tails à la Tartare.

Three ox tails, two eggs, one cupful of bread crumbs, salt, pepper, one quart of stock, a bouquet of sweet herbs. Cut the tails in four-inch pieces, and put them on to boil with the stock and sweet herbs. Let them simmer two hours. Take up, drain, and cool. When cold, dip them in the beaten eggs and in bread crumbs. Fry in boiling fat till a golden brown. Have Tartare sauce spread on the centre of a cold dish, and arrange the ox tails on this. Garnish with parsley, and serve.

Haricot of Ox Tails.

Three ox tails, two carrots, two onions, two small white turnips, three potatoes, three table-spoonfuls of butter, two of flour, three pints of water, and salt and pepper to taste. Cut the tails in pieces about four inches long. Cut the onions very fine, and the carrots, turnips, and potatoes into large cubes. Put the butter, meat, and onion in the stewpan and fry, stirring all the time, until the onions are a golden brown; then add the flour, and stir two minutes longer. Add the water, and when it comes to a boil skim carefully. Set back where it will simmer. When it has been cooking one hour, add the carrots and turnips. Cook another hour, and then add the salt, pepper, and potatoes. Simmer twenty minutes longer. Heap the vegetables in the centre of a hot dish, and arrange the tails around them. Pour the gravy over all, and serve.

Ragout of Mutton.

Three pounds of any of the cheap parts of mutton, six table-spoonfuls of butter, three of flour, twelve button onions, or one of the common size; one large white turnip, cut into little cubes; salt, pepper, one quart of water, and a bouquet of sweet herbs. Cut the meat in small pieces. Put three table-spoonfuls each of butter and flour in the stewpan, and when hot and smooth, add the meat. Stir until a rich brown, and then add water, and set where it will simmer. Put three table-spoonfuls of butter in a frying-pan, and when hot put in the turnips and onions with a teaspoonful of flour. Stir all the time until a golden brown; then drain, and put with the meat. Simmer for an hour and a half. Garnish with rice, toasted bread, plain boiled macaroni, or mashed potatoes. Small cubes of potato can be added half an hour before dishing. Serve very hot.

Ragout of Veal.

Prepare the same as mutton, using one table-spoonful more of butter, and cooking an hour longer.

Chicken Pie.

One fowl weighing between four and five pounds, half the rule for chopped paste (see Chopped Paste), three pints of water, one fourth of a teaspoonful of pepper, one table-spoonful of salt (these last two quantities may be increased if you like), three table-spoonfuls of flour, three of butter, two eggs, one table-spoonful of onion juice, and a bouquet of sweet herbs. Clean the fowl, and cut in pieces as for serving. Put it in a stewpan with the hot water, salt, pepper, and herbs. When it comes to a boil, skim, and set back where it will simmer one hour and a half. Take up the chicken and place in a deep earthen pie dish. Draw the stewpan forward where it will boil rapidly for fifteen minutes. Skim off the fat and take out the bouquet. Put the butter in a frying-pan, and when hot add the flour. Stir until smooth, but not brown, and stir in the water in which the chicken was boiled. Cook ten minutes. Beat the eggs with one spoonful of cold water, and gradually add the gravy to them. Turn this into the pie dish. Lift the chicken with a spoon, that the gravy may fall to the bottom. Set away to cool. When cold, roll out a covering of paste a little larger than the top of the dish and about one fourth of an inch thick. Cover the pie with this, having the edges turned into the dish. Roll the remainder of the paste the same as before, and with a thimble, or something as small, cut out little pieces all over the cover. Put this perforated paste over the first cover, turning out the edges and rolling slightly. Bake one hour in a moderate oven.

Pasties of Game and Poultry.

Make three pints of force-meat. (See Force-meat for game.) Cut all the solid meat from four grouse. Lard each piece with very fine strips of pork. Put half a cupful of butter and a finely-cut onion in a frying-pan. Stir until the onion is yellow; then put in the grouse, and cook slowly, with the cover on, for forty minutes. Stir occasionally. Take up the grouse, and put three table-spoonfuls of flour with the butter remaining in the pan. Stir until brown; add one quart of stock, two table-spoonfuls of glaze, a bouquet of sweet herbs, and four cloves. Simmer twenty minutes, and strain. Butter a four-quart earthen dish, and cover the bottom and sides with the force-meat. Put in a layer of the grouse, and moisten well with the gravy, which must be highly seasoned with salt and pepper; then put in the yolks of six hard-boiled eggs, and the whites, cut into rings. Moisten with gravy, and add another layer of grouse, and of eggs and gravy. Twelve eggs should be used. Make a paste as for chicken pie. Cover with this, and bake one hour and a half. Serve either hot or cold.

Any kind of meat pasties can be made in the same manner. With a veal pasty put in a few slices of cooked ham.

Cold Game Pie.

Make three pints of force-meat. (See Force-meat for game.) Cut all the meat from two partridges or grouse, and put the bones on to boil with three quarts of water and three pounds of a shank of veal. Fry four large slices of fat salt pork, and as soon as brown take up, and into the fat put one onion, cut in slices. When this begins to turn yellow, take up, and put the meat of the birds in the pan. Dredge well with salt, pepper, and flour, and stir constantly for four minutes; then take up, and put away to cool. Make a crust as directed for raised pies. Butter the French pie mould very thoroughly, and line with paste. Spread upon the paste — both upon the sides and bottom of the mould — a thin layer of fat salt pork, then a layer of force-meat, one of grouse, again one of force-meat, and so on until the pie is filled. Leave a space of about half an inch at the edge of the mould, and heap the filling in the centre. Moisten with half a cupful of well-seasoned stock. Roll the remainder of the paste into the shape of the top of the mould. Wet the paste at the edge of the mould with beaten egg; then put on the top, and press the top and side parts together. Cut a small piece of paste from the centre of the top crust, add a little more paste to it, and roll a little larger than the opening, which it is to cover. Cut the edges with the jagging iron, and, with the other end of the iron, stamp leaves or flowers. Place on the top of the pie. Bake in a slow oven three hours and a half. While the pie is baking the sauce can be prepared. When the bones and veal have been cooking two hours, add two cloves, a bouquet of sweet herbs, and the fried onions. Cook one hour longer; then salt and pepper well, and strain. The water should be reduced in boiling to one quart. When the pie is baked, take the centre piece from the cover, and slightly press the tunnel into the opening. Pour slowly one pint of the hot gravy through this. Put back the cover, and set away to cool. The remainder of the gravy must be turned into a flat dish and put in a cold place to harden. When the pie is served, place the mould in the oven, or steamer, for about five minutes; then draw out the wires and open it. Slip the pie on to a cold dish, and garnish with the jellied gravy and parsley. This is nice for suppers or lunches. All kinds of game and meat can be prepared in the same manner.

Pâté de Foies Gras.

Make a paste with one quart of flour, as for raised pies, and put away in a cool place. Put four fat goose livers in a pint of sweet milk for two or three hours, to whiten them. Chop *very fine* two pounds of fresh pork, cut from the loin (it must not be too fat), and one pound of clear veal. Put one and a half cupfuls of milk on to boil with a blade of mace, an onion, two cloves, a small piece of nutmeg, and a bouquet of sweet herbs. Cook all these for ten minutes; then strain the milk upon four table-spoonfuls of butter and two of flour, which have been well mixed. Add to this the chopped pork and veal and one of the livers, chopped fine; stir over the fire for ten minutes, being careful not to brown. Season well with pepper and salt, add four well-beaten eggs, and stir half a minute longer; then put away to cool. Cut half a pound of salt pork in slices as thin as shavings. Butter a French pie mould, holding about three quarts. Form three fourths of the paste into a ball. Sprinkle the board with flour, and roll the paste out until about one fourth of an inch thick. Take it up by the four corners and place it in the mould. Be very careful not to break it. With the hand, press the paste on the sides and bottom. The crust must come to the top of the mould. Put a layer of the pork shavings on the sides and bottom, then a thick layer of the force-meat. Split the livers, and put half of them in; over them sprinkle one table-spoonful of onion juice, salt, pepper, and, if you like, a table-spoonful of capers. Another layer of force-meat, again the liver and seasoning, and then the force-meat. On this last layer put salt pork shavings. Into the remaining paste roll three table-spoonfuls of washed butter, and roll the paste, as nearly as possible, into the shape of the top of the pie mould. Cut a small piece from the centre. The filling of the pie should have been heaped a little toward the centre, leaving a space of about one inch and a half at the edges. Brush with beaten egg the paste that is in this space. Put on the top crust, and, with the forefinger and thumb, press the two crusts together. Roll the piece of paste cut from the centre of the cover a little larger, and cover the opening with it. From some puff-paste trimmings, cut out leaves, and decorate the cover with them. Place in a moderate oven, and bake slowly two hours. Have a pint and a half of hot veal stock (which will become jellied when cold) well seasoned with pepper, salt, whole spice, and onion. When the *pâté* is taken from the oven, take off the small piece that was put on the centre of the cover. Insert a tunnel in the opening and pour the hot stock through it. Replace the cover, and set away to cool. When the *pâté* is to be served, place it in the oven for about five minutes, that it may slip from the mould easily. Draw out the wires which fasten the sides of the mould, and slide the *pâté* upon the platter. Garnish the dish with parsley and small strips of cucumber pickles.

Truffles and mushrooms can be cut up and put in the *pâté* in layers, the same as the liver and at the same time. The Strasburg fat livers (*foies gras*) come in little stone pots, and cost from a dollar to two dollars per pot.

Chartreuse of Chicken.

Make the force-meat as for *quenelles* of chicken. Simmer two large chickens in white stock for half an hour. Take up, and let cool. Have a pickled tongue boiled tender. Cut thin slices from the breast of the chickens, and cut these in squares. Cut the tongue in slices, and these in turn in squares the same size as the chicken. Butter a four-quart mould, and arrange the chicken and tongue handsomely on the bottom and sides, being careful to have the pieces fit closely together. Have note paper cut to fit the bottom and sides. Butter it well, and cover about an inch deep with the force-meat. Take up the bottom piece by the four corners and fit it into the mould, the meat side down. Pour a little hot water into any kind of flat-bottomed tin basin, and put this in the mould and move it over the papers, to melt the butter; then lift out the paper. Place the papers on the side in the same way as on the bottom, and melt the butter by rolling a bottle of hot water over them. Remove these papers, and set the mould in a cold place until the filling is ready. Cut from the tenderest part of the chicken enough meat to make two quarts. Cut four large or six small mushrooms and four truffles in strips. Put half a cupful of butter, half a large onion, four cloves, a blade of mace, a slice of carrot, one of turnip, and a stalk of celery in a saucepan, and cook five minutes, stirring all the while; then add five table-spoonfuls of flour. Stir until it begins to brown, when add one quart of the stock in which the chickens were cooked, a bouquet of sweet herbs, and salt and pepper. Simmer twenty minutes; strain, and add to the chicken. Return to the fire, and simmer twenty minutes longer, and set away to cool. When cold, put a layer of the chicken in the mould, and a light layer of the truffles and mushrooms. Continue this until the form is nearly full, and then cover with the remainder of the force-meat. Spread buttered paper upon it, and put in a cool place until cooking time, when steam two hours. Turn carefully upon the dish. Brush over with three table-spoonfuls of melted glaze. Pour one pint of supreme sauce around it, and serve.

The force-meat must be spread evenly on the paper, and smoothed with a knife that has been dipped in hot water. All kinds of meat *chartreuses* can be made in this manner.

Chartreuse of Vegetables and Game.

Six large carrots, six white turnips, two large heads of cabbage, two onions, two quarts of stock, three grouse, one pint of brown sauce, four table-spoonfuls of glaze, two cloves, a bouquet of sweet herbs, one pound of mixed salt pork, and one cupful of butter. Scrape and wash the carrots, and peel and wash the turnips. Boil for twenty minutes in salted water. Pour off the water, and add three pints of stock and a teaspoonful of sugar. Simmer gently one hour. Take up, drain, and set away to cool. Cut the cabbage in four parts. Wash, and boil twenty minutes in salted water. Drain in the colander, and return to the fire with a pint of stock, the cloves, herbs, and onions, tied in a piece of muslin, a quarter of a cupful of butter, and the pork and grouse. Cover the saucepan, and place where the contents will just simmer for two hours and a half. When cooked, put the grouse and pork on a dish to cool. Turn the cabbage into the colander, first taking out the spice and onion. Press all the juice from the cabbage and chop *very* fine. Season with salt and pepper, and put away to cool. Butter a plain mould holding about four quarts. Butter note paper, cut to fit the sides and bottom, and line the mould with it. Cut the cold turnips and carrots in thick slices, and then in pieces all the same size and shape, but of any design you wish. Line the sides and bottom of the mould with these, being particular to have the pieces come together. Have the yellow and white arranged in either squares or rows. With the chopped cabbage put half a pint of the brown sauce and two spoonfuls of the glaze. Stir over the fire for six minutes. Spread a thick layer of this on the vegetables, being careful not to displace them. Cut each grouse into six pieces. Season with salt and pepper, and pack closely in the mould. Moisten with the remaining half-pint of brown sauce. Cover with the remainder of the cabbage. Two hours before serving time, place in a steamer and cook. While the *chartreuse* is steaming, make the sauce. Put two table-spoonfuls of butter in a stewpan, and when hot add two table-spoonfuls of flour. Stir until a dark brown; then add the stock in which the cabbage was cooked, and enough of that in which the turnips and carrots were cooked to make a quart. Stir until it boils; add two spoonfuls of glaze, and set back where it will just simmer for one hour. Skim off the fat, and strain. When the *chartreuse* is done, take up and turn gently upon the dish. Lift the mould *very* carefully. Take off the paper. Pour two table-spoonfuls of the sauce on the *chartreuse* and the remainder around it. The vegetable *chartreuse* can be made with any kind of game or meat.

Chartreuse of Chicken and Macaroni.

One large fowl, about four and a half or five pounds, boiled tender; half a box of gelatine, one cupful of broth in which the chicken was boiled, one cupful of cream, salt, pepper, fourteen ounces of macaroni. Just cover the fowl with boiling water, and simmer until very tender, the time depending upon the age, but being from one to two hours if the bird is not more than a year old. Take off all the skin and fat, and cut the meat in thin, delicate pieces. Soak the gelatine two hours in half a cupful of cold water, and dissolve it in the cupful of boiling broth; add to the cream, and season highly. Have the chicken well seasoned, also. Put the macaroni in a large flat pan with boiling water to cover, and boil rapidly for three minutes. Drain off the water, and place the macaroni on a board, having about twelve pieces in a bunch. Cut in pieces about three fourths of an inch long. Butter a two-quart mould (an oval charlotte-russe mould is the best) very thickly, and stick the macaroni closely over the bottom and sides. When done, put the chicken in lightly and evenly, and add the sauce very gradually. Steam one hour. Serve either cold or hot. Great care must be taken in dishing. Place the platter over the mould and turn platter and mould simultaneously. Let the dish rest a minute, and then gently remove the mould. Serve immediately. A long time is needed to line the mould with the macaroni, but this is such a handsome, savory dish as to pay to have it occasionally. If you prefer, you can use all broth, and omit the cream.

Galatine of Turkey.

Bone the turkey, and push the wings and legs inside of the body. Make three pints of ham force-meat. Cut a cold boiled tongue in thin slices. Season the turkey with salt and pepper, and spread on a board, inside up. Spread a layer of the force-meat on this, and then a layer of tongue. Continue this until all the tongue and force-meat are used. Roll the bird into a round form, and sew up with mending cotton. Wrap tightly in a strong piece of cotton cloth, which must be either pinned or sewed to keep it in position. Put in a porcelain kettle the bones of the turkey, two calf's feet, four pounds of the knuckle of veal, an onion, two slices of turnip, two of carrot, twenty pepper-corns, four cloves, two stalks of celery, one table-spoonful of salt, and three quarts of water. When this comes to a boil, skim, and put the turkey in. Set back where it will just simmer for three hours. Take up and remove the wrapping, put on a clean piece of cloth that has been wet in cold water, and place in a dish. Put three bricks in a flat baking-pan, and place on top of the bird. Set away in a cool place over night. In the morning take off the weights and cloth. Place on a dish, the smooth side up. Melt four table-spoonfuls of glaze, and brush the turkey with it. Garnish with the jelly, and serve. Or, the galatine can be cut in slices and arranged on a number of dishes, if for a large party. In that case, place a little jelly

WASHBURN CROSBY COMPANY,

PROPRIETORS WASHBURN FLOUR MILLS,

MINNEAPOLIS, MINNESOTA.

THE WASHBURN MILLS MAKE:

10,000 bbls. of Flour per day,

60,000 bbls. per week,

3,120,000 bbls. per year.

THE WASHBURN MILLS are the largest flour mills in the world.

THE WASHBURN MILLS have a floor surface of ten acres. The combined steam and water power is equal to 7500 horse power.

THE WASHBURN MILLS require 200 cars every day to take wheat into, and flour and offal out of them.

THE WASHBURN MILLS are the only flour mills in the world having a railroad track through them.

THE WASHBURN MILLS flour has taken the highest award wherever entered for competition.

❖ CAUTION. ❖

Every Barrel or Sack of Washburn's Flour bears the firm name in full, WASHBURN CROSBY CO. None other genuine.

ENTERTAINING JUVENILES.

Schoolboys of Rookesbury;

Or, The Boys of the Fourth Form. An entertaining story of the mishaps and adventures of several boys during a term at an English school. Edited by LAURENCE H. FRANCIS. Fully illustrated with original drawings.
1 vol., small quarto, illuminated board cover, ... $1.25

Queen Hildegarde.

By LAURA E. RICHARDS, author of "Four Feet, Two Feet, and No Feet." A new edition of this popular girl's book, — a second "Little Women," — containing nineteen illustrations from new and original drawings.
1 vol., small quarto, illuminated board covers, ... $1.50

" We should like to see the sensible, heroine loving girl in her early teens who would not like this book. Not to like it would simply argue a screw loose somewhere." — BOSTON POST.

The Days of Chivalry;

Or, PAGE, SQUIRE AND KNIGHT. A highly interesting and instructive, historical romance of the Middle Ages. by W. H. DAVENPORT ADAMS, author of "Success in Life," "The Land of the Incas," etc. Thoroughly illustrated with 113 drawings.
1 vol., small quarto, illuminated board covers, ... $1.50

The Red Mountain of Alaska.

By WILLIS BOYD ALLEN. An exciting narrative of a trip through this most interesting but little known country, with accurate description of the same. Full of adventures, vividly portrayed by choice, original illustrations, by F. T. Merrill and others.
1 vol., 8vo, cloth, gilt, ... $2.50

" It throws ' Robinson Crusoe,' the ' Swiss Family Robinson,' and all those fascinating phantasies, hopelessly into the shade, and will hold many a boy spellbound, through many an evening, of many a winter." — CHICAGO TRIBUNE.

Hunting in the Jungle

WITH GUN AND GUIDE. From Les Animaux Sauvages, by WARREN F. KELLOGG. An exciting and amusing series of adventures in search of large game — gorillas, elephants, tigers and lions — fully illustrated with over a hundred original drawings by celebrated artists, engraved on wood by the best modern book illustrators.
1 vol., 8vo, chromo-lithographed board covers, ... $1.75
1 vol., 8vo, cloth, gilt, ... 2.50

Our New Way 'Round the World.

By CHARLES CARLETON COFFIN, author of "The Story of Liberty," "The Boys of '61," "Following the Flag," "The Boys of '76," "Winning His Way," "My Days and Nights on the Battlefield," etc., etc. A new REVISED edition of this standard book of travel, which is interesting and useful to young and old; with a large number of additional illustrations.
1 vol., 8vo, chromo-lithographed board covers, ... $1.75
1 vol., 8vo, cloth, gilt, ... 2.50

Travels in Mexico.

By F. A. OBER. A brilliant record of a remarkable journey from Yucatan to the Rio Grande Historic ruins, tropic wilds, silver hills are described with eloquence. No country possesses so rich a field for the historian, antiquarian, fortune-hunter, and traveller.
1 vol., 8vo, chromo-lithographed board covers, ... $1.75
1 vol., 8vo, cloth, gilt, ... 2.50

Dickens's Child's History of England.

Holiday edition, with 100 fine illustrations, by De Neuville, Emile Bayard, F. Lix, and others.
1 vol., 8vo, chromo-lithographed board covers, ... $1.75
1 vol., 8vo, cloth, gilt, ... 2.50

The Young Moose Hunters.

By C. A. STEPHENS, author of the "Knockabout Club in the Tropics," etc., etc. With numerous full-page original illustrations made expressly for this edition. An exciting account of a hunting trip through the Maine woods.
1 vol., small quarto, illuminated board covers, ... $1.50

Six Girls.

By FANNY BELLE IRVING. A charming story of every-day home life, pure in sentiment and healthy in tone. A beautiful book for girls. Fully illustrated from original designs.
1 vol., small quarto, illuminated board covers and linings, ... $1.50

Hans Christian Andersen's Fairy Tales.

The standard authorized edition. A new translation from the original Danish edition, complete and unabridged, fully illustrated with engravings made from the original drawings, with an appropriate cover designed by L. S. IPSEN.
1 vol., quarto, cloth, ... $2.25

ESTES & LAURIAT, Publishers, Boston, Mass.

in the centre of each slice, and garnish the border of the dish with jelly and parsley. The time and materials given are for a turkey weighing about nine pounds. Any kind of fowl or bird can be prepared in the same manner.

To make the jelly: Draw forward the kettle in which the turkey was cooked, and boil the contents rapidly for one hour. Strain, and put away to harden. In the morning scrape off all the fat and sediment. Put the jelly in a clean saucepan with the whites and shells of two eggs that have been beaten with four table-spoonfuls of cold water. Let this come to a boil, and set back where it will just simmer for twenty minutes. Strain through a napkin, and set away to harden.

Galatine of Veal.

Bone a breast of veal. Season well with salt and pepper. Treat the same as turkey, using, however, two pounds of boiled ham instead of the tongue. Cook four hours.

Chicken in Jelly.

For each pound of chicken, a pint of water. Clean the chicken, and put to boil. When it comes to a boil, skim carefully; and simmer gently until the meat is very tender, — about an hour and a half. Take out the chicken, skin, and take all the flesh from the bones. Put the bones again in the liquor, and boil until the water is reduced one half. Strain, and set away to cool. Next morning skim off all the fat. Turn the jelly into a clean saucepan, carefully removing all the sediment; and to each quart of jelly add one fourth of a package of gelatine (which has been soaked an hour in half a cupful of cold water), an onion, a stalk of celery, twelve pepper-corns, a small piece of mace, four cloves, the white and shell of one egg, and salt and pepper to taste. Let it boil up; then set back where it will simmer twenty minutes. Strain the jelly through a napkin. In a three-pint mould put a layer of jelly about three fourths of an inch deep. Set in ice water to harden. Have the chicken cut in long, thin strips, and well seasoned with salt and pepper; and when the jelly in the mould is hard, lay in the chicken, lightly, and cover with the liquid jelly, which should be cool, but not hard. Put away to harden. When ready to serve, dip the mould in warm water and then turn into the centre of a flat dish. Garnish with parsley, and, if you choose, with Tartare or mayonnaise sauce.

Chicken Chaud Froid.

Skin two chickens, and cut in small pieces as for serving. Wash, and put them in a stewpan with enough white stock to cover, and one large onion, a clove, half a blade of mace, a bouquet of sweet herbs, and half a table-spoonful of salt. Let this come to a boil; then skim carefully, and set back where it will simmer for one hour. Take up the chicken, and set the stewpan where the stock will boil rapidly. Put three table-spoonfuls of butter in the frying-pan, and when it melts stir in two table-spoonfuls of flour, and cook until smooth, but not brown. Stir this into the stock, of which there must be not more than a pint; add four table-spoonfuls of glaze, and boil up once. Taste to see if seasoned enough; if it is not, add more salt and pepper. Now add half a cupful of cream, and let boil up once more. Have the chicken in a deep dish. Pour this sauce on it, and set away to cool. At serving time, have large slices of cold boiled sweet potatoes, fried in butter till a golden brown, handsomely arranged on a warm dish. On them place the chicken, which must be very cold. On each piece of the meat put a small teaspoonful of Tartare sauce. Heap the potatoes around the edge of the dish, garnish with parsley, and serve.

To Remove a Fillet from a Fowl or Bird.

Draw the skin off of the breast, and then run a sharp knife between the flesh and the ribs and breast-bone. You will in this way separate the two fillets from the body of the bird. The legs and wings of the largest birds and fowl can be boned, and stuffed with force-meat, and then prepared the same as, and served with, the fillet. The body of the bird can be used for soups. Fillets from all kinds of birds can be prepared the same as those from chickens.

Chicken Fillets, Larded and Breaded.

Lard the fillets, having four fine strips of pork for each one, and season with salt and pepper. Dip in beaten egg and in fine bread crumbs. Fry ten minutes in boiling fat. Serve on a hot dish with a spoonful of Tartare sauce on each.

Chicken Fillets, Braised.

Lard the fillets as for breading. For each one lay a slice of fat pork in the bottom of the braising-pan, and on this a very small piece of onion. Dredge the fillets well with salt, pepper, and flour, and place them on the pork and onion. Cover the pan, and set on the stove. Cook slowly half an hour; then add one pint of light stock or water and the bones of one of the chickens. Cover the pan, and place in a moderate oven for one hour, basting frequently with the gravy. If the gravy should cook away, add a little more stock or water (there should be nearly a pint of it at the end of the hour). Take up the fillets, and drain; then cover them with soft butter, and dredge lightly with flour. Broil till a light brown. Serve on a hot dish with the sauce poured around. Or, they can be dressed on a mound of mashed potato, with a garnish of any green vegetable at the base, the sauce to be poured around it.

To make the sauce: Skim all the fat from the gravy in which the fillets were cooked. Cook one table-spoonful of butter and one heaping tea-spoonful of flour together until a light brown; then add the gravy, and boil up once. Taste to see if seasoned enough, and strain.

Chicken Fillets, Sauté.

Flatten the fillets by pounding them lightly with the vegetable masher. Season with pepper and salt, and dredge well with flour. Put in the frying-pan one table-spoonful of butter for each fillet, and when hot put the fillets in, and cook rather slowly twenty minutes. Brown on both sides. Take up, and keep hot while making the sauce. If there are six fillets, add two table-spoonfuls of butter to that remaining in the frying-pan, and when melted stir in one table-spoonful of flour. Stir until it begins to brown slightly; then slowly add one and a half cupfuls of cold milk, stirring all the while. Let this boil one minute. Season with salt, pepper, and, if you like, a little mustard. Fill the centre of a hot dish with green peas or mashed potatoes, against which rest the fillets, and pour the sauce around. Serve very hot.

Chicken Curry.

One chicken, weighing three pounds; three fourths of a cupful of butter, two large onions, one heaping table-spoonful of curry powder, three tomatoes, or one cupful of the canned article, enough cayenne to cover a silver three-cent piece, salt, one cupful of milk. Put the butter and the onions, cut fine, on to cook. Stir all the while until brown; then put in the chicken, which has been cut in small pieces, the curry, tomatoes, salt, and pepper. Stir well. Cover tightly, and let simmer one hour, stirring occasionally; then add the milk. Boil up once, and serve with boiled rice. This makes a very rich and hot curry, but, for the real lover of the dish, none too much so.

Veal Curry.

Two pounds of veal, treated in the same manner, but cooked two hours. Mutton and lamb can be used in a like way.

Chicken Quenelles.

One large chicken or tender fowl, weighing about three pounds; six table-spoonfuls of butter, one table-spoonful of chopped salt pork, three eggs, one teaspoonful of onion juice, one of lemon juice, half a cupful of white stock or cream, one cupful of stale bread, one of new milk, and salt and pepper to taste. Skin the chicken, take all the flesh from the bones, and chop and pound *very* fine. Mix the pork with it, and rub through a flour sieve. Cook the bread and milk together for ten minutes, stirring often, to get smooth. Add this to the chicken, and then add the seasoning, stock or cream, yolks of eggs, one by one, and lastly the whites, which have been beaten to a stiff froth.

Cover the sides and bottom of a frying-pan with soft butter. Take two table-spoons and a bowl of boiling water. Dip one spoon in the water, and then fill it with force-meat, heaping it; then dip the other spoon in the hot water, and turn the contents of the first into it. This gives the *quenelle* the proper shape; and it should at once be slipped into the frying-pan. Continue the operation until all the meat is shaped. Cover the quenelles with white stock, boiling, and slightly salted, and cook gently twenty minutes. Take them up, and drain for a minute; then arrange on a border of mashed potatoes or fried bread. Pour a spoonful of either Bechamel, mushroom, or olive sauce on each, and the remainder in the centre of the dish. Serve hot.

Chicken Quenelles, Stuffed.

Prepare the force-meat as for *quenelles*. Soak four table-spoonfuls of gelatine for one hour in cold water to cover. Put two table-spoonfuls of butter in a frying-pan, and when hot add one table-spoonful of flour. Stir until smooth, but not brown; then gradually stir in one pint of cream. Add one table-spoonful of lemon juice, a speck of mace, and plenty of salt and pepper. Cook for two minutes. Stir in the soaked gelatine, and remove from the fire. Into this sauce stir one pint and a half of cold chicken, cut *very* fine. Set away to cool. Butter eighteen small egg cups, and cover the sides and bottoms with a thick layer of the force-meat. Fill the centre with the prepared force-meat, which should be quite firm. Cover with chicken. Place the cups in a steamer and cover them with sheets of thick paper. Put on the cover of the steamer, and place upon a kettle of boiling water for half an hour. Do not let the water boil too rapidly. Take up, and put away to cool. When cold, dip the *quenelles* twice in beaten egg and in bread crumbs. Fry in boiling fat for three minutes. Serve hot with a garnish of stoned olives.

Chicken Quenelles, Breaded.

Prepare the *quenelles* as before, and when they have been boiled, drain, and let them grow cold. Dip in beaten egg, and roll in bread crumbs; place in the frying-basket and plunge into boiling fat. Cook three minutes. Serve with fried parsley, or any kind of brown sauce.

Veal Quenelles.

One pound of clear veal, one cupful of white sauce, six table-spoonfuls of butter, one cupful of bread crumbs, one of milk, four eggs, salt, pepper, a slight grating of nutmeg, and the juice of half a lemon. Make and use the same as chicken *quenelles*.

Chicken Pillau.

Cut a chicken into pieces the size you wish to serve at the table. Wash clean, and put in a stewpan with about one eighth of a pound of salt pork, which has been cut in small pieces. Cover with cold water, and boil gently until the chicken begins to grow tender, which will be in about an hour, unless the chicken is old. Season rather highly with salt and pepper, add three teacupfuls of rice, which has been picked and washed, and let boil thirty or forty minutes longer. There should be a good quart of liquor in the stewpan when the rice is added. Care must be taken that it does not burn. Instead of chicken any kind of meat may be used.

Chicken Soufflé.

One pint of cooked chicken, finely chopped; one pint of cream sauce, four eggs, one teaspoonful of chopped parsley, one teaspoonful of onion juice, salt, pepper. Stir the chicken and seasoning into the boiling sauce. Cook two minutes. Add the yolks of the eggs, well beaten, and set away to cool. When cold, add the whites, beaten to a stiff froth. Turn into a buttered dish, and bake half an hour. Serve with mushroom or cream sauce. This dish must be served the moment it is baked. Any kind of delicate meat can be used, the soufflé taking the name of the meat of which it is made.

Fried Chicken.

Cut the chicken into six or eight pieces. Season well with salt and pepper. Dip in beaten egg, and then in fine bread crumbs in which there is one teaspoonful of chopped parsley for every cupful of crumbs. Dip again in the egg and crumbs. Fry ten minutes in boiling fat. Cover the centre of a cold dish with Tartare sauce. Arrange the chicken on this, and garnish with a border of pickled beets. Or, it can be served with cream sauce.

Blanquette of Chicken.

One quart of cooked chicken, cut in delicate pieces; one large cupful of white stock, three table-spoonfuls of butter, a heaping table-spoonful of flour, one teaspoonful of lemon juice, one cupful of cream or milk, the yolks of four eggs, salt, pepper. Put the butter in the saucepan, and when hot add the flour. Stir until smooth, but not brown. Add the stock, and cook two minutes; then add the seasoning and cream. As soon as this boils up, add the chicken. Cook ten minutes. Beat the yolks of the eggs with four table-spoonfuls of milk. Stir into the blanquette. Cook about half a minute longer. This can be served in a rice or potato border, in a *croustade*, on a hot dish, or with a garnish of toasted or fried bread.

Blanquette of Veal and Ham.

Half a pint of boiled ham, one pint and a half of cooked veal, one pint of cream sauce, one teaspoonful of lemon juice, the yolks of two uncooked eggs, salt, pepper, two hard-boiled eggs. Have the veal and ham cut in delicate pieces, which add with the seasoning to the sauce. When it boils up, add the yolks, which have been beaten with four table-spoonfuls of milk. Cook half a minute longer. Garnish with the hard-boiled eggs.

Salmis of Game.

Take the remains of a game dinner, say two or three grouse. Cut all the meat from the bones, in as handsome pieces as possible, and set aside. Break up the bones, and put on to boil with three pints of water, and two cloves. Boil down to a pint and a half. Put three table-spoonfuls of butter and two onions, cut in slices, on to fry. Stir all the time until the onions begin to brown; then add two spoonfuls of flour, and stir until a rich dark brown. Strain the broth on this. Stir a minute, and add one teaspoonful of lemon juice, and salt and pepper to taste; if you like, one table-spoonful of Leicestershire sauce, also. Add the cold game, and simmer fifteen minutes. Serve on slices of fried bread. Garnish with fried bread and parsley.

This dish can be varied by using different kinds of seasoning, and by serving sometimes with rice, and sometimes with mashed potatoes, for a border. Half a dozen mushrooms is a great addition to the dish, if added about five minutes before serving. A table-spoonful of curry powder, mixed with a little cold water, and stirred in with the other seasoning, will give a delicious curry of game. When curry is used, the rice border is the best of those mentioned above.

Game Cutlets à la Royale.

One quart of the tender parts of cold game, cut into dice; one generous pint of rich stock, one third of a box of gelatine, one quart of any kind of force-meat, four cloves, one table-spoonful of onion juice, two of butter, one of flour, three eggs, one pint of bread or cracker crumbs, salt, pepper. Soak the gelatine for one hour in half a cupful of cold water. Put the butter in a frying-pan, and when hot add the flour. Stir until smooth and brown, and add the stock and seasoning. Simmer ten minutes; strain upon the game, and simmer fifteen minutes longer. Beat an egg, and add to the gelatine. Stir this into the game and sauce, and take from the fire instantly. Place the stewpan in a basin of cold water, and stir until it begins to cool; then turn the mixture into a shallow baking-pan, having it about an inch thick. Set on the ice to harden. When hard, cut into cutlet-shaped pieces with a knife that has been dipped in hot water. When all the mixture is cut, put the pan in another of warm water for half a minute. This will loosen the cutlets from the bottom of the pan. Take them out carefully, cover every part of each cutlet with force-meat, and set on ice until near serving time. When ready to cook them, beat the two eggs with a spoon. Cover the cutlets with this and the crumbs. Place a few at a time in the frying-basket, and plunge them into boiling fat. Fry two minutes. Drain, and place on brown paper,

until all are cooked. Arrange them in a circle on a hot dish. Pour mushroom sauce in the centre, garnish with parsley, and serve. Poultry cutlets can be prepared and served in the same way.

Cutlets à la Duchesse.

Two pounds of lamb, mutton or veal cutlets, one large cupful of cream, one table-spoonful of onion juice, four table-spoonfuls of butter, one of flour, two whole eggs, the yolks of four more, two table-spoonfuls of finely chopped ham, one of lemon juice, and salt and pepper to taste. Put two table-spoonfuls of the butter in the frying-pan. Season the cutlets with salt and pepper, and when the butter is hot, put them in it. Fry gently for five minutes, if lamb or mutton; but if veal, put a cover on the pan, and fry very slowly for fifteen minutes. Set away to cool. Put the remainder of the butter in a small frying-pan, and when hot stir in the flour. Cook one minute, stirring all the time, and being careful not to brown. Stir in the cream. Have the ham, the yolks of eggs, and the onion and lemon juice beaten together. Stir this mixture into the boiling sauce. Stir for about one minute, and remove from the fire. Season well with pepper and salt. Dip the cutlets in this sauce, being careful to cover every part, and set away to cool. When cold, dip them in beaten egg and in bread crumbs. Fry in boiling fat for one minute. Arrange them in a circle on a hot dish, and have green peas in the centre and cream sauce poured around.

Cutlets served in Papillotes.

Fold and cut half-sheets of thick white paper, about the size of commercial note, so that when opened they will be heart-shaped. Dip them in melted butter, and set aside. After trimming all the fat from lamb or mutton chops, season them with pepper and salt. Put three table-spoonfuls of butter in the frying-pan, and when melted, lay in the chops, and cook slowly for fifteen minutes. Add one teaspoonful of finely chopped parsley, one teaspoonful of lemon juice, and one table-spoonful of Halford sauce. Dredge with one heaping table-spoonful of flour, and cook quickly five minutes longer. Take up the cutlets, and add to the sauce in the pan four table-spoonfuls of glaze and four of water. Stir until the glaze is melted, and set away to cool. When the sauce is cold, spread it on the cutlets. Now place these, one by one, on one side of the papers, having the bones turned toward the centre. Fold the papers and carefully turn in the edges. When all are done, place them in a pan, and put into a moderate oven for ten minutes; then place them in a circle, and fill the centre of the dish with thin fried, or French fried potatoes. Serve very hot. The quantities given above are for six cutlets.

Veal Cutlets with White Sauce.

One and a half pounds of cutlets, two table-spoonfuls of butter, a slice of carrot, and a small slice of onion. Put the butter and the vegetables, cut fine, in a sauce-pan. Season the cutlets with salt and pepper, and lay them on the butter and vegetables. Cover tightly, and cook slowly for half an hour; then take out, and dip in egg and bread crumbs, and fry in boiling fat till a golden brown. Or, dip the cutlets in soft butter and then in flour, and broil. Serve with white sauce poured around. Put a quart of green peas, or points of asparagus, in the centre of the dish, and arrange the cutlets around them. Pour on the sauce. This gives a handsome dish. Or, serve with olive sauce.

Mutton Cutlets, Crumbed.

Season French chops with salt and pepper, dip them in melted butter, and roll in *fine* bread crumbs. Broil for eight minutes over a fire not too bright, as the crumbs burn easily. Serve with potato balls heaped in the centre of the dish.

Mutton Cutlets, Breaded.

Trim the cutlets, and season with salt and pepper. Dip in beaten egg and in bread crumbs, and fry in boiling fat. If three quarters of an inch thick, they will be done rare in six minutes, and well done in ten. Arrange in the centre of a hot dish, and pour tomato sauce around them. One pint of sauce is enough for two pounds of cutlets.

Stewed Steak with Oysters.

Two pounds of rump steak, one pint of oysters, one table-spoonful of lemon juice, three of butter, one of flour, salt, pepper, one cupful of water. Wash the oysters in the water, and drain into a stew-pan. Put this liquor on to heat. As soon as it comes to a boil, skim, and set back. Put the butter in a frying-pan, and when hot, put in the steak. Cook ten minutes. Take up the steak, and stir the flour into the butter remaining in the pan. Stir until a dark brown. Add the oyster liquor, and boil one minute. Season with salt and pepper. Put back the steak, cover the pan, and simmer half an hour; then add the oysters and lemon juice. Boil one minute. Serve on a hot dish with points of toast for a garnish.

Rice Borders.

These are prepared in two ways. The first is to boil the rice as fo. a vegetable, and, with a spoon, heap it lightly around the edge of the fricassee, ragout, etc. The second method is a little more difficult. Put one cupful of rice on to boil in three cupfuls of cold water. When it has been boiling half an hour, add two table-spoonfuls of butter and one heaping teaspoonful of salt. Set back where it will just simmer, and cook one hour longer. Mash *very fine* with a spoon, add two well-beaten eggs, and stir for three minutes. Butter a plain border mould, and fill with the rice. Place in the heater for ten minutes. Turn upon a hot dish. Fill the centre with a fricassee, salmis, or blanquette, and serve hot. A mould with a border two inches high and wide, and having a space in the centre five and a half inches wide and eleven long, is pretty and convenient for rice and potato borders, and also for jelly borders, with which to decorate salads, boned chicken, creams, etc.

Potato Border.

Six potatoes, three eggs, one table-spoonful of butter, one of salt, half a cupful of boiling milk. Pare, boil, and mash the potatoes. When fine and light, add the butter, salt, and pepper, and two well-beaten eggs. Butter the border mould and pack the potato in it. Let this stand on the kitchen table ten minutes; then turn out on a dish and brush over with one well-beaten egg. Brown in the oven. Fill the centre with a curry, fricassee, salmis, or blanquette.

To Make a Croustade.

The bread for the *croustade* must not be too light, and should be at least three days old. If the loaf is round, it can be carved into the form of a vase, or if long, into the shape of a boat. Have a very sharp knife, and cut slowly and carefully, leaving the surface as smooth as possible. There are two methods by which it can be browned: one is to plunge it into a deep pot of boiling fat for about one minute; the other is to butter the entire surface of the bread and put it into a hot oven, being careful not to let it burn. Care must be taken that the inside is as brown as the outside; if not, the sauce will soak through the *croustade* and spoil it. Creamed oysters, stewed lobster, chicken, or any kind of meat that is served in a sauce, can be served in the *croustade*.

Cheese Soufflé.

Two table-spoonfuls of butter, one heaping table-spoonful of flour, half a cupful of milk, one cupful of grated cheese, three eggs, half a teaspoonful of salt, a speck of cayenne. Put the butter in a saucepan, and when hot add the flour, and stir until smooth, but not browned. Add the milk and seasoning. Cook two minutes; then add the yolks of the eggs, well beaten, and the cheese. Set away to cool. When cold, add the whites, beaten to a stiff froth. Turn into a buttered dish, and bake from twenty to twenty-five minutes. Serve the moment it comes from the oven. The dish in which this is baked should hold a quart. An escalop dish is the best.

Rissoles.

Roll the trimmings from pie crust into a sheet about a sixth of an inch thick. Cut this in cakes with the largest patty cutter. Have any kind of meat or fish prepared as for croquettes. Put a heaping teaspoonful on each cake. Brush the edges of the paste with beaten egg, and then fold and press together. When all are done, dip in beaten egg and fry brown in boiling fat. They should cook about eight minutes. Serve *hot*.

Fritter Batter.

One pint of flour, half a pint of milk, one table-spoonful of salad oil or butter, one teaspoonful of salt, two eggs. Beat the eggs light. Add the milk and salt to them. Pour half of this mixture on the flour, and when beaten light and smooth add the remainder and the oil. Fry in boiling fat. Sprinkle with sugar, and serve on a hot dish. This batter is nice for all kinds of fritters.

Fritter Batter, No. 2.

One pint of flour, one teaspoonful of salt, one of sugar, one of cream of tartar, half a teaspoonful of soda, one table-spoonful of oil, one egg, half a pint of milk. Mix the flour, salt, sugar, cream of tartar, and soda together, and rub through a sieve. Beat the egg very light, and add the milk. Stir half of this on the flour, and when the batter is light and smooth add the remainder, and finally the oil.

Chicken Fritters.

Cut cold roasted or boiled chicken or fowl in small pieces, and place in an earthen dish. Season well with salt, pepper, and the juice of a fresh lemon. Let the meat stand one hour; then make a fritter batter, and stir the pieces into it. Drop, by the spoonful, into boiling fat, and fry till a light brown. Drain, and serve immediately. Any kind of cold meat, if tender, can be used in this way.

Apple Fritters.

Pare and core the apples, and cut in slices about one third of an inch thick. Dip in the batter, and fry six minutes in boiling fat. Serve on a hot dish. The apples may be sprinkled with sugar and a little nutmeg, and let stand an hour before being fried. In that case sprinkle them with sugar when you serve them.

Fruit Fritters.

Peaches, pears, pineapples, bananas, etc., either fresh or canned, are used for fritters. If you choose, when making fruit fritters, you can add two table-spoonfuls of sugar to the batter.

Oyster Fritters.

One pint of oysters, two eggs, one pint of flour, one heaping teaspoonful of salt, one table-spoonful of salad oil, enough water with the oyster liquor to make a scant half-pint. Drain and chop the oysters. Add the water and salt to the liquor. Pour part of this on the flour, and when smooth add the remainder. Add the oil and the eggs, well beaten. Stir the oysters into the batter. Drop small spoonfuls of this into boiling fat, and fry until brown. Drain, and serve hot.

Clam Fritters.

Drain and chop a pint of clams, and season with salt and pepper. Make a fritter batter as directed, using, however, a *heaping* pint of flour, as the liquor in the clams thins the batter. Stir the clams into this, and fry in boiling fat.

Cream Fritters.

One pint of milk, the yolks of six and whites of two eggs, two table-spoonfuls of sugar, half a pint of flour, three heaping table-spoonfuls of butter, half a teaspoonful of salt, a slight flavoring of lemon, orange, nutmeg, or anything else you please. Put half of the milk on in the double boiler, and mix the flour to a smooth paste with the other half. When the milk boils, stir this into it. Cook for five minutes, stirring constantly; then add the butter, sugar, salt, and flavoring. Beat the eggs well, and stir them into the boiling mixture. Cook one minute. Butter a shallow cake-pan, and pour in the mixture. Have it about half an inch deep in the pan. Set away to cool. When cold, cut into small squares. Dip these in beaten egg and in crumbs, place in the frying-basket, and plunge into boiling fat. Fry till a golden brown. Arrange on a hot dish, sprinkle sugar over them, and serve *very hot*.

Potato Fritters.

One pint of boiled and mashed potato, half a cupful of hot milk, three table-spoonfuls of butter, three of sugar, two eggs, a little nutmeg, one teaspoonful of salt. Add the milk, butter, sugar, and seasoning to the mashed potato, and then add the eggs well beaten. Stir until very smooth and light. Spread, about half an inch deep, on a buttered dish, and set away to cool. When cold, cut into squares. Dip in beaten egg and in bread crumbs, and fry brown in boiling fat. Serve immediately.

Croquettes.

Care and practice are required for successfully making croquettes. The meat must be chopped fine, all the ingredients be thoroughly mixed, and the whole mixture be as moist as possible without spoiling the shape. Croquettes are formed in pear, round, and cylindrical shapes. The last is the best, as the croquettes can be moister in this form than in the two others.

To shape: Take about a table-spoonful of the mixture, and with both hands shape in the form of a cylinder. Handle as gently and carefully as if a tender bird. Pressure forces the particles apart, and thus breaks the form. Have a board sprinkled lightly with bread or cracker crumbs, and roll the croquettes *very gently* on this. Remember that the slightest pressure will break them. Let them lie on the board until all are finished; when, if any have become flattened, roll them into shape again. Cover a board *thickly* with crumbs. Have beaten eggs, slightly salted, in a deep plate. Hold a croquette in the left hand, and with a brush, or the right hand, cover it with the egg; then roll in the crumbs. Continue this until they are all crumbed. Place a few at a time in the frying-basket (they should not touch each other), and plunge into boiling fat. Cook till a rich brown. It will take about a minute and a half. Take up, and lay on brown paper in a warm pan.

Royal Croquettes.

Three small or two large sweetbreads, one boiled chicken, one large table-spoonful of flour, one pint of cream, half a cupful of butter, one table-spoonful of onion juice, one table-spoonful of chopped parsley, one teaspoonful of mace, the juice of half a lemon, and salt and pepper to taste. Let the sweetbreads stand in boiling water five minutes. Chop very fine, with the chicken, and add seasoning. Put two table-spoonfuls of the butter in a stewpan with the flour. When it bubbles, add the cream, gradually; then add the chopped mixture, and stir until thoroughly heated. Take from the fire, add the lemon juice, and set away to cool. Roll into shape with cracker crumbs. Dip in six beaten eggs and then in cracker crumbs. Let them stand until dry, when dip again in egg, and finally in bread crumbs — not too fine. All the crumbs should first be salted and peppered. Fry quickly in boiling fat.

Royal Croquettes, No. 2.

Half a boiled chicken, one large sweetbread, cleaned, and kept in hot water for five minutes; a calf's brains, washed, and boiled five minutes; one teaspoonful of chopped parsley, salt, pepper, half a pint of cream, one egg, quarter of a cupful of butter, one table-spoonful of corn-starch. Chop the chicken, brains, and sweetbread very fine, and add the egg well beaten. Mix the corn-starch with a little of the cream. Have the remainder of the cream boiling, and stir in the mixed corn-starch; then add the butter and the chopped mixture, and stir over the fire until it bubbles. Set aside to cool. Shape, and roll twice in egg and in cracker crumbs. Put in the frying-basket, and plunge into boiling fat. They should brown in less than a minute. — [Mrs. Furness, of Philadephia.

Oyster Croquettes.

Half a pint of raw oysters, half a pint of cooked veal, one heaping table-spoonful of butter, three table-spoonfuls of cracker crumbs, the yolks of two eggs, one table-spoonful of onion juice. Chop the oysters and veal very fine. Soak the crackers in oyster liquor, and then mix all the ingredients, and shape. Dip in egg and roll in cracker crumbs, and fry as usual. The butter should be softened before the mixing.

Lobster Croquettes.

Chop fine the meat of a two-pound lobster; take also two table-spoonfuls of butter, enough water or cream to make very moist, one egg, salt and pepper to taste, and half a table-spoonful of flour. Cook butter and flour together till they bubble. Add the cream or water (about a scant half-cupful), then the lobster and seasoning, and, when hot, the egg well beaten. Set away to cool. Shape, dip in egg and cracker crumbs, and fry as usual.

Salmon Croquettes.

One pound of cooked salmon (about a pint and a half when chopped), one cupful of cream, two table-spoonfuls of butter, one of flour, three eggs, one pint of crumbs, pepper, salt. Chop the salmon fine. Mix the flour and butter together. Let the cream come to a boil, and stir in the flour, butter, salmon, and seasoning. Boil for one minute. Stir into it one well-beaten egg, and remove from the fire. When cold, shape, and proceed as for other croquettes.

Shad Roe Croquettes.

One pint of cream, four table-spoonfuls of corn-starch, four shad roe, four table-spoonfuls of butter, one teaspoonful of salt, the juice of two lemons, a slight grating of nutmeg, and a speck of cayenne. Boil the roe fifteen minutes in salted water; then drain and mash. Put the cream on to boil. Mix the butter and corn-starch together, and stir into the boiling cream. Add the seasoning and roe. Boil up once, and set away to cool. Shape and fry as directed. — [Miss Lizzie Devereux.

Rice and Meat Croquettes.

One cupful of boiled rice, one cupful of finely chopped cooked meat, — any kind; one teaspoonful of salt, a little pepper, two table-spoonfuls of butter, half a cupful of milk, one egg. Put the milk on to boil, and add the meat, rice, and seasoning. When this boils, add the egg, well beaten; stir one minute. After cooling, shape, dip in egg and crumbs, and fry as before directed.

Rice Croquettes.

One large cupful of cooked rice, half a cupful of milk, one egg, one table-spoonful of sugar, one of butter, half a teaspoonful of salt, a slight grating of nutmeg. Put milk on to boil, and add rice and seasoning. When it boils up, add the egg, well beaten. Stir one minute; then take off and cool. When cold, shape, and roll in egg and crumbs, as directed. Serve very hot. Any flavoring can be substituted for the nutmeg.

Potato Croquettes.

Pare, boil, and mash six good-sized potatoes. Add one table-spoonful of butter, two thirds of a cupful of hot cream or milk, the whites of two eggs, well beaten, and salt and pepper to taste. If you wish, use also a slight grating of nutmeg, or a teaspoonful of lemon juice. Let the mixture cool slightly, then shape, roll in egg and crumbs, and fry.

Chicken Croquettes.

One solid pint of finely chopped cooked chicken, one table-spoonful of salt, half a teaspoonful of pepper, one cupful of cream or chicken stock, one table-spoonful of flour, four eggs, one teaspoonful of onion juice, one table-spoonful of lemon juice, one pint of crumbs, three table-spoonfuls of butter. Put the cream or stock on to boil. Mix the flour and butter together, and stir into the boiling cream; then add the chicken and seasoning. Boil for two minutes, and add two of the eggs, well beaten. Take from the fire immediately, and set away to cool. When cold, shape and fry. Many people think a teaspoonful of chopped parsley an improvement.

Other Croquettes.

Veal, mutton, lamb, beef, and turkey can be prepared in the same manner as chicken. Very dry, tough meat is not suitable for croquettes. Tender roasted pieces give the finest flavor.

Large Vol-au-Vent.

Make puff or chopped paste, according to the rule given, and let it get chilled through; roll it again four times, the last time leaving it a piece about seven inches square. Put in the ice chest for at least half an hour; then roll into a ten-inch square. Place on this a plate or a round tin, nine and a half inches in diameter, and, with a sharp knife, cut around the edge. Place another plate, measuring seven inches or a little more, in the centre. Dip a case-knife in hot water and cut around the plate, having the knife go two thirds through the paste. Place the paste in a flat baking-pan and put in a hot oven. After twelve or fifteen minutes, close the drafts, to slacken the heat, and cook half an hour longer, being careful not to let it burn. As soon as the vol-au-vent is taken from the oven, lift out the centre piece with a case-knife, and take out the uncooked paste with a spoon. Return the cover. At the time of serving, place in the oven to heat through; then fill and cover, and serve while hot. The vol-au-vent can be made and baked the day before using, if more convenient. Heat it and fill as directed.

Vol-au-Vent of Chicken.

Cut into dice one and a half pints of cooked chicken, and season with salt and pepper. Make a cream sauce, which season well with salt and pepper; and, if you like, add half a teaspoonful of onion juice and the same quantity of mixed mustard. Heat the chicken in this, and fill the vol-au-vent. All kinds of poultry and other meats can be used for a vol-au-vent with this sauce.

Vol-au-Vent of Sweetbreads.

Clean and wash two sweetbreads, and boil twenty minutes in water to cover. Drain and cool them, and cut into dice. Heat in cream sauce, and fill the vol-au-vent. Serve hot.

Vol-au-Vent of Salmon.

Heat one pint and a half of cooked salmon in cream sauce. Fill the vol-au-vent, and serve hot. Any rich, delicate fish can be served in a vol-au-vent.

Vol-au-Vent of Oysters.

Prepare the vol-au-vent as directed. Put one quart of oysters on to boil in their own liquor. As soon as a scum rises, skim it off, and drain the oysters. Return half a pint of the oyster liquor to the saucepan. Mix two heaping table-spoonfuls of butter with a scant one of flour, and when light and creamy, gradually turn on it the boiling oyster liquor. Season well with salt, pepper, and, if you like, a little nutmeg or mace (it must be only a "shadow"). Boil up once, and add three table-spoonfuls of cream and the oysters. Stir over the fire for half a minute. Fill the case, cover, and serve immediately.

Vol-au-Vent of Lobster.

Rub together four table-spoonfuls of butter and one and a half of flour. Pour on this, gradually, one pint of boiling white stock. Let it boil up once, and add the juice of a lemon, salt, and a speck of cayenne; add, also, the yolks of two eggs, beaten with a spoonful of cold water, and the meat of two small lobsters, cut into dice. Stir for one minute over the fire. Fill the case, put on the cover, and serve.

Patties.

Make puff paste as directed. (See Puff Paste.) After it has been rolled four times, put it on ice to harden. When hard, roll again twice. The last time leave the paste about an inch thick. Put in the ice chest to get very firm; then put on the board, and gently roll it down to three quarters of an inch in thickness. Great care must be taken to have every part equally thick. Cut out pieces with a round tin cutter three and a half inches in diameter, and place in the pans. Take another cutter two and a half inches in diameter, dip it in hot water, place in the centre of the patty, and cut about two thirds through. In doing this, do not press down directly, but use a rotary motion. These centre pieces, which are to form the covers, easily separate from the rest when baked. Place in a very hot oven. When they have been baking ten minutes, close the drafts, to reduce the heat; bake twenty minutes longer. Take from the oven, remove the centre pieces, and, with a teaspoon, dig out the uncooked paste. Fill with prepared fish or meat, put on the covers, and serve. Or, if more convenient to bake them early in the day, or, indeed, the previous day, put them in the oven twelve minutes before serving, and they will be nearly as nice as if fresh baked. The quantities given will make eighteen patties.

Chicken Patties.

Prepare the cream the same as for oysters, and add to it one pint of cold chicken, cut into dice. Boil three minutes. Fill the shells and serve. Where it is liked, one teaspoonful of onion juice is an improvement. Other poultry and all game can be served in patties the same as chicken.

Veal Patties.

Put in a stewpan a generous half-pint of white sauce with a pint of cooked veal, cut into dice, and a teaspoonful of lemon juice. Stir until very hot. Fill the shells, and serve.

Lobster Patties.

One pint of lobster, cut into dice; half a pint of white sauce, a speck of cayenne, one eighth of a teaspoonful of mustard. Heat all together. Fill the shells and serve.

Oyster Patties.

One pint of small oysters, half a pint of cream, a large teaspoonful of flour, salt, pepper. Let the cream come to a boil. Mix the flour with a little cold milk, and stir into the boiling cream. Season with salt and pepper. While the cream is cooking, let the oysters come to a boil in their own liquor. Skim carefully, and drain off all the liquor. Add the oysters to the cream, and boil up once. Fill the patty shells, and serve. The quantities given are enough for eighteen shells.

Crust Patties.

Cut a loaf of stale bread in slices an inch thick. With the patty cutter press out as many pieces as you wish patties, and with a smaller cutter press half through each piece. Place this second cutter as near the centre as possible when using. Put the pieces in the frying-basket, and plunge into boiling fat for half a minute. Take out and drain, and with a knife remove the centre crusts and take out the soft bread; then fill, and put on the centre pieces.

Filling for crusts: Put two table-spoonfuls of butter in the frying-pan, and when hot add one of flour. Stir until smooth and brown. Add one cupful of stock. Boil one minute, and stir in one pint of cooked veal, cut rather fine. Season with salt, pepper, and a little lemon juice. When hot, fill the crusts. Any kind of cold meat can be served in this manner.

Sweetbreads.

Sweetbreads are found in calves and lambs. The demand for calves' sweetbreads has grown wonderfully within the past ten years. In all our large cities they sell at all times of the year for a high price, but in winter and early spring they cost more than twice as much as they do late in the spring and during the summer. The throat and heart sweetbreads are often sold as one, but in winter, when they bring a very high price, the former is sold for the same price as the latter. The throat sweetbread is found immediately below the throat. It has an elongated form, is not so firm and fat, and has not the fine flavor of the heart sweetbread. The heart sweetbread is attached to the last rib, and lies near the heart. The form is somewhat rounded, and it is smooth and firm.

To Clean Sweetbreads.

Carefully pull off all the tough and fibrous skin. Place them in a dish of cold water for ten minutes or more, and they are then ready to be boiled. They must always be boiled twenty minutes, no matter what the mode of cooking is to be.

Sweetbreads Larded and Baked.

When the sweetbreads have been cleaned, draw through each one four very thin pieces of pork (about the size of a match). Drop them into cold water for five or ten minutes, then into hot water, and boil twenty minutes. Take out, spread with butter, dredge with salt, pepper, and flour, and bake twenty minutes in a quick oven. Serve with green peas, well drained, seasoned with salt and butter, and heaped in the centre of the dish. Lay the sweetbreads around them, and pour a cream sauce around the edge of the dish. Garnish with parsley. One pint of cream sauce is sufficient for eight or ten sweetbreads.

Sweetbread Sauté.

One sweetbread, after being boiled, split and cut in four pieces. Season with salt and pepper. Put in a small frying-pan one small table-spoonful of butter, and the same quantity of flour. When hot, put in the sweetbreads; turn constantly until a light brown. They will fry in about eight minutes. Serve with cream sauce or tomato sauce.

Broiled Sweetbreads.

Split the sweetbread after being boiled. Season with salt and pepper, rub thickly with butter, and sprinkle with flour. Broil over a rather quick fire, turning constantly. Cook about ten minutes, and serve with cream sauce.

Breaded Sweetbreads.

After being boiled, split them, and season with salt and pepper; then dip in beaten egg and cracker crumbs. Fry a light brown in hot lard. Serve with tomato sauce.

Sweetbreads in Cases.

Cut the sweetbreads, after being boiled, in very small pieces. Season with salt and pepper, and moisten well with cream sauce. Fill the paper cases, and cover with bread crumbs. Brown, and serve.

Pancakes.

Six eggs, a pint of milk, one heaping teaspoonful of salt, one cupful of flour, one table-spoonful of sugar, one of melted butter or of salad oil. Beat the eggs very light, and add the milk. Pour one third of this mixture on the flour, and beat until perfectly smooth and light; then add the remainder and the other ingredients. Heat and butter an omelet pan. Pour into it a thin layer of the mixture. When brown on one side, turn, and brown the other. Roll up, sprinkle with sugar, and serve hot. Or, cover with a thin layer of jelly, and roll. A number of them should be served on one dish.

SALADS.

A SALAD should come to the table fresh and crisp. The garnishes should be of the lightest and freshest kind. Nothing is more out of place than a delicate salad covered with hard-boiled eggs, boiled beets, etc. A salad with which the mayonnaise dressing is used should have only the delicate white leaves of the celery, or the small leaves from the heart of the lettuce, and these should be arranged in a wreath at the base, with a few tufts here and there on the salad. The contrast between the creamy dressing and the light green is not great, but it is pleasing. In arranging a salad on a dish, or in a bowl, handle it very lightly. Never use pressure to get it into form. When a jelly border is used with salads, some of it should be helped with the salad. The small round radishes

may be arranged in the dish with a lettuce salad. In washing lettuce great care must be taken not to break or wilt it. The large dark green leaves are not nice for salad. As lettuce is not an expensive vegetable, it is best, when the heads are not round and compact, to buy an extra one and throw the large tough leaves away. In winter and early spring, when lettuce is raised in hot-houses, it is liable to have insects on it. Care must be taken that all are washed off. Only the white, crisp parts of celery should be used in salads. The green, tough parts will answer for stews and soups. Vegetable salads can be served for tea and lunch, and with, or after, the meats at dinner. The hot cabbage, red cabbage, celery, cucumber, and potato salads are particularly appropriate for serving with meats. The lettuce salad, with the French dressing, and the dressed celery, are the best to serve after the meats. A rich salad, like chicken, lobster, or salmon, is out of place at a company dinner. It is best served for suppers and lunches. The success of a salad (after the dressing is made) depends upon keeping the lettuce or celery crisp, and not adding meat or dressing to it until the time for serving.

Mayonnaise Dressing.

A table-spoonful of mustard, one of sugar, one tenth of a teaspoonful of cayenne, one teaspoonful of salt, the yolks of three uncooked eggs, the juice of half a lemon, a quarter of a cupful of vinegar, a pint of oil, and a cupful of whipped cream. Beat the yolks and dry ingredients, until they are very light and thick, with either a silver or wooden spoon,—or, better still, with a Dover beater of second size. The bowl in which the dressing is made should be set in a pan of ice water during the beating. Add a few drops of oil at a time, until the dressing becomes very *thick* and rather hard. After it has reached this stage, the oil can be added more rapidly. When it gets so thick that the beater turns hard, add a little vinegar. When the last of the oil and vinegar has been added, it should be *very* thick. Now add the lemon juice and whipped cream, and place on ice for a few hours, unless you are ready to use it. The cream may be omitted without injury.

Salad Dressing made at the Table.

The yolk of a raw egg, a table-spoonful of mixed mustard, one fourth of a teaspoonful of salt, six table-spoonfuls of oil. Stir the yolk, mustard, and salt together with a fork until they begin to thicken. Add the oil, gradually, stirring all the while. More or less oil can be used.

Cream Salad Dressing.

Two eggs, three table-spoonfuls of vinegar, one of cream, one teaspoonful of sugar, one fourth of a teaspoonful of salt, one fourth of a teaspoonful of mustard. Beat two eggs well. Add the sugar, salt, and mustard, then the vinegar, and the cream. Place the bowl in a basin of boiling water, and stir until about the thickness of rich cream. If the bowl is thick and the water boils all the time, it will take about five minutes. Cool, and use as needed.

Red Mayonnaise Dressing.

Lobster "coral" is pounded to a powder, rubbed through a sieve, and mixed with mayonnaise dressing. This gives a dressing of a bright color. Or, the juice from boiled beets can be used instead of "coral."

Green Mayonnaise Dressing.

Mix enough spinach green with mayonnaise sauce to give it a bright green color. A little finely chopped parsley can be added.

Aspic Mayonnaise Dressing.

Melt, but heat only slightly, one cupful of aspic jelly; or, one cupful of consommé will answer, if it is well jellied. Put in a bowl and place in a basin of ice water. Have ready the juice of half a lemon, one cupful of salad oil, one fourth of a cupful of vinegar, one table-spoonful of sugar, one scant table-spoonful of mustard, one teaspoonful of salt, and one tenth of a teaspoonful of cayenne. Mix the dry ingredients with the vinegar. Beat the jelly with a whisk, and as soon as it begins to thicken add the oil and vinegar, a little at a time. Add the lemon juice the last thing. You must beat all the time after the bowl is placed in the ice water. This gives a whiter dressing than that made with the yolks of eggs.

Boiled Salad Dressing.

Three eggs, one table-spoonful each of sugar, oil, and salt, a scant table-spoonful of mustard, a cupful of milk, and one of vinegar. Stir oil, salt, mustard, and sugar in a bowl until perfectly smooth. Add the eggs, and beat well; then add the vinegar, and finally the milk. Place the bowl in a basin of boiling water, and stir the dressing until it thickens like soft custard. The time of cooking depends upon the thickness of the bowl. If a common white bowl is used, and it is placed in water that is boiling at the time and is kept constantly boiling, from eight to ten minutes will suffice; but if the bowl is very thick, from twelve to fifteen minutes will be needed. The dressing will keep two weeks if bottled tightly and put in a cool place.

Sour Cream Salad Dressing.

One cupful of sour cream, one teaspoonful of salt, a speck of cayenne, one table-spoonful of lemon juice, three of vinegar, one teaspoonful of sugar. Mix all together thoroughly. This is best for vegetables.

Sardine Dressing.

Pound in a mortar, until perfectly smooth, the yolks of four hard-boiled eggs and three sardines, which have been freed of bones, if there were any. Add the mixture to any of the thick dressings, like the mayonnaise or the boiled. This dressing is for fish.

Salad Dressing without Oil.

The yolks of four uncooked eggs, one table-spoonful of salt, one heaping teaspoonful of sugar, one heaping teaspoonful of mustard, half a cupful of clarified chicken fat, a quarter of a cupful of vinegar, the juice of half a lemon, a speck of cayenne. Make as directed for mayonnaise dressing.

Salad Dressing made with Butter.

Four table-spoonfuls of butter, one of flour, one table-spoonful of salt, one of sugar, one heaping teaspoonful of mustard, a speck of cayenne, one cupful of milk, half a cupful of vinegar, three eggs. Let the butter get hot in a saucepan. Add the flour, and stir until smooth, being careful not to brown. Add the milk, and boil up. Place the saucepan in another of hot water. Beat the eggs, salt, pepper, sugar, and mustard together, and add the vinegar. Stir this into the boiling mixture, and stir until it thickens like soft custard, which will be in about five minutes. Set away to cool; and when cold, bottle, and place in the ice chest. This will keep two weeks.

Bacon Salad Dressing.

Two table-spoonfuls of bacon or pork fat, one of flour, one of lemon juice, half a teaspoonful of salt, one teaspoonful of sugar, one of mustard, two eggs, half a cupful of water, half a cupful of vinegar. Have the fat hot. Add the flour, and stir until smooth, but not brown. Add the water, and boil up once. Place the saucepan in another of boiling water. Have the eggs and seasoning beaten together. Add the vinegar to the boiling mixture, and stir in the beaten egg. Cook four minutes, stirring all the while. Cool and use. If corked tightly, this will keep two weeks in a cold place.

French Salad Dressing.

Three table-spoonfuls of oil, one of vinegar, one salt-spoonful of salt, one half a salt-spoonful of pepper. Put the salt and pepper in a cup, and add one table-spoonful of the oil. When thoroughly mixed, add the remainder of the oil and the vinegar. This is dressing enough for a salad for six persons. If you like the flavor of onion, grate a little juice into the dressing. The juice is obtained by first peeling the onion, and then grating with a coarse grater, using a good deal of pressure. Two strokes will give about two drops of juice, — enough for this rule.

Chicken Salad.

Have cold roasted or broiled chicken free of skin, fat, and bones. Place on a board, and cut in long, thin strips, and cut these into dice. Place in an earthen bowl (there should be two quarts), and season with four table-spoonfuls of vinegar, two of oil, one teaspoonful of salt, and one half of a teaspoonful of pepper. Set away in a cold place for two or three hours. Scrape and wash enough of the tender white celery to make one quart. Cut this, with a sharp knife, in pieces about half an inch thick. Put these in the ice chest until serving time. Make the mayonnaise dressing. Mix the chicken and celery together, and add half of the dressing. Arrange in a salad bowl or on a flat dish, and pour the remainder of the dressing over it. Garnish with white celery leaves. Or, have a jelly border, and arrange the salad in this. Half celery and half lettuce is often used for chicken salad. Many people, when preparing for a large company, use turkey instead of chicken, there being so much more meat in the same number of pounds of the raw material; but the salad is not nearly so nice as with chicken. If, when the chicken or fowl is cooked, it is allowed to cool in the water in which it is boiled, it will be juicier and tenderer than if taken from the water as soon as done.

Lobster Salad.

Cut up and season the lobster the same as chicken. Break the leaves from a head of lettuce, one by one, and wash them singly in a large pan of cold water. Put them in a pan of ice water for about ten minutes, and then shake in a wire basket to free them of water. Place in the ice chest until serving time. When ready to serve, put two or three leaves together in the form of a shell, and arrange these shells on a flat dish. Mix one half of the mayonnaise dressing with the lobster. Put a table-spoonful of this in each cluster of leaves. Finish with a teaspoonful of the dressing on each spoonful of lobster. This is an exceedingly inviting dish. Another method is to cut or tear the leaves rather coarse, and mix with the lobster. Garnish the border of the dish with whole leaves. There should be two thirds lobster to one third lettuce.

Salmon Salad.

One quart of cooked salmon, two heads of lettuce, two table-spoonfuls of lemon juice, one of vinegar, two of capers, one teaspoonful of salt, one third of a teaspoonful of pepper, one cupful of mayonnaise dressing, or the French dressing. Break up the salmon with two silver forks. Add to it the salt, pepper, vinegar, and lemon juice. Put in the ice chest, or some other cold place, for two or three hours. Prepare the lettuce as directed for lobster salad. At serving time, pick out leaves enough to

border the dish. Cut or tear the remainder in pieces, and arrange these in the centre of a flat dish. On them heap the salmon lightly, and cover with the dressing. Now sprinkle on the capers. Arrange the whole leaves at the base, and, if you choose, lay one fourth of a thin slice of lemon on each leaf.

Oyster Salad.

One pint of celery, one quart of oysters, one third of a cupful of mayonnaise dressing, three table-spoonfuls of vinegar, one of oil, half a teaspoonful of salt, one eighth of a teaspoonful of pepper, one table-spoonful of lemon juice. Let the oysters come to a boil in their own liquor. Skim well and drain. Season them with the oil, salt, pepper, vinegar, and lemon juice. When cold, put in the ice chest for at least two hours. Scrape and wash the whitest and tenderest part of the celery, and, with a sharp knife, cut in very thin slices. Put in a bowl with a large lump of ice, and set in the ice chest until serving time. When ready to serve, drain the celery, and mix with the oysters and half of the dressing. Arrange in the dish, pour the remainder of the dressing over and garnish with white celery leaves.

Sardine Salad.

Arrange one quart of any kind of cooked fish on a bed of crisp lettuce. Split six sardines, and if there are any bones, remove them. Cover the fish with the sardine dressing. Over this put the sardines, having the ends meet in the centre of the dish. At the base of the dish make a wreath of thin slices of lemon. Garnish with parsley or lettuce, and serve immediately.

Shad Roe Salad.

Three shad roe, boiled in salted water twenty minutes. When cold, cut in thin slices. Season and set away, the same as salmon. Serve the same as salmon, except omit the capers, and use chopped pickled beet.

Salads of Fish.

All kinds of cooked fish can be served in salads. Lettuce is the best green salad to use with them, but all green vegetables, when cooked and cold, can be added to the fish and dressing. The sardine and French dressings are the best to use with fish.

Polish Salad.

One quart of cold game or poultry, cut very fine; the French dressing, four hard-boiled eggs, one large or two small heads of lettuce. Moisten the meat with the dressing, and let it stand in the ice chest two or three hours. Rub the yolks of the eggs to a powder, and chop the whites very fine. Wash the lettuce and put in the ice chest until serving time. When ready to serve, put the lettuce leaves together and cut in long, narrow strips with a sharp knife, or tear it with a fork. Arrange on a dish, heap the meat in the centre, and sprinkle the egg over all.

Beef Salad.

One quart of cold roasted or stewed beef — it must be very tender, double the rule for French dressing, one table-spoonful of chopped parsley, and one of onion juice, to be mixed with the dressing. Cut the meat in thin slices, and then into little squares. Place a layer in the salad bowl, sprinkle with parsley and dressing, and continue this until all the meat is used. Garnish with parsley, and keep in a cold place for one or two hours. Any kind of meat can be used instead of beef.

Meat and Potato Salad.

Prepare the meat as directed for beef salad, using, however, one half the quantity. Add one pint of cold boiled potatoes, cut in thin slices, and dressing. Garnish, and set away as before. These salads can be used as soon as made, but the flavor is improved by their standing an hour or more.

Bouquet Salad.

Four hard-boiled eggs, finely chopped; one head of lettuce, or one pint of water-cresses; a large bunch of nasturtium blossoms or butter-cups, the French dressing, with the addition of one teaspoonful of sugar. Wash the lettuce or cresses, and throw into ice water. When crisp, take out, and shake out all the water. Cut or tear in pieces. Put a layer in the bowl, with here and there a flower, and sprinkle in half of the egg and half the dressing. Repeat this. Arrange the flowers in a wreath, and put a few in the centre. Serve immediately.

Cauliflower Salad.

Boil one large cauliflower with two quarts of water and one table-spoonful of salt, for half an hour. Take up and drain. When cold, divide into small tufts. Arrange on the centre of a dish, and garnish with a border of strips of pickled beet. Pour cream dressing, or a cupful of mayonnaise dressing, over the cauliflower. Arrange a star of the pickled beet in the centre. Serve immediately.

Asparagus Salad.

Boil two bunches of asparagus with one quart of water and one table-spoonful of salt, for twenty minutes. Take up and drain on a sieve. When cold, cut off the tender points, and arrange them on the dish. Pour on cream salad dressing.

Asparagus and Salmon Salad.

Prepare the asparagus as before directed. Season a quart of cooked salmon with one teaspoonful of salt, one third of a teaspoonful of pepper, three table-spoonfuls of oil, one of vinegar, and two of lemon juice. Let this stand in the ice chest at least two hours. Arrange the salmon in the centre of the dish and the asparagus points around it. Cover the fish with one cupful of mayonnaise dressing. Garnish the dish with points of lemon. Green peas can be used instead of asparagus.

Cucumber Salad.

Cut about one inch off of the point of the cucumber, and pare. (The bitter juice is in the point, and if this is not cut off before paring, the knife carries the flavor all through the cucumber.) Cut in thin slices, cover with cold water, and let stand half an hour. Drain, and season with French dressing. If oil is not liked it can be omitted.

Tomato Salad.

Pare ripe tomatoes (which should be very cold), and cut in thin slices. Arrange on a flat dish. Put one teaspoonful of mayonnaise dressing in the centre of each slice. Place a delicate border of parsley around the dish, and a sprig here and there between the slices of tomato.

Cabbage Salad.

One large head of cabbage, twelve eggs, two small cupfuls of sugar, two teaspoonfuls of salt, one table-spoonful of melted butter, two teaspoonfuls of mustard, one cupful of vinegar, or more, if you like. Divide the cabbage into four pieces, and wash well in cold water. Take off all the wilted leaves and cut out the tough, hard parts. Cut the cabbage very fine with a *sharp* knife. Have the eggs boiled hard, and ten of them chopped fine. Add these and the other ingredients to the cabbage. Arrange on a dish and garnish with the two remaining eggs and pickled beets.

Hot Cabbage Salad.

One quart of finely shaved cabbage, two table-spoonfuls of bacon or pork fat, two large slices of onion, minced *very fine ;* one teaspoonful of salt, one fourth of a teaspoonful of pepper, half a cupful of vinegar, one teaspoonful of sugar. Fry the onion in the fat until it becomes yellow; then add the other ingredients. Pour the hot mixture on the cabbage. Stir well, and serve at once. Lettuce can be served in the same manner.

Vegetable Salad.

A spoonful of green parsley, chopped fine with a knife; six potatoes, half of a small turnip, half of a carrot, one small beet. Cut the potatoes in small slices, the beet a little finer, and the turnip and carrot very fine. Mix all thoroughly. Sprinkle with a scant teaspoonful of salt, unless the vegetables were salted in cooking, and add the whole French dressing, or half a cupful of the boiled dressing. Keep very cool until served.

Red Vegetable Salad.

One pint of cold boiled potatoes, one pint of cold boiled beets, one pint of uncooked red cabbage, six table-spoonfuls of oil, eight of red vinegar (that in which beets have been pickled), two teaspoonfuls of salt (unless the vegetables have been cooked in salted water), half a teaspoonful of pepper. Cut the potatoes in *thin* slices and the beets fine, and slice the cabbage as thin as possible. Mix all the ingredients. Let stand in a cold place one hour; then serve. Red cabbage and celery may be used together. Use the French dressing.

Potato Salad.

Ten potatoes, cut fine ; the French dressing, with four or five drops of onion juice in it, and one table-spoonful of chopped parsley.

Potato Salad, No. 2.

One quart of potatoes, two table-spoonfuls of grated onion, two of chopped parsley, four of chopped beet, and enough of any of the dressings to make moist. The sardine is the best for this. Pare and cut the potatoes in thin slices, while hot. Mix the other ingredients with them, and put away in a cool place until serving time. This is better for standing two or three hours.

Cooked Vegetables in Salad.

Nearly every kind of cooked vegetables can be served in salads. They can be served separately or mixed. They must be cold and well drained before the dressing is added. Any of the dressings given, except sardine, can be used.

Dressed Celery.

Scrape and wash the celery. Let it stand in ice water twenty minutes, and shake dry. With a sharp knife, cut it in pieces about an inch long. Put in the ice chest until serving time ; then moisten well with mayonnaise dressing. Arrange in the salad bowl or on a flat dish. Garnish with a border of white celery leaves or water-cresses. When served on a flat dish, points of pickled beets, arranged around the base, make an agreeable change.

Lettuce Salad.

Two small, or one large head of lettuce. Break off all the leaves carefully, wash each separately, and throw into a pan of ice water, where they should remain an hour. Put them in a wire basket or coarse towel, and *shake* out all the water. Either cut the leaves with a sharp knife, or tear them in large pieces. Mix the French dressing with them, and serve immediately. Beets, cucumbers, tomatoes, cauliflower, asparagus, etc., can each be served as a salad, with French or boiled dressing. Cold potatoes, beef, mutton, or lamb, cut fine, and finished with either dressing, make a good salad.

MEAT AND FISH SAUCES.

Brown Sauce.

ONE pound of round beef, one pound of veal, cut from the lower part of the leg ; eight table-spoonfuls of butter, one onion, one large slice of carrot, four cloves, a small piece of mace, five table-spoonfuls of flour, salt and pepper to taste, four quarts of stock. Cut the meat in small pieces. Rub three spoonfuls of the butter on the bottom of a large stewpan. Put in the meat, and cook half an hour, stirring frequently. Add the vegetables, spice, a bouquet of sweet herbs, and one quart of the stock. Simmer this two hours, and add the remainder of the stock. Half a dozen mushrooms will improve the flavor greatly. Put the remainder of the butter in a frying-pan, and when hot add the flour. Stir until dark brown, and as soon as it begins to boil add to the sauce. Simmer one hour longer. Season with salt and pepper, and strain through a fine French sieve or gravy strainer. Skim off the fat, and the sauce is ready to use. This will keep a week in winter. It is the foundation for all fine dark sauces, and will well repay for the trouble and expense of making.

White Sauce.

Make the white sauce the same as the brown, but use all veal and white stock. When the butter and flour are cooked together, be careful that they do not get browned.

White Sauce, No. 2.

One quart of milk, four table-spoonfuls of butter, four of flour, a small slice of onion, two sprigs of parsley, salt and pepper to taste. Put the milk, onion, and parsley on in the double boiler. Mix the butter and flour together until smooth and light. When the milk boils, stir four table-spoonfuls of it into the butter and flour, and when this is well mixed, stir it into the boiling milk. Cook eight minutes. Strain, and serve. This sauce is best with fish.

White Sauce, No. 3.

One large slice of onion, one small slice of carrot, a clove, a small piece of mace, twelve pepper-corns, two table-spoonfuls of flour, two heaping table-spoonfuls of butter, one quart of cream not very rich, salt to taste. Cook the spice and vegetables slowly in the butter for twenty minutes. Add the flour, and stir until smooth, being careful not to brown. Add the cream, gradually, stirring all the while. Boil for two minutes. Strain, and serve. This sauce is good for veal and chicken cutlets, *quenelles,* sweetbreads, etc.

White Sauce, No 4.

One pint of milk, one of cream, four table-spoonfuls of flour, the yolks of two eggs, salt and pepper to taste. Put the milk and cream on in the double boiler, reserving one cupful of the milk. Pour eight table-spoonfuls of the milk on the flour, stir until perfectly smooth, and add the remainder of the milk. Stir this into the other milk when it boils. Stir the sauce for two minutes ; then cover, and cook eight minutes longer. Season well with salt and pepper. Beat the yolks of the eggs with four spoonfuls of cream or milk. Stir into the sauce, and remove from the fire immediately. The eggs may be omitted, if you choose. One table-spoonful of chopped parsley, stirred into the sauce just before taking from the fire, is an improvement. This sauce is nice for all kinds of boiled fish, but particularly for boiled salt fish.

Bechamel Sauce.

One pint of white sauce, one pint of rich cream, salt, pepper. Let the sauce and cream come to a boil separately. Mix them together, and boil up once. Strain, and serve.

Cream Bechamel Sauce.

Three table-spoonfuls of butter, three scant ones of flour, ten peppercorns, a small piece of mace, half an onion, a large slice of carrot, two cupfuls of white stock, one of cream, salt, a little nutmeg, two sprigs of parsley, one of thyme, and one bay leaf. Tie the parsley, bay leaf, and thyme together. Rub the butter and flour to a smooth paste. Put all the ingredients, except the cream, in a stewpan, and simmer half an hour, stirring frequently ; add the cream, and boil up once. Strain, and serve.

Allemande Sauce.

One pint of white sauce, the yolks of six eggs, the juice of half a lemon, one table-spoonful of mushroom ketchup, one table-spoonful of butter, half a cupful of cream, salt, pepper, a grating of nutmeg. Let the sauce come to a boil. Place the saucepan in another of boiling water, and add all the seasoning except the lemon. Beat the yolks of eggs and the cream together, and add to the sauce. Stir three minutes. Take off, add the lemon juice, and strain.

Cream Sauce.

One pint of cream, one generous table-spoonful of flour, and salt and pepper to taste. Let the cream come to a boil. Have the flour mixed smooth with half a cupful of cold cream, reserved from the pint, and stir it into the boiling cream. Add seasoning, and boil three minutes. This sauce is good for delicate meats, fish, and vegetables, and to pour around croquettes and baked and Quaker omelets.

Cream Sauce, No. 2.

One cupful of milk, a teaspoonful of flour, and a table-spoonful of butter, salt, and pepper. Put the butter in a small frying-pan, and when hot, *but not brown*, add the flour. Stir until smooth; then gradually add the milk. Let it boil up once. Season to taste with salt and pepper, and serve. This is nice to cut cold potatoes into and let them just heat through. They are then creamed potatoes. It also answers as a sauce for other vegetables, omelets, fish, and sweetbreads, or, indeed, for anything that requires a white sauce. If you have plenty of cream, use it, and omit the butter.

Polish Sauce.

One pint of stock, two table-spoonfuls of butter, four of grated horse-radish, one of flour, one of chopped parsley, the juice of one lemon, one teaspoonful of sugar, salt, pepper. Cook the butter and flour together until smooth, but not brown. Add the stock; and when it boils, add all the other ingredients except the parsley. Boil up once, and add the parsley. This sauce is for roast veal.

Robert Sauce.

Two cupfuls of stock, two small onions, four table-spoonfuls of butter, one heaping table-spoonful of flour, one teaspoonful of dry mustard, one of sugar, a speck of cayenne, two table-spoonfuls of vinegar, salt. Cut the onions into dice, and put on with the butter. Stir until they begin to color; then add the flour, and stir until brown. As soon as it boils, add the stock and other ingredients, and simmer five minutes. Skim and serve.

Supreme Sauce.

Add to one pint of white sauce three finely chopped mushrooms, the juice of half a lemon, and one table-spoonful of butter. Simmer all together ten minutes. Rub through the strainer and use.

Olive Sauce.

Two dozen queen olives, one pint of rich stock, the juice of one lemon, two table-spoonfuls of salad oil, one of flour, salt, pepper, a small slice of onion. Let the olives stand in hot water half an hour, to extract the salt. Put the onion and oil in the stewpan, and as soon as the onion begins to color add the flour. Stir until smooth, and add the stock. Set back where it will simmer. Pare the olives, round and round, close to the stones, and have the pulp in a single piece. If this is done carefully with a sharp knife, in somewhat the same way that an apple skin is removed whole, the olives will still have their natural shape after the stones are taken out. Put them in the sauce, add the seasoning, and simmer twenty minutes. Skim carefully, and serve. If the sauce is liked thin, half the amount of flour given can be used. This sauce is for roast ducks and other game.

Flemish Sauce.

Cut a cupful of the red part of a carrot into *very small* dice. Cover with boiling water, and simmer one hour. Put three table-spoonfuls of butter, two of flour, a slice of carrot, an onion cut fine, a blade of mace, and twenty pepper-corns in a saucepan. Stir over the fire one minute, and add two cupfuls of stock. Simmer gently half an hour. Add a cupful of cream, boil up once, and strain. Now add the cooked carrot, one table-spoonful of chopped parsley, two of chopped cucumber pickles, and, if you like, one of grated horseradish. Taste to see if salt enough.

Chestnut Sauce.

One pint of shelled chestnuts, one quart of stock, one teaspoonful of lemon juice, one table-spoonful of flour, two of butter, salt, pepper. Boil the chestnuts in water for about three minutes; then plunge them into cold water, and rub off the dark skins. Put them on to cook with the stock, and boil gently until they will mash readily (it will take about an hour). Mash as fine as possible. Put the butter and flour in a saucepan and cook until a dark brown. Stir into the sauce, and cook two minutes. Add the seasoning, and rub all through a sieve. This sauce is for roast turkey. When to be served with boiled turkey, use only a pint and a half of stock; rub the butter and flour together, and stir into the boiling mixture; rub through the sieve as before; add half a pint of cream to the sauce; return to the fire, boil up once, and serve. The chestnuts used are twice as large as the native fruit. All first-class provision dealers and grocers keep them.

Celery Sauce.

Cut the tender parts of a head of celery *very fine*. Pour on water enough to cover them, and no more. Cover the saucepan, and set where it will simmer one hour. Mix together two table-spoonfuls of flour and four of butter. When the celery has been boiling one hour, add to it the butter and flour, one pint of milk or cream, and salt and pepper. Boil up once, and serve.

Brown Mushroom Sauce.

One forty-cent can of French mushrooms, two cupfuls of stock, two table-spoonfuls of flour, four of butter, salt, pepper. Melt the butter. Add the flour, and stir until a very dark brown; then gradually add the stock. When this boils up, add the liquor from the mushrooms. Season, and simmer twenty minutes. Skim off any fat that may rise to the top. Add the mushrooms, and simmer five minutes longer. Too much cooking toughens the mushrooms. This sauce is to be served with any kind of roasted, broiled, or braised meats. It is especially nice with beef.

Brown Mushroom Sauce, No. 2.

One pint of stock, two cloves, one small slice each of turnip, carrot, and onion, three table-spoonfuls of butter, two of flour, half a can of mushrooms, or one eighth of a pound of the fresh vegetable. Cut the vegetables in small pieces, and fry in the butter with the cloves until brown. Add the flour, and stir until dark brown; then gradually add the stock. Chop the mushrooms, stir into the sauce, and simmer half an hour. Rub through the sieve. Use the same as the other brown mushroom sauce.

White Mushroom Sauce.

Make a mushroom sauce like the first, using one cupful of white stock and one cupful of cream, and cooking the butter only until smooth. Do not let it become browned.

Beurre Noir.

Two table-spoonfuls of butter, one of vinegar, one of chopped parsley, one teaspoonful of lemon juice, half a teaspoonful of salt, one quarter of a teaspoonful of pepper. Put the butter in a frying-pan, and when *very* hot add the parsley and then the other ingredients. Boil up once. This sauce is for fried and broiled fish, and it is poured over the fish before sending to the table.

Maître d'Hôtel Butter.

Four table-spoonfuls of butter, one of vinegar, one of lemon juice, half a teaspoonful of salt, one quarter of a teaspoonful of pepper, one teaspoonful of chopped parsley. Beat the butter to a cream, and gradually beat in the seasoning. This sauce is spread on fried and broiled meats and fish instead of butter. It is particularly nice for fish and beefsteak.

Maître d'Hôtel Sauce.

One pint of white stock, the yolks of three eggs, one heaping table-spoonful of corn-starch. Put the stock on to boil, reserving one third of a cupful for the corn-starch. Mix the corn-starch with the cold stock and stir into the boiling. Boil gently for five minutes. Prepare the *maître d'hôtel* butter as directed in the rule, and add to it the yolks of the eggs. Gradually stir into this the boiling mixture. After placing the saucepan in another of boiling water, stir constantly for three minutes. Take off, and serve.

Hollandaise Sauce.

Half a tea-cupful of butter, the juice of half a lemon, the yolks of two eggs, a speck of cayenne, half a cupful of boiling water, half a teaspoonful of salt. Beat the butter to a cream; then add the yolks, one by one, the lemon juice, pepper and salt. Place the bowl in which these are mixed in a sauce-pan of boiling water. Beat with an egg-beater until the sauce begins to thicken (about a minute), and add the boiling water, beating all the time. When like a soft custard it is done. The bowl, if thin, must be kept over the fire only about five minutes, provided the water boils all the time. The sauce should be poured around meat or fish when it is on the dish.

Lobster Sauce.

One small lobster, four table-spoonfuls of butter, two of flour, one fifth of a teaspoonful of cayenne, two table-spoonfuls of lemon juice, one pint of boiling water. Cut the meat into dice. Pound the "coral" with one table-spoonful of the butter. Rub the flour and the remainder of the butter to a smooth paste. Add the water, pounded "coral" and butter, and the seasoning. Simmer five minutes, and then strain on the lobster. Boil up once, and serve. This sauce is for all kinds of boiled fish.

Butter Sauce.

Two table-spoonfuls of flour, half a cupful of butter, and one pint of boiling water. Work the flour and butter together until light and creamy, and gradually add the boiling water. Stir constantly until it comes to a boil, but do not let it boil. Take from the fire, and serve. A table-spoonful of lemon juice and a speck of cayenne may be added if you choose. A table-spoonful of chopped parsley also gives an agreeable change.

White Oyster Sauce.

One pint of oysters, three table-spoonfuls of butter, one heaping table-spoonful of flour, one of lemon juice, salt, pepper, a speck of cayenne. Wash the oysters in enough water, with the addition of the oyster liquor, to make a pint. Work the butter and flour to a smooth paste. Let the water and oyster juice come to a boil. Skim, and pour on the flour and butter. Let come to a boil, and add the oysters and seasoning. Boil up once, and serve. Half a cupful of the water may be omitted and half a cupful of boiling cream added at the last moment.

Brown Oyster Sauce.

The same ingredients as for the white sauce. Put the butter and flour in the saucepan and stir until a dark brown. Add the skimmed liquor, boil up, and add the other ingredients. Boil up once more, and serve. In the brown sauce stock can be used instead of water. The sauce is served with broiled or stewed beefsteak.

Shrimp Sauce.

Make a butter sauce, and add to it two table-spoonfuls of essence of anchovy and half a pint of canned shrimp. Stir well, and it is ready to serve.

Anchovy Sauce.

Make the butter sauce, and stir into it four table-spoonfuls of essence of anchovy and one of lemon juice.

Egg Sauce.

Six hard-boiled eggs, chopped fine with a silver knife or spoon; half a cupful of boiling cream or milk, and the butter sauce. Make the sauce, add the boiling cream or milk, and then the eggs. Stir well, and serve.

Fine Herbs Sauce.

One table-spoonful of chopped onion, two of chopped mushroom, one of chopped parsley, two of butter, salt, pepper, one pint of white sauce, No. 3. Put the butter and chopped ingredients in a saucepan and stir for one minute over the fire. Add the sauce, and boil up once.

Caper Sauce.

Make a butter sauce, and stir into it one table-spoonful of lemon juice, two of capers, and one of essence of anchovy.

Mustard Sauce.

Stir three table-spoonfuls of mixed mustard and a speck of cayenne into a butter sauce. This is nice for devilled turkey and broiled smoked herrings.

Curry Sauce.

One table-spoonful of butter, one of flour, one teaspoonful of curry powder, one large slice of onion, one large cupful of stock, salt and pepper to taste. Cut the onion fine, and fry brown in the butter. Add the flour and curry powder. Stir for one minute, add the stock, and season with the salt and pepper. Simmer five minutes; then strain and serve. This sauce can be served with a broil or *sauté* of meat or fish.

Vinaigrette Sauce.

One teaspoonful of white pepper, one of salt, half a teaspoonful of mustard, half a cupful of vinegar, one table-spoonful of oil. Mix the salt, pepper, and mustard together; then *very* slowly add the vinegar, and, after mixing well, add the oil. The sauce is to be eaten on cold meats or on fish.

Piquant Sauce.

Two cupfuls of brown sauce, one of consommé (common stock will do), four table-spoonfuls of vinegar, two of chopped onion, two of chopped capers, two of chopped cucumber pickles, one fourth of a teaspoonful of cayenne, one teaspoonful of sugar, salt to taste. Cook the onion and vinegar in a saucepan for three minutes; then add the sauce, consommé, sugar, salt, and pepper. Boil rapidly for five minutes, stirring all the while. Add the capers and pickles, and boil three minutes longer.

Tomato Sauce.

One quart of canned tomatoes, two table-spoonfuls of butter, two of flour, eight cloves, and a small slice of onion. Cook the tomato, onion, and cloves ten minutes. Heat the butter in a small frying-pan, and add the flour. Stir over the fire until smooth and brown, and then stir into the tomatoes. Cook two minutes. Season to taste with salt and pepper, and rub through a strainer fine enough to keep back the seeds. This sauce is nice for fish, meat, and macaroni.

Tartare Sauce.

The yolks of two uncooked eggs, half a cupful of oil, three table-spoonfuls of vinegar, one of mustard, one teaspoonful of sugar, one quarter of a teaspoonful of pepper, one teaspoonful of salt, one of onion juice, one table-spoonful of chopped capers, one of chopped cucumber pickles. Make the same as mayonnaise dressing. Add the chopped ingredients the last thing. This sauce can be used with fried and broiled meats and fish, and with meats served in jelly.

Champagne Sauce.

Mix thoroughly a table-spoonful of butter with one of flour. Set the saucepan on the fire, and stir constantly until the mixture is dark brown; then pour into it half a pint of boiling gravy (the liquor in which pieces of lean meat have boiled until it is very rich). Pour in this gravy slowly, and stir slowly and continually. Let boil up once, season well with pepper and salt, and strain. Add half a cupful of champagne, and serve.

Port Wine Sauce for Game.

Half a tumbler of currant jelly, half a tumbler of port wine, half a tumbler of stock, half a teaspoonful of salt, two table-spoonfuls of lemon juice, four cloves, a speck of cayenne. Simmer the cloves and stock together for half an hour. Strain on the other ingredients, and let all melt together. Part of the gravy from the game may be added to it.

Currant Jelly Sauce.

Three table-spoonfuls of butter, one onion, one bay leaf, one sprig of celery, two table-spoonfuls of vinegar, half a cupful of currant jelly, one table-spoonful of flour, one pint of stock, salt, pepper. Cook the butter and onion until the latter begins to color. Add the flour and herbs. Stir until brown; add the stock, and simmer twenty minutes. Strain, and skim off all the fat. Add the jelly, and stir over the fire until it is melted. Serve with game.

Bread Sauce for Game.

Two cupfuls of milk, one of dried bread crumbs, a quarter of an onion, two table-spoonfuls of butter, and salt and pepper. Dry the bread in a warm oven, and roll into rather coarse crumbs. Sift; and put the fine crumbs which come through, and which make about one third of a cupful, on to boil with the milk and onion. Boil ten or fifteen minutes, and add a table-spoonful of butter and the seasoning. Skim out the onion. Fry the coarse crumbs a light brown in the remaining butter, which must be very hot before they are put in. Stir over a hot fire two minutes, being watchful not to burn. Cover the breasts of the roasted birds with these, and serve the sauce poured around the birds, or in a gravy dish.

FORCE–MEAT AND GARNISHES.

Force-Meat for Game.

ONE pound of clear uncooked veal, a quarter of a pound of fat pork, one pound of boiled ham, one quart of milk, one pint of bread crumbs, half a cupful of butter, three table-spoonfuls of onion juice, one table-spoonful of salt, half a teaspoonful of pepper, six mushrooms, the yolks of four eggs, a speck each of clove, cinnamon, mace, and nutmeg. Chop the veal, pork, ham, and mushrooms *very fine*, and, with a pestle, pound to a powder. Cook the bread and milk together, stirring often, until the former is soft and smooth. Set away to cool, first adding the butter and seasoning to it. When cold, add to the powdered meat. Mix thoroughly, and rub through a sieve. Add the yolks of the eggs. This force-meat is used for borders in which to serve hot entrées of game. It is also used in game pies, and sometimes for *quenelles*. When used for a border it is put in a well-buttered mould and steamed three hours. It is then turned out on a flat dish, and the hot salmis, blanquette, or ragout is poured into the centre.

Ham Force-Meat.

Two pounds of cooked ham, chopped, and then pounded very fine; one pound of bread crumbs, one pint of milk, the yolks of four eggs, one table-spoonful of mixed mustard, one teaspoonful of salt, a speck of cayenne, one cupful of brown sauce. Make as directed for force-meat for game.

Veal Force-Meat.

Three pounds of veal, one cupful of butter, one pint of bread crumbs, one pint of milk, one pint of white sauce, two table-spoonfuls of salt, half a teaspoonful of pepper, two table-spoonfuls of Halford sauce, two of onion juice, the yolks of six eggs, half a teaspoonful of grated nutmeg, two table-spoonfuls of chopped parsley. Make and use the same as game force-meat.

Chicken Force-Meat.

Use only the breast of the chicken. Make the same as veal force-meat, using cream, however, with the bread crumbs, instead of milk. This force-meat is for the most delicate entrées only. Either the chicken or veal can be formed into balls about the size of a walnut, and fried or poached for soups.

Fish Force-Meat.

This can be made the same as veal force-meat. Salmon and halibut will be found the best kinds of fish to use for it. The force-meat is for entrées of fish.

Force-meat is sometimes formed into a square or oval piece for the centre of the dish. It should be about an inch and a half thick. Place on a buttered sheet or plate and steam two hours. When cooked, slip on to the centre of the dish. Arrange the entrée on this, and pour the sauce around the base. Delicate cutlets, sweetbreads, etc., can be used here. Veal or chicken force-meat is the best for all light entrées.

Jelly Border.

Make one quart of aspic jelly. Set the plain border mould (see Rice Borders, under Entrées) in a pan with a little ice and water. Pour enough of the liquid jelly into the mould to make a layer half an inch deep. Let this get hard. When hard, decorate with cooked carrot and beet, and the white of a hard-boiled egg. These must all be cut in pretty shapes with the vegetable cutter, and arranged on the jelly. Very carefully add two table-spoonfuls of jelly, and let it harden. Fill with the remainder of the jelly, and set away to harden. At serving time put the mould for half a minute in a pan of warm water. Wipe it, and turn the jelly on a cold flat dish. Fill the centre with salad, boned fowl, or anything else you choose.

Marinade for Fish.

One quart of cider, two slices of carrot, one large onion, four cloves, a bouquet of sweet herbs, two table-spoonfuls of butter, two of salt, half a teaspoonful of pepper, and the same quantity of mustard. Cook the onion and carrot in the butter for ten minutes, and add the other ingredients. Cover the saucepan, and simmer one hour and a half. This is for stewing fish. It should be strained on the fish, and that should simmer forty minutes.

Cold Marinade.

A bouquet of sweet herbs, the juice of half a lemon, two table-spoonfuls of oil, six of vinegar, one of onion juice, a speck of cayenne, one teaspoonful of salt, one fourth of a teaspoonful of pepper, one tenth of a teaspoonful of ground clove. Mix all together. Sprinkle on the meat or fish, which should stand ten or twelve hours. This is particularly for fish, chops, steaks, and cutlets which are to be either fried or broiled. Any of the flavorings that are not liked may be omitted. When cooked meats or fish are sprinkled with salt, pepper, and vinegar, as for salads, they are said to be marinated.

To Get Onion Juice.

Peel the onion, and grate on a large grater, using a good deal of pressure.

To Fry Parsley.

Wash the parsley, and wipe dry. Put in the frying-basket and plunge into boiling fat for half a minute.

To Make Spinach Green.

Wash a peck of spinach. Pour on it two quarts of boiling water. Let it stand one minute. Pour off the water, and pound the spinach to a soft pulp. Put this in a coarse towel and squeeze all the juice into a small frying-pan. (Two people, by using the towel at the same time, will extract the juice more thoroughly than one can.) Put the pan on the fire, and stir until the juice is in the form of curd and whey. Turn this on a sieve, and when all the liquor has been drained off, scrape the dry material from the sieve, and put away for use. Another mode is to put with the juice in the frying-pan three table-spoonfuls of sugar. Let this cook five minutes; then bottle for use. This is really the more convenient way. Spinach green is used for coloring soups, sauces, and creams.

Points of Lemon.

Cut fresh lemons in thin slices, and divide these slices into four parts. This gives the points. They are used as a garnish for salads and made dishes.

To Make a Bouquet of Sweet Herbs.

Put two sprigs of parsley on the table, and across them lay two bay leaves, two sprigs of thyme, two of summer savory, and two *leaves* of sage. Tie all the other herbs (which are dry) with the parsley. The bouquet is for soups, stews, game, and meat jellies. When it can be obtained, use tarragon also.

VEGETABLES.

ALL green vegetables must be washed thoroughly in cold water, and dropped into water which has been salted and is just beginning to boil. There should be a table-spoonful of salt for every two quarts of water. If the water boils a long time before the vegetables are put in, it loses all its gases, and the mineral ingredients are deposited on the bottom and sides of the kettle, so that the water is flat and tasteless: the vegetables will not look green, nor have a fine flavor. The time of boiling green vegetables depends very much upon the age, and how long they have been gathered. The younger and more freshly gathered, the more quickly they are cooked. The following is a time-table for cooking.

Potatoes, boiled	30 minutes.
Potatoes, baked	45 minutes.
Sweet Potatoes, boiled	45 minutes.
Sweet Potatoes, baked	1 hour.
Squash, boiled	25 minutes.
Squash, baked	45 minutes.
Green Peas, boiled	20 to 40 minutes.
Shell Beans, boiled	1 hour.
String Beans, boiled	1 to 2 hours.
Green Corn	25 minutes to 1 hour.

Asparagus	15 to 30 minutes.
Spinach	1 to 2 hours.
Tomatoes, fresh	1 hour.
Tomatoes, canned	30 minutes.
Cabbage	45 minutes to 2 hours.
Cauliflower	1 to 2 hours.
Dandelions	2 to 3 hours.
Beet Greens	1 hour.
Onions	1 to 2 hours.
Beets	1 to 5 hours.
Turnips, white	45 minutes to 1 hour.
Turnips, yellow	1 1-2 to 2 hours.
Parsnips	1 to 2 hours.
Carrots	1 to 2 hours.

Nearly all these vegetables are eaten dressed with salt, pepper, and butter, but sometimes a small piece of lean pork is boiled with them, and seasons them sufficiently.

Potatoes.

No other vegetable is in America so commonly used and abused. The most inexperienced housekeeper takes it as a matter of course that she or her cook cannot fail of boiling potatoes properly. The time of cooking the potato, unlike that of nearly all other vegetables, does not vary with age or freshness; so there need never be a failure. In baking, the heat of the oven is not always the same, and the time of cooking will vary accordingly. The potato is composed largely of starch. Cooking breaks the cells and sets this starch free. If the potato is removed from heat and moisture as soon as this occurs, it will be dry and mealy, but if it is allowed to boil or bake, even for a few minutes, the starch will absorb the moisture, and the potato will become soggy and have a poor flavor.

Boiled Potatoes.

Twelve medium-sized potatoes, one table-spoonful of salt, boiling water to cover. Pare the potatoes, and, if old, let them stand in cold water an hour or two, to freshen them. Boil fifteen minutes; then add the salt, and boil fifteen minutes longer. Pour off *every drop* of water. Take the cover from the saucepan and shake the potatoes in a current of cold air (at either the door or window). Place the saucepan on the back part of the stove, and cover with a clean coarse towel until serving time. The sooner the potatoes are served, the better. This rule will insure perfectly sweet and mealy potatoes, if they were good and ripe at first.

Mashed Potatoes.

Twelve potatoes, one and a half table-spoonfuls of salt, one table-spoonful of butter, half a cupful of boiling milk. Pare and boil as directed for boiled potatoes, and mash fine and light. Add the salt and butter. Beat well; then add the milk, and beat as you would for cake. This will give a light and delicate dish of potatoes. The potatoes must be perfectly smooth before adding the other ingredients.

Purée of Potato.

Prepare the potatoes as directed for mashed potatoes, except use a generous cupful of milk and half a teaspoonful of pepper. If the purée is to serve as a foundation for dry meats, like grouse, veal, or turkey, use a cupful of rich stock instead of the milk. This preparation, spread on a hot platter, with any kind of cold meat or fish that has been warmed in a little sauce or gravy heaped in the centre of it, makes a delightful dish for lunch or dinner.

Potato Puffs.

Prepare the potatoes as directed for mashed potato. While *hot*, shape in balls about the size of an egg. Have a tin sheet well buttered, and place the balls on it. As soon as all are done, brush over with beaten egg. Brown in the oven. When done, slip a knife under them and slide them upon a hot platter. Garnish with parsley, and serve immediately.

Riced Potato.

Have a flat dish and the colander hot. With a spoon, rub mashed potato through the colander on to the hot dish. Be careful that the colander does not touch the potato on the dish. It is best to have only a few spoonfuls of the potato in it at one time. When all has been pressed through, place the dish in the oven for five minutes.

Potato à la Royale.

One pint of hot boiled potatoes, a generous half-cupful of cream or milk, two table-spoonfuls of butter, the whites of four eggs and yolk of one, salt and pepper to taste. Beat the potato very light and fine. Add the seasoning, milk and butter, and lastly the whites of the eggs, beaten to a stiff froth. Turn into a buttered escalop dish. Smooth with a knife and brush over with the yolk of the egg, which has been well beaten. Brown quickly, and serve. It will take ten minutes to brown. The dish in which it is baked should hold a little more than a quart.

Potatoes à l'Italienne.

Prepare the potatoes as for serving *à la royale*. Add one table-spoonful of onion juice, one of finely chopped parsley, and half a cupful of finely chopped cooked ham. Heap lightly in the dish, but do not smooth. Sprinkle on this one table-spoonful of grated Parmesan cheese. Brown quickly, and serve. The cheese may be omitted if not liked.

USE THE

WORLD RENOWNED

WASHBURN CROSBY CO.

FLOUR.

THE PERFECT BREAD FLOUR.

The Washburn Crosby Co.

FLOUR

WILL YIELD FROM

40 TO 60 POUNDS MORE BREAD TO THE BARREL

THAN FLOUR MADE FROM WINTER WHEAT.

ONE TRIAL AND YOU WILL USE NO OTHER.

Thin Fried Potatoes.

Pare and cut raw potatoes *very thin*, with either the vegetable slicer or a sharp knife. Put them in cold water and let them stand in a cold place (the ice chest is best) from ten to twenty-four hours. This draws out the starch. Drain them well. Put about one pint in the frying-basket, plunge into boiling lard, and cook about ten minutes. After the first minute set back where the heat will decrease. Drain, and dredge with salt. Continue this until all are fried. Remember that the fat must be hot at first, and when it has regained its heat after the potatoes have been added, must be set back where the potatoes will not cook fast. If the cooking is too rapid they will be brown before they have become crisp. Care must also be taken, when the potatoes are first put in the frying-kettle, that the fat does not boil over. Have a fork under the handle of the basket, and if you find that there is danger, lift the basket partly out of the kettle. Continue this until all the water has evaporated; then let the basket remain in the kettle. If many potatoes are cooked in this way for a family, quite an amount of starch can be saved from the water in which they were soaked by pouring off the water and scraping the starch from the bottom of the vessel. Dry, and use as any other starch.

French Fried Potatoes.

Pare small uncooked potatoes. Divide them in halves, and each half in three pieces. Put in the frying-basket and cook in boiling fat for ten minutes. Drain, and dredge with salt. Serve hot with chops or beef-steak. Two dozen pieces can be fried at one time.

Potatoes à la Parisienne.

Pare large uncooked potatoes. Cut little balls out of these with the vegetable scoop. Six balls can be cut from one large potato. Drop them in ice water. When all are prepared, drain them, and put in the frying-basket. This can be half full each time, — that is, about three dozen balls can be put in. Put the basket carefully into the fat, the same as for thin fried potatoes. Cook ten minutes. Drain. Dredge with salt, and serve very hot. These are nice to serve with a fillet of beef, beefsteak, chops, or game. They may be arranged on the dish with the meats, or served in a separate dish.

Potato Balls Fried in Butter.

Cut little balls from cooked potatoes with the vegetable scoop. After all the salt has been washed from one cupful of butter (chicken fat will do instead), put this in a small frying-pan. When hot, put in as many potato balls as will cover the bottom, and fry until a golden brown. Take up, drain, and dredge with salt. Serve very hot. These balls can be cut from raw potatoes, boiled in salted water five minutes, and fried in the butter ten minutes. When boiled potatoes are used, the part left after the balls have been cut out will answer for creamed or Lyonnaise potatoes; but when raw potatoes are used, the part left should be put into cold water until cooking time, and can be used for mashed or riced potatoes.

Potatoes Baked with Roast Beef.

Pare rather small potatoes, and boil for twelve minutes in salted water. Take up and put on the grate with roast beef. Bake twenty-five or thirty minutes. Arrange on the dish with the beef, or, if you prefer, on a separate dish.

Broiled Potatoes.

Cut cold boiled potatoes in slices a third of an inch thick. Dip them in melted butter and *fine* bread crumbs. Place in the double broiler and broil over a fire that is not too hot. Garnish with parsley, and serve on a hot dish. Or, season with salt and pepper, toast till a delicate brown, arrange on a hot dish, and season with butter.

Lyonnaise Potatoes.

One quart of cold boiled potatoes, cut into dice; three table-spoonfuls of butter, one of chopped onion, one of chopped parsley, salt, pepper. Season the potatoes with the salt and pepper. Fry the onions in the butter, and when they turn yellow add the potatoes. Stir with a fork, being careful not to break them. When hot, add the parsley, and cook two minutes longer. Serve immediately on a hot dish.

Duchess Potatoes.

Cut cold boiled potatoes into cubes. Season well with salt and pepper, and dip in melted butter and lightly in flour. Arrange them on a baking sheet, and bake fifteen minutes in a quick oven. Serve *very* hot.

Housekeeper's Potatoes.

One quart of cold boiled potatoes, cut into dice; one pint of stock, one table-spoonful of chopped parsley, one of butter, one teaspoonful of lemon juice, salt, pepper. Season the potatoes with the salt and pepper, and add the stock. Cover, and simmer twelve minutes. Add lemon juice, butter, and parsley, and simmer two minutes longer.

Potatoes à la Maître d'Hôtel.

One quart of cold boiled potatoes, cut into dice; one scant pint of milk, one table-spoonful of chopped parsley, three of butter, one tea-spoonful of lemon juice, salt, pepper, the yolks of two eggs, one teaspoonful of flour. Mix the butter, flour, lemon juice, parsley, and yolks of eggs together. Season the potatoes with salt and pepper. Add the milk, and put on in the double boiler. Cook five minutes; then add the other ingredients, and cook five minutes longer. Stir often.

Stewed Potatoes.

One quart of cold boiled potatoes, cut into little dice; one pint and a half of milk, one table-spoonful of parsley, one of flour, two of butter, salt, pepper. Put the potatoes in the double boiler, and dredge them with the salt, pepper, and flour. Add the parsley, butter, and milk. Cover, and put on to boil. Cook twelve minutes. Serve very hot.

Creamed Potatoes.

One quart of cold boiled potatoes, cut in very *thin* slices; one pint of cream sauce, salt, pepper. Season the potatoes with salt and pepper, and turn them into the sauce. Cover the stewpan, and cook until the potatoes are hot, — no longer. Serve immediately in a hot dish. They will heat in the double boiler in six minutes, and will not require stirring.

Escaloped Potatoes.

Cut one quart of cold boiled potatoes in *very thin* slices, and season well with salt and pepper. Butter an escalop dish. Cover the bottom with a layer of cream sauce, add a layer of the potatoes, sprinkle with chopped parsley, and moisten with sauce. Continue this until all the material is used. Have the last layer one of cream sauce. Cover the dish with fine bread crumbs, put a table-spoonful of butter in little bits on the top, and cook twenty minutes. It takes one pint of sauce, one table-spoonful of parsley, half a cupful of bread crumbs, one teaspoonful of salt, and as much pepper as you like. This dish can be varied by using a cupful of chopped ham with the potatoes. Indeed, any kind of meat can be used.

Potato Soufflé.

Six large, smooth potatoes, half a cupful of boiling milk, one table-spoonful of butter, the whites of four eggs, salt and pepper to taste. Wash the potatoes clean, being careful not to break the skin. Bake forty-five minutes. Take the potatoes from the oven, and with a sharp knife cut them in two, lengthwise. Scoop out the potato with a spoon, and put it in a hot bowl. Mash light and fine. Add the seasoning, butter, and milk, and then half the whites of the eggs. Fill the skins with the mixture. Cover with the remaining white of the egg, and brown in the oven. Great care must be taken not to break the skins.

Sweet Potatoes.

Sweet potatoes require from forty-five to fifty-five minutes to boil, and from one hour to one and a quarter to bake. The time given will make the potatoes moist and sweet. If, however, they are preferred dry and mealy, fifteen minutes less will be enough.

French Fried Sweet Potatoes.

Prepare and fry the same as the white potatoes. Or, they can first be boiled half an hour, and then pared, cut, and fried as directed. The latter is the better way, as they are liable to be a little hard if fried when raw.

Cold Boiled Sweet Potatoes.

Cut cold boiled sweet potatoes in thick slices, and season well with salt and pepper. Have the bottom of the frying-pan covered with either butter, or pork, ham, or chicken fat. Put enough of the sliced potatoes in the pan to just cover the bottom. Brown one side, and turn, and brown the other. Serve in a hot dish. Cold potatoes can be served in cream, cut in thick slices and toasted; cut in thick slices, dipped in egg and bread crumbs, and fried brown; and can be fried in batter.

Plain Boiled Macaroni.

Two quarts of boiling water, one table-spoonful of salt, and twelve sticks of macaroni. Break and wash the macaroni, throw it into the salt and water, and boil *rapidly* for twenty-five minutes. Pour off the water, season with salt, pepper, and butter, and serve.

Macaroni in Gravy.

Twelve sticks of macaroni, one and a half pints of stock, one scant table-spoonful of flour, one generous table-spoonful of butter, salt, pepper. Break and wash the macaroni. Put it in a saucepan with the stock. Cover, and simmer half an hour. Mix the butter and flour together. Stir this and the seasoning in with the macaroni. Simmer ten minutes longer, and serve. A table-spoonful of grated cheese may be added.

Macaroni with Cream Sauce.

Boil the macaroni as directed for the plain boiled dish. Drain, and serve with half a pint of cream sauce.

Macaroni with Tomato Sauce.

Boil and drain as directed for plain boiled macaroni. Pour over it one pint of tomato sauce.

Macaroni with Cheese.

Prepare the macaroni with the cream sauce. Turn into a buttered escalop dish. Have half a cupful of grated cheese and half a cupful of bread crumbs mixed. Sprinkle over the macaroni, and place in the oven and brown. It will take about twenty minutes.

Macaroni à l'Italienne.

Twelve sticks of macaroni (a quarter of a pound), half a pint of milk, two table-spoonfuls of cream, two of butter, one of flour, some salt, white pepper, and cayenne, and a quarter of a pound of cheese. Break and wash the macaroni, and boil it rapidly for twenty minutes in two quarts of water. Put the milk on in the double boiler. Mix the butter and flour together, and stir into the boiling milk. Add the seasoning, cream, and cheese. Drain, and dish the macaroni. Pour the sauce over it, and serve immediately. One table-spoonful of mustard can be stirred into the sauce if you like. If the sauce and macaroni are allowed to stand long after they are put together, the dish will be spoiled. If they cannot be served immediately, keep both hot in separate dishes.

Stuffed Tomatoes.

Twelve large, smooth tomatoes, one teaspoonful of salt, a little pepper, one table-spoonful of butter, one of sugar, one cupful of bread crumbs, one teaspoonful of onion juice. Arrange the tomatoes in a baking-pan. Cut a thin slice from the smooth end of each. With a small spoon, scoop out as much of the pulp and juice as possible without injuring the shape. When all have been treated in this way, mix the pulp and juice with the other ingredients, and fill the tomatoes with this mixture. Put on the tops, and bake slowly three quarters of an hour. Slide the cake turner under the tomatoes and lift gently on to a flat dish. Garnish with parsley, and serve.

Stuffed Tomatoes, No. 2.

Twelve tomatoes, two cupfuls of bread crumbs, one of stock, four table-spoonfuls of butter, one of flour, salt, pepper, one teaspoonful of onion juice. Cut slices from the stem end of the tomatoes. Remove the juice and pulp with a spoon, and dredge the inside with salt and pepper. Put two table-spoonfuls of the butter in a frying-pan, and when hot stir in the bread crumbs. Stir constantly until they are brown and crisp, and fill the tomatoes with them. Cover the openings with fresh crumbs and bits of butter. Bake slowly half an hour. Fifteen minutes before the tomatoes are done, make the sauce in this manner: Put one table-spoonful of butter in the frying-pan, and when hot add the flour. Stir until brown and smooth; then add the stock, tomato juice, and pulp. Stir until it boils up, and add the onion juice, salt, and pepper. Simmer ten minutes, and strain. Lift the tomatoes on to a flat dish with the cake turner. Pour the sauce around, garnish with parsley, and serve. Any kind of meat, chopped fine and seasoned highly, can be used in place of the crumbs.

Escaloped Tomatoes.

One pint of fresh or canned tomatoes, one generous pint of bread crumbs, three table-spoonfuls of butter, one of sugar, one scant table-spoonful of salt, one fourth of a teaspoonful of pepper. Put a layer of the tomato in an escalop dish. Dredge with salt and pepper, and dot butter here and there. Now put in a layer of crumbs. Continue this until all the ingredients are used, having crumbs and butter for the last layer. If fresh tomatoes have been used, bake one hour, but if canned, bake half an hour.

Broiled Tomatoes.

Cut the tomatoes in halves. Sprinkle the inside of the slices with *fine* bread crumbs, salt, and pepper. Place them in the double broiler, and broil over the fire for ten minutes, having the outside next the fire. Carefully slip them on a hot dish (stone china), and put bits of butter here and there on each slice. Put the dish in the oven for ten minutes, and then serve. Or, if you have a range or gas stove, brown before the fire or under the gas.

Fried Tomatoes.

Slice ripe tomatoes and dip them in well-beaten eggs, which have been seasoned with salt, pepper, and sugar (one teaspoonful of sugar to each egg), and then in fine bread or cracker crumbs. Have two table-spoonfuls of butter in a frying-pan, and when hot put in as many slices of tomato as will cover the bottom. Fry for ten minutes, five for each side. Serve on thin slices of toast.

To Peel Tomatoes.

Put the tomatoes in a frying-basket and plunge them into boiling water for about three minutes. Drain, and peel.

Baked Onions.

Peel large onions, and boil one hour in plenty of water, slightly salted. Butter a shallow dish or a deep plate, and arrange the onions in it. Sprinkle with pepper and salt, put a teaspoonful of butter in the centre of each onion, and cover lightly with crumbs. Bake slowly one hour. Serve with cream sauce.

Stuffed Onions.

Boil as for baking. Cut out the heart of the onions and fill the space with any kind of cold meat, chopped fine, and highly seasoned. To each pint of meat add one egg and two thirds of a cupful of milk or cream. When the onions are filled put a bit of butter (about a teaspoonful) on each one. Cover with crumbs, and bake one hour. Serve with cream sauce.

Parsnips Fried in Butter.

Scrape the parsnips, and boil gently forty-five minutes. When cold, cut in long slices about one third of an inch thick. Season with salt and pepper. Dip in melted butter and in flour. Have two table-spoonfuls of butter in the frying-pan, and as soon as hot put in enough parsnips to cover the bottom. Fry brown on both sides, and serve on a hot dish.

Parsnips Fried in Molasses.

Have one cupful of molasses in a large frying-pan. When boiling, put in slices of parsnips that have been seasoned with salt, and cooled. Fry brown, and serve hot.

Parsnip Balls.

Mash one pint of boiled parsnips. Add two table-spoonfuls of butter, one heaping teaspoonful of salt, a little pepper, two table-spoonfuls of cream or milk, and one beaten egg. Mix all the ingredients except the egg. Stir on the fire until the mixture bubbles; then add the egg, and set away to cool. When cold, make into balls one third the size of an egg. Dip them in beaten egg and in crumbs. Put in the frying-basket and plunge into boiling fat. Cook till a rich brown.

Escaloped Parsnip.

Prepare the parsnips as for the balls, omitting the egg. Turn into a buttered dish, cover with crumbs, dot with butter, and brown in the oven.

Asparagus with Cream.

Have the asparagus tied in bundles. Wash, and plunge into boiling water in which there is a teaspoonful of salt for every quart of water. Boil rapidly for fifteen minutes. Take up, and cut off the tender heads. Put them in a clean saucepan with one generous cupful of cream or milk to every quart of asparagus. Simmer ten minutes. Mix one table-spoonful of butter and a generous teaspoonful of flour together. When creamy, stir in with the asparagus. Add salt and pepper to taste, and simmer five minutes longer.

Green Peas à la Française.

Boil green peas until tender, and drain. For every quart, put in a saucepan two table-spoonfuls of butter, one of flour, and half a teaspoonful of sugar. Stir until all are thoroughly mixed. Add the peas, and stir over the fire for five minutes. Add one cupful of white stock or cream, and simmer ten minutes. The canned peas can be prepared in the same manner.

Minced Cabbage.

Drain boiled cabbage in the colander. Put it in the chopping-tray and chop fine. For each quart of the chopped cabbage, put two table-spoonfuls of butter and one of flour in the frying-pan. As soon as smooth and hot, put in the cabbage, which season well with salt, pepper, and, if you like it, two table-spoonfuls of vinegar. Stir constantly for five or eight minutes. When done, heap on a dish. Make smooth with a knife, and garnish with hard-boiled eggs.

Minced Spinach.

Boil the spinach in salt and water until tender. Drain in the colander, and chop fine in the tray. Season well with pepper and salt. For each quart of the chopped spinach, put two table-spoonfuls of butter and one of flour in a frying-pan. When this has cooked smooth, and before it has become brown, add the spinach. Stir for five minutes; then add half a cupful of cream or milk, and stir three minutes longer. Arrange in a mound on a hot dish. Garnish with a wreath of slices of hard-boiled eggs at the base, and finish the top with another wreath. Serve hot. Lettuce can be cooked and served in the same manner. It must be boiled about twenty minutes to be tender.

Cauliflower with Cream Sauce.

Take off the green leaves and the stalk of the cauliflower. Wash, and put on to cook in boiling water. Boil gently for half an hour. Turn off the water, and add one pint of milk, one pint of boiling water, and one table-spoonful of salt. Simmer half an hour longer. Take up with a skimmer, being careful not to break it. Pour over this a cream sauce, and serve.

Escaloped Cauliflower.

Cook the cauliflower one hour in salt and water. Drain, and break apart. Put a layer of the cauliflower in an escalop dish, moisten it with Bechamel or cream sauce, and sprinkle in a little grated cheese. Put in another layer of cauliflower, and continue, as directed before, until all of the vegetable is used. There should be two table-spoonfuls of grated cheese and one pint of sauce to each head of cauliflower. Cover with bread crumbs and cheese, and dot with bits of butter. Bake half an hour in a moderate oven.

Stewed Celery with Cream Sauce.

Wash and scrape the tender white part of two heads of celery. Cut them in pieces about two inches long. Cover with boiling water and simmer gently half an hour. Season well with salt. Drain off the water in which the celery was cooked. Add a pint of cream sauce, and serve.

Celery Stewed in Stock.

Scrape, wash, and cut the white part of two heads of celery. Put in a stewpan with one pint of stock, and simmer half an hour. Mix together two table-spoonfuls of butter, and one of flour. Stir this in with the celery. Season with salt, and simmer five minutes longer.

Stewed Okra.

After the ends of the pods have been cut off, wash, and put on with just enough water to prevent burning (about a cupful to a quart of the okra) and a teaspoonful of salt. Simmer gently thirty minutes. Season with pepper and butter, and with more salt if necessary.

Okra Stewed with Tomatoes.

Cut the okra in thin slices, and pare and slice the tomatoes. Have one pint of tomatoes to two of okra. Put the vegetables in a stewpan with one teaspoonful of salt and a little pepper. Simmer half an hour. Add one table-spoonful of butter, and more salt, if needed.

Escaloped Okra and Tomatoes.

Prepare the same as stewed okra and tomatoes. When they have been stewing fifteen minutes add the butter and pepper, and turn into a deep dish. Cover with bread or cracker crumbs, dot with butter, and bake half an hour.

Fried Egg Plant.

Cut the plant in slices about one third of an inch thick. Pare these, and lay in a flat dish. Cover with boiling water, to which has been added one table-spoonful of salt for every quart of water. Let this stand one hour. Drain, and pepper the slices slightly, and dip in beaten egg and bread crumbs (two eggs and a pint of crumbs for a good-sized plant). Fry in boiling fat for eight or ten minutes. The slices will be soft and moist when done. Or, the slices can be seasoned with pepper, and fried in just enough pork fat to brown them. The egg plant is sometimes stewed, and sometimes baked, but there is no other mode so good as frying.

Boiled Rice.

One cupful of rice, one quart of boiling water, one scant table-spoonful of salt. Wash the rice in three waters, and put in the double kettle with the salt and boiling water. Boil rapidly fifteen minutes; then pour off *all* the water. Cover tightly, return to the fire, and cook twenty minutes longer. The water in the under boiler must boil rapidly all the time. Rice cooked in this manner will have every grain separate.

Corn Oysters.

One cupful of flour, half a cupful of melted butter, three table-spoonfuls of milk, two teaspoonfuls of salt, one fourth of a teaspoonful of pepper, one pint of grated corn. Pour the corn on the flour, and beat well; then add the other ingredients, and beat rapidly for three minutes. Have fat in the frying-pan to the depth of about two inches. When smoking hot, put in the batter by the spoonful. Hold the spoon close to the fat and the shape of the oyster will be good. Fry about five minutes.

New Bedford Corn Pudding.

Twelve ears of corn, four eggs, a generous pint and a half of milk, a generous teaspoonful of salt, four table-spoonfuls of sugar. Grate the corn, beat the eggs with a spoon, and mix all the ingredients together. Butter a deep earthen dish, and pour the mixture into it. Bake slowly two hours. Serve hot. When the corn is old, it will take one quart of milk. If very young and milky, one pint of milk will be sufficient.

Pickled Beets.

Cut boiled beets in slices. Lay these in a large glass jar or earthen pot. For every beet, put in one slice of onion, one table-spoonful of grated horseradish, six cloves, and vinegar enough to cover. The beets will be ready to use in ten or twelve hours. They will not keep more than a week.

Baked Beans.

Pick one quart of beans free from stones and dirt. Wash, and soak in cold water over night. In the morning pour off the water. Cover with hot water, put two pounds of corned beef with them and boil until they begin to split open (the time depends upon the age of the beans, but it will be from thirty to sixty minutes). Turn them into the colander, and pour over them two or three quarts of cold water. Put about half of the beans in a deep earthen pot, then put in the beef, and finally the remainder of the beans. Mix one teaspoonful of mustard and one table-spoonful of molasses with a little water. Pour this over the beans, and then add boiling water to just cover. Bake *slowly* ten hours. Add a little water occasionally.

PIES AND PUDDINGS.

Puff Paste.

ONE quart of pastry flour, one pint of butter, one table-spoonful of salt, one of sugar, and a quarter cupful of ice water. Wash the hands with soap and water, and dip them first in very hot, and then in cold water. Rinse a large bowl or pan with boiling water and then with cold. Half fill it with cold water. Wash the butter in this, working it with the hands until it is light and waxy. This frees it of the salt and buttermilk, and lightens it, so that the pastry is more delicate. Shape the butter into two thin cakes, and put in a pan of ice water to harden. Mix the salt and sugar with the flour. With the hands, rub one third of the butter into the flour. Add the water, stirring with a knife. Stir quickly and vigorously until the paste is a smooth ball. Sprinkle the board *lightly* with flour. Turn the paste on this, and pound quickly and lightly with the rolling-pin. Do not break the paste. Roll from you and to one side; or, if easier to roll from you all the while, turn the paste around. When it is about one fourth of an inch thick, wipe the remaining butter, break it in bits, and spread these on the paste. Sprinkle lightly with flour. Fold the paste, one third from each side, so that the edges meet. Now fold from the ends, but do not have these meet. Double the paste, pound lightly, and roll down to about one third of an inch in thickness. Fold as before, and roll down again. Repeat this three times if for pies, and six times if for *vol-au-vents*, patties, tarts, etc. Place on the ice, to harden, when it has been rolled the last time. It should be in the ice chest at least an hour before being used. In hot weather, if the paste sticks when being rolled down, put it on a tin sheet and place on ice. As soon as it is chilled, it will roll easily. The less flour you use in rolling out the paste, the tenderer it will be. No matter how carefully every part of the work may be done, the paste will not be good if much flour is used.

Chopped Paste.

One quart of pastry flour, two cupfuls of unwashed butter, one teaspoonful of salt, one table-spoonful of sugar, and a scant cupful of ice water. Put the flour, salt, sugar, and butter in the chopping-tray. Chop all together until the butter is thoroughly mixed with the flour; then add the water, and continue chopping. When well mixed, sprinkle the board with flour, turn the paste on it, and roll into a flat piece. Place in a pan on the ice. When hard, use the same as puff paste. It can be used as soon as mixed, but will not, of course, be so nice.

French Paste for Raised Pies.

One quart of pastry flour, one table-spoonful of sugar, one teaspoonful of salt, one scant cupful of butter, one egg, one teacupful of water. Rub the butter, salt, and sugar into the flour. Beat the egg, and add the water to it. Stir this into the flour and butter. Stir this mixture until it is a smooth paste; then put on the board, and roll the same as puff paste. This paste must be rolled eight times.

To Make a Pie.

Butter the pie plate (tin is the best), and cover with paste that has been rolled very thin. Roll a strip of paste long enough to go around the plate, and cut in strips an inch wide. Wet the edge of the plate with water, and put a strip of paste on it. Fill with any kind of prepared fruit. Have the paste in a roll, and cut enough from the end to cover the pie. Sprinkle the board lightly with flour, and place the paste upon it. Flour the rolling-pin with the hand. Roll from you and to one side until the paste is the right size. It must be much larger than the plate. In the centre cut a slit about half an inch long. Cover the pie, having the paste "*fulled*" on, as it shrinks in the baking. The oven must be hot at first, and after the first fifteen minutes the drafts must be closed. A mince pie will require one hour to bake, and an apple pie fifty minutes. Peach and nearly all other fruit pies require the same time.

Mince Pie Meat.

Boil a beef tongue, weighing six pounds, and six pounds of the vein of a round of beef (these should just simmer). After skinning the tongue, chop it and the beef very fine, and add five pounds of beef suet, chopped fine; five pounds of stoned raisins, three of dried currants, one and a half of citron cut fine, nine of sugar, one and a half pints of molasses, two quarts of the liquor in which the meat was boiled, one quart of brandy, one pint of white wine, a cupful of salt, half a cupful of cinnamon, one fourth of a cupful of cloves, one fourth of a cupful of allspice, three nutmegs, a table-spoonful of mace. Put all in a large pan, and let stand over night. Put what you wish to bake in another pan with half as much stewed and sweetened apple as you have meat, and let it stand one hour. Put the remainder of the meat in a jar. Cover with a paper dipped in brandy, and then cover tightly, to exclude the air. Set in a cool place for future use. — [Mrs. M. L. W.

Squash Pies.

Five pints of stewed and strained squash, two quarts of boiling milk, one and a half nutmegs, four teaspoonfuls of salt, five cupfuls of sugar, nine eggs, four table-spoonfuls of Sicily Madeira, and two of rose-water. Gradually pour the boiling milk on the squash, and stir continually. Add the nutmeg, rose-water, and sugar. When cold, add the eggs, well beaten; and just before the mixture is put in the plates, add the Madeira. Butter deep plates, and line with a plain paste. Fill with the mixture, and bake in a moderate oven for forty minutes. — [Mrs. M. L. W.

Sweet Potato Pies.

When the potatoes are dry and mealy, take a quart after they have been pared, boiled, and mashed, a quart of milk, four eggs, salt, nutmeg, cinnamon, and sugar to taste. Bake the same as squash pies. If the potatoes are very moist, use less milk.

Lemon Pie.

The juice and rind of one lemon, two eggs, eight heaping table-spoonfuls of sugar, one small teacupful of milk, one teaspoonful of corn-starch. Mix the corn-starch with a little of the milk. Put the remainder on the fire, and when boiling stir in the corn-starch. Boil one minute. Let this cool, and add the yolks of the eggs, four heaping table-spoonfuls of the sugar, and the grated rind and juice of the lemon, all well beaten together. Have a deep pie-plate lined with paste, and fill with this mixture. Bake slowly half an hour. Beat the whites of the eggs to a stiff froth, and gradually beat into them the remainder of the sugar. Cover the pie with this, and brown slowly.

Orange Pies.

Two cupfuls of sugar, two of flour, five eggs, one teaspoonful of cream of tartar, half a teaspoonful of soda, the juice and rind of one orange. These are for the cake. Beat the eggs very light; then add the sugar, and beat until frothy. Now add the orange. Mix the soda and cream of tartar with the flour, and rub through a sieve on to the beaten eggs and sugar. Stir well, and bake in deep tin plates. There will be enough for six plates. When baked, put a thin layer of the icing between the cakes, and cover the pie with icing. There should be three cakes in a pie.

Icing: The whites of four eggs, one teacupful of powdered sugar, the juice and rind of two oranges. After beating the whites to a stiff froth, beat in the sugar, and then the rind and juice of the oranges. When the pies are iced, dry them in the heater.

Chocolate Pies.

Make plain cup-cake, and bake in Washington-pie plates, having the cake thick enough to split. After splitting, spread one half with a filling made as below, place the top piece on, and sprinkle with powdered sugar. The cake should always be fresh.

Filling: One square of Baker's chocolate, one cupful of sugar, the yolks of two eggs, one third of a cupful of boiling milk. Mix scraped chocolate and sugar together; then add, very slowly, the boiling milk, and then the eggs, and simmer ten minutes, being careful that it does not burn. Flavor with vanilla. Have fully cold before using.

HOT PUDDINGS.

Custard Soufflé.

Two scant table-spoonfuls of butter, two table-spoonfuls of flour, two table-spoonfuls of sugar, one cupful of milk, four eggs. Let the milk come to a boil. Beat the flour and butter together; add to them, gradually, the boiling milk, and cook eight minutes, stirring often. Beat the sugar and the yolks of the eggs together. Add to the cooked mixture, and set away to cool. When cool, beat the whites of the eggs to a stiff froth, and add to the mixture. Bake in a buttered pudding-dish for twenty minutes in a moderate oven. Serve *immediately* with creamy sauce.

Cabinet Pudding.

One quart of milk, four eggs, four table-spoonfuls of sugar, half a teaspoonful of salt, one table-spoonful of butter, three pints of stale sponge-cake, one cupful of raisins, chopped citron and currants. Have a little more of the currants than of the two other fruits. Beat the eggs, sugar, and salt together, and add the milk. Butter a three-pint pudding-mould (the melon shape is nice), sprinkle the sides and bottom with the fruit, and put in a layer of cake. Again sprinkle in fruit, and put in more cake. Continue this until all the materials are used. Gradually pour on the custard. Let the pudding stand two hours, and steam an hour and a quarter. Serve with wine or creamy sauce.

English Plum Pudding.

A pound of suet, chopped fine; a pint of sugar, one pound of grated stale bread, one pound of raisins, two of currants, a glass of brandy, two teaspoonfuls of ginger, two nutmegs, half a pint of milk, a little salt. Beat well, and steam five hours. Serve with rich sauce.

Rachel Pudding.

One quart of bread crumbs, one of apples, cut very fine; half a cupful of suet, chopped very fine; one cupful of English currants, the rind and juice of two lemons, four eggs, well beaten. Mix thoroughly. Grease a pudding-mould, and put the mixture in it. Steam three hours, and serve with rich wine sauce.

Chocolate Pudding.

One quart of milk, four table-spoonfuls of corn-starch, four of sugar, four of scraped chocolate, two of boiling water, two eggs, one teaspoonful of salt. Reserve one cupful of the milk, and put the remainder on to boil. Put the sugar, chocolate, and water in a saucepan, or, better still,

a small frying-pan, and stir over a *hot* fire for about a minute, when the mixture should be smooth and glossy. Stir this into the boiling milk. Mix the corn-starch with cold milk. Beat the egg, and add to the corn-starch and milk; add also the salt. Stir this into the *boiling* milk, and beat well for about three minutes. Turn the mixture into a melon mould that has been dipped in cold water. Let the pudding stand in the mould about fifteen minutes. Turn into the pudding-dish, and heap whipped cream around it. Serve sugar and cream with it; or vanilla sauce will answer.

Chocolate Roll Pudding.

This pudding consists of cake, frosting, and sauce. It is very nice. Beat the whites of three eggs to a stiff froth, and add the yolks. Beat into the eggs one cupful of sugar and one of flour. As soon as all are thoroughly mixed, stir in half a cupful of cold water, in which has been dissolved soda about the size of a pea. Pour thin into a buttered pan, and bake in a moderate oven from twelve to fifteen minutes. When baked, sprinkle the top with two table-spoonfuls of milk.

Frosting: Beat the whites of six eggs to a froth, and divide into two parts. Put a teaspoonful of sugar to one half, and one teaspoonful of sugar and three of grated chocolate to the other. Take the cake from the pan and put it on a flat dish or tin sheet. Spread half of each mixture over the top. Return to the oven for about five minutes, to harden the frosting. Take out and roll up. Put the remainder of the frosting on the top and sides of the roll. Put again in the oven to harden the frosting. Take out, and slide on a flat dish. Pour the sauce around, and serve. The yolks of the eggs may be used for puddings or custards.

Sauce: One egg, one teacupful of powdered sugar, five table-spoonfuls of boiling milk, one teaspoonful of vanilla extract. Beat the white of the egg to a stiff froth, and gradually beat in the sugar. Add the yolk of the egg, the vanilla, and lastly the boiling milk.

Ground Rice Pudding.

One quart of milk, five table-spoonfuls of ground rice, four of sugar, one teaspoonful of salt, six eggs, half a cupful of butter. Put the milk in the double boiler, reserving half a cupful. Mix the rice and cold milk together, and stir into the milk in the boiler when this is hot. Stir constantly for five minutes. Add the salt, butter, and sugar, and set away to cool. When cold, add the eggs, well beaten. Bake one hour in a moderate oven. Serve with creamy sauce.

Rice Pudding.

One cupful of rice, one quart of milk, one cupful of raisins, one heaping teaspoonful of salt, one cupful of water, one quart of soft custard. Wash the rice, and let it soak two hours in cold water. Turn off the water, and put the rice in the double boiler with the cupful of water. Cook half an hour; then add the salt, raisins, and milk, and cook an hour longer. Butter a melon mould and pack the rice in it. Let it stand twenty minutes. Turn out on a deep dish, decorate with bits of bright jelly, pour the custard around, and serve. The custard should be *cold* and the pudding *hot*. The raisins can be omitted if not liked.

German Puffs.

The yolks of six eggs, five table-spoonfuls of flour, one of melted butter, one pint of milk, half a teaspoonful of salt. Beat the yolks of the eggs light, add the milk to them, and pour part of this mixture on the flour. Beat light and smooth; then add the remainder of the eggs and milk, and the salt and butter. Butter muffin pans, and half fill them with the batter. The quantities given will make twelve puffs. Bake twenty minutes in a quick oven. Serve on a hot platter with the sauce poured over them.

Sauce: The whites of six eggs, one cupful of powdered sugar, the juice of two oranges or of one lemon. After beating the whites to a stiff froth, gradually beat in the sugar, and then the juice of the fruit.

Down-East Pudding.

One pint of molasses, one quart of flour, one table-spoonful of salt, one teaspoonful of soda, three pints of blackberries. Boil three hours, and serve with sauce made in the following manner:—

One teacupful of powdered sugar, half a cupful of butter, one egg, two teaspoonfuls of *boiling* water, one of brandy. Beat the butter to a cream, and add, very gradually, the sugar and brandy. Beat in the yolk of the egg, and when perfectly creamy add the white, which has been beaten to a froth; then add the water, and stir very carefully.

Amber Pudding.

One dozen large, tart apples, one cupful of sugar, the juice and rind of two lemons, six eggs, four table-spoonfuls of butter, enough puff or chopped paste to line a three-pint pudding-dish. Pare and quarter the apples. Pare the thin rind from the lemon, being careful not to cut into the white part. Put the butter, apple, and lemon rind and juice in a stewpan with half a cupful of water. Cover tightly, and simmer about three quarters of an hour. Rub through a sieve, add the sugar, and set away to cool. Line the dish with *thin* paste. Beat the yolks of the eggs, and stir this into the cooled mixture. Turn this into the lined dish. Bake slowly for half an hour. Beat the whites to a stiff froth, and gradually beat into them three table-spoonfuls of powdered sugar. Cover the pudding with this. Return to the oven and cook twelve minutes with the door open. Serve either hot or cold.

Fig Pudding.

One cupful of molasses, one of chopped suet, one of milk, three and a quarter of flour, two eggs, one teaspoonful of soda, one of cinnamon, half a teaspoonful of nutmeg, one pint of figs. Mix together the molasses, suet, spice, and the figs, cut fine. Dissolve the soda with a table-spoonful of hot water, and mix with the milk. Add to the other ingredients. Beat the eggs light, and stir into the mixture. Add the flour, and beat thoroughly. Butter two small or one large brown-bread mould. Turn the mixture into the mould or moulds, and steam five hours. Serve with creamy or wine sauce.

Date Pudding.

Make the same as fig pudding, but use a pint of dates instead of the figs.

Apple Tapioca Pudding.

One large cupful of tapioca, three pints of water, one cupful of sugar, one teaspoonful of salt, one teaspoonful of essence of lemon, three pints of pared and quartered apples. Wash the tapioca and soak over night in three pints of cold water (three hours will do if there is no more time). Put the tapioca in the double boiler and cook until it looks clear. It will take from twenty to thirty minutes. When cooked enough, add the sugar, salt, and lemon, and then the apples. Turn into a buttered dish and bake an hour and a quarter. Let it stand in a cool room half an hour before serving. Serve with sugar and cream.

Baked Apple Pudding.

Fill a three-quart earthen dish with pared and quarted apples. Sprinkle on these one cupful of sugar, a slight grating of nutmeg, one table-spoonful of butter, and half a cupful of water. Cover, and bake thirty minutes. Make half the rule for chopped paste. Roll a piece of the paste into a strip that will reach around the pudding-dish. This strip should be about two inches deep. Roll the remainder of the paste to cover the dish. Take the pudding-dish from the oven, slip the strip of paste between the apple and the dish, and put on the top crust. Return to the oven, and bake one hour longer. Serve with a cream sauce.

Dutch Apple Pudding.

One pint of flour, one teaspoonful of cream of tartar, half a teaspoonful of soda, half a teaspoonful of salt, an egg, a generous two thirds of a cupful of milk, two table-spoonfuls of butter, four large apples. Mix the salt, soda, and cream of tartar with the flour, and rub through the sieve. Beat the egg light, and add the milk. Rub the butter into the flour. Pour the milk and egg on this, and mix quickly and thoroughly. Spread the dough about half an inch deep on a buttered baking-pan. Have the apples pared, cored, and cut into eighths. Stick these pieces in rows into the dough. Sprinkle with two table-spoonfuls of sugar. Bake in a quick oven for about twenty-five minutes. This pudding is to be eaten with sugar and cream, or a simple sauce.

Apple Soufflé.

One pint of steamed apple, one table-spoonful of melted butter, half a cupful of sugar, the whites of six eggs and the yolks of three, a slight grating of nutmeg. Stir into the hot apple the butter, sugar, and nutmeg, and the yolks of the eggs, well beaten. When this is cold, beat the whites of the eggs to a stiff froth, and stir into the mixture. Butter a three-pint dish, and turn the soufflé into it. Bake thirty minutes in a moderate oven. Serve immediately with any kind of sauce.

Apple and Rice Pudding.

One cupful and a half of uncooked rice, and two dozen apples. Wash the rice well, and soak two hours in cold water. Peel and quarter the apples. Wet the pudding-cloth and spread it in the colander. Cover with two thirds of the rice. Lay in the apples, having them packed as closely as possible. Sprinkle the remainder of the rice over them. Tie as tightly as possible, and plunge into boiling water. Boil one hour. Serve with molasses sauce.

Eve's Pudding.

Six eggs, six apples, six ounces of bread, six ounces of currants, half a teaspoonful of salt, nutmeg. Boil three hours, or steam four. Serve with wine sauce.

Batter and Fruit Pudding.

One pint of milk, one pint of flour, four eggs, one table-spoonful of butter, one teaspoonful of salt, one pint of fruit, pared and quartered (apples or peaches are best). Beat the eggs well with a spoon, and add the milk to them. Turn part of this mixture on the flour, and beat to a light, smooth batter. Add the remainder of the milk and eggs, and the salt. Butter a pudding dish and pour in the batter. Sprinkle in the fruit. Bake half an hour. Serve with foaming sauce the moment it comes from the oven.

Amherst Pudding.

Three fourths of a cupful of butter, three fourths of a pint of sugar, four eggs, five table-spoonfuls of strained apple, the grated rind and the juice of a lemon, and nutmeg and rosewater if you like. Bake half an hour in a moderate oven, in a shallow pudding-dish that has been lined with a rich paste, rolled very thin. Let it become partially cooled before serving.

Swiss Pudding.

One teacupful of flour, four table-spoonfuls of butter, three of sugar, one pint of milk, five eggs, the rind of a lemon. Grate the rind of the lemon (the yellow part only, remember) into the milk, which put in the double boiler. Rub the flour and butter together. Pour the boiling milk on this, and return to the boiler. Cook five minutes, stirring the first two. Beat the yolks of the eggs and the sugar together, and stir into the boiling mixture. Remove from the fire immediately. When cold, add the whites of the eggs, beaten to a stiff froth. Have a three-quart mould, well buttered. Turn the mixture into this, and steam forty minutes. Turn on a hot dish, and serve without delay. Creamy sauce, or a tumbler of currant jelly, melted with the juice of two lemons, should be served with it.

Delicate Indian Pudding.

One quart of milk, two heaping table-spoonfuls of Indian meal, four of sugar, one of butter, three eggs, one teaspoonful of salt. Boil the milk in the double boiler. Sprinkle the meal into it, stirring all the while. Cook twelve minutes, stirring often. Beat together the eggs, salt, sugar, and half a teaspoonful of ginger. Stir the butter into the meal and milk. Pour this gradually on the egg mixture. Bake slowly one hour.

Indian and Apple Pudding.

One cupful of Indian meal, one cupful of molasses, two quarts of milk, two teaspoonfuls of salt, three table-spoonfuls of butter, or one of finely chopped suet; one quart of pared and quartered apples (sweet are best, but sour will do), half a teaspoonful of ginger, half a teaspoonful of grated nutmeg. Put the milk on in the double boiler. When it boils, pour it gradually on the meal. Pour into the boiler again and cook half an hour, stirring often. Add the molasses, butter, seasoning, and apples. Butter a deep pudding-dish, pour the mixture into it, and bake slowly three hours. Make half the rule if the family is small.

COLD PUDDINGS.

Royal Pudding.

ONE quart of milk, half a cupful of sago, two table-spoonfuls of butter, one tea-cupful of granulated sugar, half a teaspoonful of salt, four eggs, four table-spoonfuls of raspberry jam, four table-spoonfuls of wine. Put the milk in the double boiler, and just before it comes to a boil stir in the sago. Cook until it thickens (about half an hour), stirring frequently; then add the butter, sugar, and salt. Let it cool; and when cold, add the yolks of the eggs, well beaten, and the wine. Turn into a buttered pudding-dish, and bake half an hour. Set away to cool. When cold, spread the jam over it. Beat the whites of the eggs to a stiff froth, and stir into them four table-spoonfuls of powdered sugar. Spread this on the pudding. Brown quickly, and serve. The pudding can be made the day before using. In this case, put the whites of the eggs in the ice chest, and make the méringue and brown just before serving.

Cold Tapioca Pudding.

Soak a cupful of tapioca over night in a quart of cold water. In the morning drain off all the water. Put the tapioca and a quart and half a pint of milk in the double boiler. After cooking forty-five minutes, add a teaspoonful of salt. Stir well, and cook fifteen minutes longer. Wet a mould or bowl in cold water. Turn the pudding into this, and set away to cool. Serve with sugar and cream. This pudding is also nice hot.

Danish Pudding.

One cupful of tapioca, three generous pints of water, half a teaspoonful of salt, half a tea-cupful of sugar, one tumbler of any kind of bright jelly. Wash the tapioca, and soak in the water all night. In the morning put on in the double boiler, and cook one hour. Stir frequently. Add the salt, sugar, and jelly, and mix thoroughly. Turn into a mould that has been dipped in cold water, and set away to harden. Serve with cream and sugar.

Black Pudding.

One quart of blueberries, one pint of water, one cupful of sugar, a five-cent baker's loaf, butter. Stew the berries, sugar, and water together. Cut the bread in thin slices, and butter these. Put a layer of the bread in a deep dish, and cover it with some of the hot berries. Continue this until all the bread and fruit is used, and set away to cool. The pudding should be perfectly cold when served. Serve with cream and sugar. Any other small berries can be used instead of blueberries.

Almond Pudding.

One pint of shelled almonds, two dozen macaroons, the grated rind of a lemon, half a cupful of sugar, half a cupful of butter, the yolks of six eggs, one quart of milk, one pint of cream, one table-spoonful of rice flour. Blanch the almonds and pound them in a mortar. Put the milk in a double boiler, reserving half a cupful. Add the pounded almonds to it. Mix the rice flour with the half-cupful of cold milk, and stir into the boiling milk. Cook six minutes, and put away to cool. When about half cooled, add the sugar and butter, which should have been beaten together until light. When cold, add the yolks of the eggs, well beaten, the macaroons, which have been dried and rolled fine, and the cream. Butter a pudding-dish that will hold a little more than two quarts; or, two small ones will do. Turn the mixture into this, and bake slowly forty-five minutes. Serve cold.

Jenny Lind Pudding.

One dozen sponge fingers, one dozen macaroons, one dozen cocoanut cakes, one quart of custard, two cupfuls of freshly-grated cocoanut. Make a quart of soft custard, and season with one teaspoonful of lemon extract or two table-spoonfuls of wine. When cold, pour on the cakes, which have been arranged in a deep glass dish. Sprinkle the grated cocoanut over this, and serve. If you have not the fresh cocoanut use one cupful of the prepared.

Peach Méringue Pudding.

Three dozen ripe peaches, one and a third cupfuls of granulated sugar, six table-spoonfuls of powdered sugar, one quart of milk, three tea-spoonfuls of corn-starch, six eggs. Put one cupful of the granulated sugar and one pint of water on to boil. Peel and quarter the peaches. When the sugar and water begins to boil, put in one third of the peaches, and simmer eight minutes. Take them up, and put in another third. Continue this until all the fruit is done. Boil the syrup until it becomes thick. Pour over the peaches and set away to cool. Separate the whites and yolks of the six eggs, and put the whites in the ice chest. Beat together the yolks and one third of a cupful of sugar. Put a pint and a half of milk in the double boiler. Mix three teaspoonfuls of corn-starch with half a pint of cold milk, and when the other milk is boiling stir this into it. Stir for three minutes; then put on the cover and cook three minutes longer. Pour the boiling mixture gradually on the beaten eggs and sugar. Return to the boiler and cook four minutes, stirring all the while. Take from the fire, add half a teaspoonful of salt, and set away to cool. This is the sauce. Twenty minutes before serving heap the peaches in the centre of a shallow dish. Beat the whites of the eggs to a stiff froth, and gradually beat in five table-spoonfuls of powdered sugar. Cover the peaches with this. Place a board in the oven, put the dish on it, and cook until a light brown. Season the sauce with one fourth of a teaspoonful of almond extract, and pour around the pudding. Serve.

The peaches and sauce must be cold. If the oven is hot, and the board is placed under the dish, the browning of the méringue will not heat the pudding much.

Apple Méringue Pudding.

Two quarts of pared and quartered apples, a lemon, two cupfuls of granulated sugar and six table-spoonfuls of powdered, six eggs, one quart of milk, three teaspoonfuls of corn-starch. Pare the thin yellow rind off of the lemon, being careful not to cut into the white part, and put it in a saucepan with one and two thirds cupfuls of the granulated sugar. Boil ten minutes; then put in the apples and juice of the lemon. Cover, and simmer half an hour. The apples should be tender, but not much broken. Take them up, and boil the syrup until thick. When it is reduced enough, pour it over the apples, and put these away to cool. Make the sauce and finish the pudding the same as for peach méringue, flavoring the sauce, however, with extract of lemon.

Frozen Cabinet Pudding.

Two dozen stale lady-fingers, one cupful of English currants, one pint of cream, one pint of milk, one *small* tea-cupful of sugar, three eggs, three table-spoonfuls of wine. Put the milk in the double boiler. Beat the eggs and sugar together, and gradually pour the hot milk on them. Return to the boiler and cook two minutes, stirring all the while. Pour the hot custard on the lady-fingers, add the currants, and set away to cool. When cold, add the wine and the cream, whipped to a froth. Freeze the same as ice cream. When frozen, wet a melon mould in cold water, sprinkle a few currants on the sides and bottom, and pack with the frozen mixture. Pack the mould in salt and ice for one hour. At serving time, wipe it, and dip in warm water for a moment. Turn out the pudding on a dish, pour apricot sauce around it, and serve.

Frozen Cabinet Pudding, No. 2.

One dozen macaroons, one dozen and a half sponge fingers, one dozen cocoanut cakes, one cupful of English currants, one quart of custard. Wet a melon mould in cold water. Sprinkle the sides and bottom with currants. Arrange layers of the mixed cakes, which sprinkle with currants. Continue this until all the cake and currants are used. Put a pint and a half of milk in the double boiler. Beat together four eggs and two table-spoonfuls of sugar. When the milk is hot, stir in one third of a package of gelatine, which has been soaking one hour in half a cupful of milk. Add the beaten egg and sugar, and cook four minutes stirring all the while. Take off, and add one fourth of a teaspoonful of salt and one teaspoonful of vanilla, or two table-spoonfuls of wine. Pour this, a few spoonfuls at a time, on the cake. Set away to cool. When cold, cover with thick white paper, and put on the tin cover. Pack the mould in salt and ice for four or six hours. At serving time, wipe the mould free of salt and ice, and dip for a moment in warm water. Take off the cover and paper, and turn out. Serve with quince sauce.

Peach Pudding.

Pare and cut fine one dozen ripe peaches. Sprinkle with three table-spoonfuls of sugar, and let them stand one hour. Make a custard the same as for frozen cabinet pudding, No. 2. Have the peaches in a deep glass dish, and, as soon as the custard is partly cooled, turn it on them. Set away in a cold place for six or eight hours. When convenient, it is well to make this pudding the day before using.

Orange Pudding.

One pint of milk, the juice of six oranges and rind of three, eight eggs, half a cupful of butter, one large cupful of granulated sugar, a quarter of a cupful of powdered sugar, one table-spoonful of ground rice, paste to line the pudding-dish. Mix the ground rice with a little of the cold milk. Put the remainder of the milk in the double boiler, and when it boils stir in the mixed rice. Stir for five minutes; then add the butter, and set away to cool. Beat together the sugar, the yolks of the eight eggs, and whites of four. Grate the rind and squeeze the juice of the oranges into this. Stir all into the cooked mixture. Have a pudding-dish, holding about three quarts, lined with paste. Pour the preparation into this, and bake in a moderate oven for forty minutes. Beat the remaining four whites of the eggs to a stiff froth, and gradually beat in the powdered sugar. Cover the pudding with this. Return to the oven, and cook ten minutes, having the door open. Set away to cool. It must be ice cold when served.

Orange Pudding, No. 2.

One cupful and a half of granulated sugar, six table-spoonfuls of the powdered, six eggs, six large or eight small sweet oranges, half a package of gelatine, one quart of boiling milk. Soak the gelatine for two hours in one cupful of the milk. Put the remaining milk in the double boiler. Beat together the yolks of the eggs and the granulated sugar. When the milk boils, stir in the gelatine, and then the beaten yolks and sugar. Stir constantly until the mixture begins to thicken (which will be about five minutes); then remove from the fire and put away to cool. Pare the oranges, and free them of seeds and tough parts. Put them in a large glass dish, and when the custard has cooled pour it over the fruit. Let this stand in a cold place six or eight hours. Beat the whites of the eggs to a stiff froth, and gradually beat in the powdered sugar. Cover the pudding with this, and serve.

Royal Diplomatic Pudding.

Soak half a box of gelatine in half a cupful of cold water one or two hours. Pour on this two thirds of a pint of boiling water, and add the juice of a lemon, a cupful of sugar, and half a pint of wine. Stir, and strain. Have two moulds, one holding two quarts, the other a quart. Put a layer of jelly in the large mould, and place on ice. When hard, garnish with candied cherries, cut in two. Pour in a few spoonfuls of liquid jelly, *not hot*, to hold the cherries, and then pour in enough to cover them. When the jelly is perfectly hard, set the small mould in the centre of the large one, and fill the space between with jelly. Fill the small mould with ice, and set both in a basin of ice-water. When the jelly is again hard, remove the ice from the small mould, which fill with warm water, and lift it out carefully. The vacant space is to be filled with custard made by the following recipe: The yolks of five eggs, half a cupful of sugar, two table-spoonfuls of wine, one teaspoonful of vanilla extract, half a box of gelatine, soaked in half a cupful of cold water, a scant cupful of milk. Put the milk to boil. Add the gelatine, and the eggs and sugar, beaten together. Strain, and add the wine and vanilla. When the custard begins to thicken, add half a pint of cream, whipped to a stiff froth. Pour the custard into the space mentioned, and let it stand until it hardens. Turn the pudding out of the mould, and serve with soft custard poured around it.

Orange Diplomatic Pudding.

Make one quart of orange jelly. Arrange this in the mould and make a filling the same as for royal diplomatic pudding. Flavor the filling, and the custard for the sauce, with orange.

Lemon Diplomatic Pudding.

Make one quart of lemon jelly, and prepare the mould with it the same as for the royal diplomatic pudding. Make a lemon sponge, with which fill the cavity. When hard, serve with a custard flavored with lemon.

Bird's Nest Pudding.

Half a package of Cox's sparkling gelatine, six oranges, three cupfuls and a half of sugar, one pint of blanc-mange. Take the peel from the oranges in quarters. Put it in two quarts of water, and let it stand over night. In the morning drain off the water. Cut the peel in thin strips with the scissors. Put it in cold water and boil until tender. Make a syrup of half a cupful of sugar and a pint of water. Drain the straws of orange peel on a sieve. Put them in this syrup and simmer half an hour. Turn into a bowl, and let stand until next day. Put one pint of sugar and one pint of water on to boil. Cook rapidly for twenty minutes; the syrup will then fall from the spoon in threads. Put the straws in this and boil half an hour. Take out, and drain on a sieve. As they dry, put them in a dish, which place in the warm oven. These are for the nests. For the jelly, soak the gelatine two hours in half a cupful of cold water; then pour on it enough boiling water to make, with the juice of the oranges, two cupfuls and a half. Add one small cupful of sugar and the orange juice. Stir well, and strain through a napkin into a shallow dish. In one end of each of six eggs make a hole, about the size of a cent. Break the yolks with a skewer, and pour the eggs into a bowl. (They may be used for puddings and custards.) Wash and drain the shells. Fill them with the blanc-mange. Have a pan filled with meal, in which to stand the shells. Set away to cool. Break the jelly in pieces with a fork, and put in a flat glass dish. Arrange the straws in the form of nests, six in number, and arrange them on the jelly. Place the eggs in these, and serve.

Quince Iced Pudding.

Beat three eggs very light; then add one cupful and a half of powdered sugar, and beat until foamy. Put two cupfuls of sifted pastry flour in the sieve, and add one teaspoonful of cream of tartar and half a teaspoonful of soda. Stir half a cupful of cold water into the beaten eggs and sugar; then sift the flour on this. Mix quickly and thoroughly. Have a tin mould similar to the border moulds shown in the chapter on Kitchen Furnishing, but of oval shape, higher and plain. It should be about four inches high, and six wide and eight long, top measurement, — the mould tapering. The space between the outer and inner walls should be an inch and a half. Butter this mould and pour the cake mixture into it. Bake slowly for forty-five minutes. Let it stand in the mould until nearly cold. Turn on a flat dish. Put the whites of two eggs in a bowl, gradually beat into them one cupful and a half of powdered sugar, and season with half a teaspoonful of vanilla extract. Ice the cake with this, and set away to dry. In the mean time, make a cream with one generous quart of cream, one cupful of sugar, one table-spoonful of vanilla, and one pint of soft custard. Freeze the same as ice cream. Spread the inside of the cake with a large tumbler of quince jelly. At serving-time pack the frozen cream in the centre of the cake. Heap whipped cream on the top and at the base, and serve immediately. This is an elegant pudding, and is not difficult to make.

Princess Pudding.

Soak for an hour in a pint of cold water one box of Cox's sparkling gelatine, and add one pint of boiling water, one pint of wine, the juice of four lemons, and three large cupfuls of sugar. Beat the whites of four eggs to a stiff froth, and stir into the jelly when it begins to thicken. Pour into a large mould, and set in ice water in a cool place. When ready to serve, turn out as you would jelly, only have the pudding in a deep dish. Pour one quart of soft custard around it, and serve.

Apple Porcupine.

Sixteen large apples, two large cupfuls of granulated sugar, one lemon, one quart of water, one teacupful of powdered sugar, one quart of milk, one table-spoonful of corn-starch, half a teaspoonful of salt, six eggs, one pint of blanched almonds. Put the water and granulated sugar in a saucepan. Have ten of the apples pared and cored, and as soon as the sugar and water boils, put in as many of the apples as will cook without crowding. Simmer gently until the fruit is cooked through. When done on one side the fruit must be turned. Drain, and cool them on a dish. Cook ten apples in this manner. Have the six that remain pared and quartered, and stewed in one cupful of water. Turn the stewed apples into the syrup left from cooking the others. Add the grated rind and the juice of the lemon. Simmer until a smooth marmalade is formed. It will take about twenty minutes. Set away to cool. Put the milk on in the double boiler, reserving half a cupful. When it boils, stir in the corn-starch, which has been mixed with the cold milk. Stir well, and cook five minutes. Beat the yolks of the six eggs and the whites of two with half of the powdered sugar. Gradually pour the boiling mixture on this. Return to the boiler and cook three minutes, stirring all the time. Add the salt. Turn into a pitcher or bowl, and set away to cool. Heap the cooked apples in a mound, using the marmalade to fill up the spaces between the apples. Beat the four whites of eggs to a stiff froth, and beat the half cupful of powdered sugar into it. Cover the apples with this, and stick the almonds into it. Brown slowly in the oven. Set away to cool. At serving time, season the custard with lemon, and pour it around the porcupine.

SAUCES.

Rich Wine Sauce.

ONE cupful of butter, two of powdered sugar, half a cupful of wine. Beat the butter to a cream. Add the sugar gradually, and when very light add the wine, which has been made hot, a little at a time. Place the bowl in a basin of hot water and stir for two minutes. The sauce should be smooth and foamy.

Creamy Sauce.

Half a cupful of butter, one cupful of *powdered* sugar, one fourth of a cupful of cream or milk, four table-spoonfuls of wine, or one teaspoonful of vanilla or lemon extract. If lemon or vanilla is used, add four table-spoonfuls of cream. Beat the butter to a cream. Add the sugar, gradually, beating all the while. When light and creamy, gradually add the wine, and then the cream, a little at a time. When all is beaten smooth, place the bowl in a basin of hot water and stir until the sauce is smooth and creamy, — no longer. It will take only a few minutes. This is a delicious sauce, and if well beaten, and not kept in the hot water long enough to melt the sugar, it will be white and foamy all through.

Foaming Sauce.

One cupful of butter, two of powdered sugar, the whites of two eggs, five table-spoonfuls of wine or three of brandy, one fourth of a teacupful

of *boiling* water. Beat the butter to a cream, and gradually beat the sugar into it. Add the whites of the eggs, unbeaten, one at a time, and then the brandy or wine. When all is a light, smooth mass, add the water, beating in a little at a time. Place the bowl in a basin of hot water and stir until smooth and frothy, which will be about two minutes. This sauce is for rich puddings.

German Sauce.

One cupful of sugar, half a cupful of water, three eggs, one table-spoonful of butter, three of brandy, or a teaspoonful of any extract you like. Put the sugar and water in a saucepan and boil for fifteen minutes. Beat the yolks of the eggs, and stir them into the boiling syrup. Put the basin in another of hot water and beat the mixture with the whisk until it begins to thicken; then add the butter, the whites of the eggs beaten to a stiff froth, and the brandy. Stir one minute longer, and serve.

German Sauce No. 2.

The yolks of five and whites of three eggs, one cupful of powdered sugar, one pint of cream, and any flavor you choose. Beat together the yolks of the eggs and the sugar, and add the cream. Put this mixture in the double boiler (having first beaten the whites to a stiff froth), and stir until it begins to thicken; then add the whites and seasoning. Beat thoroughly, and serve.

Lemon Sauce.

One cupful of sugar, half a cupful of water, the rind and juice of two lemons, the yolks of three eggs. Boil together the sugar, water, lemon juice, and grated rind for twenty minutes. Beat the yolks of the eggs. Put the basin containing the boiling syrup in another of boiling water. Stir the yolks of the eggs into this, and beat rapidly for three minutes. Take up the saucepan and continue the beating for five minutes; then serve.

Cream Sauce.

One cupful of powdered sugar, one egg, two cupfuls of whipped cream. Beat the white of the egg to a stiff froth. Add the yolk and sugar, and beat well. Flavor with vanilla, lemon, or wine, and add the cream last of all. This sauce is excellent for a light pudding.

Vanilla Sauce.

The whites of two eggs and the yolk of one, half a cupful of powdered sugar, one teaspoonful of vanilla, three table-spoonfuls of milk. Beat the whites of the eggs to a stiff froth, next beat in the sugar, and then the yolk of the egg and the seasoning. Serve immediately. This sauce is for light puddings.

Molasses Sauce.

One cupful of molasses, half a cupful of water, one table-spoonful of butter, a little cinnamon or nutmeg (about half a teaspoonful), one fourth of a teaspoonful of salt, three table-spoonfuls of vinegar. Boil all together for twenty minutes. The juice of a lemon can be used instead of the vinegar. This sauce is nice for apple or rice puddings.

Caramel Sauce.

Put one cupful of sugar in a small frying-pan and stir on the fire until a dark brown, if you like a strong caramel flavor, or till a light brown, if you like a delicate flavor. Add a cupful of boiling water, and simmer fifteen minutes. Set away to cool.

Quince Sauce.

One cupful of quince preserve, one of milk, one table-spoonful of corn-starch, half a cupful of sugar. Mix the corn-starch with a little of the cold milk, and put the remainder in the double boiler. When it boils, stir in the corn-starch, and cook ten minutes; then add the sugar and the preserve, mashed fine. Cook ten minutes longer and rub through a strainer. This sauce is usually served cold, but when used with hot pudding, it too should be hot.

Apricot Sauce.

One cupful of canned apricot, one of sugar, one of milk, one table-spoonful of corn-starch, half a cupful of water. Put the milk in the double boiler. Mix the corn-starch with a few spoonfuls of cold milk, and stir into the boiling milk. Cook ten minutes. Boil the sugar and water together for twenty minutes. Rub the apricot through a sieve, and stir it into the syrup. Beat well, and then beat in the boiled milk and corn-starch. Place the saucepan in a dish of cold water and stir for about eight minutes. Set away to cool. If you have cream, use it instead of the milk. All kinds of fruit can be used in pudding sauces by following this rule. If the fruit is preserved, use less sugar; and if very acid, use more.

If it is necessary to make the wine, creamy, or foaming sauce any considerable time before dinner, do not add the hot water or hot wine, and do not place the bowl in hot water, until serving time. The vanilla and cream sauces are spoiled by standing after being made.

DESSERT.

Blanc-Mange made with Sea Moss Farina.

ONE quart of milk, one level table-spoonful of sea moss farina, half a teaspoonful of salt, three table-spoonfuls of sugar, one teaspoonful of flavor. Put the milk in the double boiler and sprinkle the farina into it, stirring all the while. Let this heat slowly. Stir often. When it boils up, and looks white, add the sugar, salt, and flavor. Strain, and turn into a mould that has been dipped in cold water. Set away to harden. It will take about three hours for this. The blanc-mange is ready to use as soon as cold.

Blanc-Mange made with Gelatine.

One package of gelatine, three pints of milk, four table-spoonfuls of sugar, half a teaspoonful of salt, one teaspoonful of extract of vanilla or of lemon. Put the gelatine with the milk and let it stand in a cold place for two hours; then put it in the double boiler, and heat quickly. Do not let it boil. Stir often; and as soon as the gelatine is melted, take off, and add the sugar, salt, and flavor. Strain, and partially cool, before putting into the moulds. It should stand six hours before serving, and it is even better, especially in summer, to make it the day before using.

Blanc-Mange made with Isinglass.

One quart of milk, three and a half sheets of Cooper's isinglass, half a teaspoonful of salt, three table-spoonfuls of sugar, and a four-inch piece of stick cinnamon. Break up the isinglass, put it and the cinnamon with the milk, and let stand in a cold place two hours; then put it in the double boiler and let it come, gradually, to the boiling point. It must not boil. Stir often while heating. As soon as the isinglass is dissolved, take from the fire, and add the salt and sugar. Strain into a tin basin, which place in a pan of cold water. Stir occasionally while cooling. When nearly cold, turn into a mould and place in the ice chest. It can be poured into the mould as soon as strained, but the cream will rise to the top in that case, unless the mixture is stirred carefully in the centre of the mould. The sheets of isinglass vary in thickness, so that it is best to take part of the thick sheets and part of the thin.

Chocolate "Blanc"-Mange.

One package of gelatine, four table-spoonfuls of sugar, one (ounce) square of Baker's chocolate, three pints of milk. Soak the gelatine two hours in the milk, and then put it in the double boiler. Scrape the chocolate fine and put it in a small frying-pan with two spoonfuls of the sugar and two of boiling water. Stir this over a hot fire until smooth and glossy (it will take about a minute), and stir into the milk. Add the remainder of the sugar, and strain. Turn into moulds, and set away to harden. This dish should be made at least eight hours before being used. If you please, you can add a teaspoonful of vanilla extract. By adding the chocolate to any of the preparations for blanc-mange while they are hot, you have a chocolate "blanc"-mange.

Cream à la Versailles.

One quart of milk, half a cupful of sugar, half a teaspoonful of vanilla extract, half a teaspoonful of salt, seven eggs, two table-spoonfuls of water. Put the sugar in a small frying-pan and stir until a very light brown. Add the water, stir a moment longer, and mix with the milk. Beat the eggs and salt with a spoon. Add this mixture and the vanilla to the milk. Butter a two-quart charlotte-russe mould lightly, and put the custard in it. Put the mould in a basin of warm (not hot) water, and bake slowly until the custard is firm in the centre. It should take forty minutes; but if the oven is quite hot, it will be done in thirty minutes. Test by putting a knife down into the centre, for if the custard is not milky, it is done. Set away in a cold place until serving time. It must be ice cold when eaten. Turn out on a flat dish, and pour caramel sauce over it.

Royal Cream.

One quart of milk, one third of a box of gelatine, four table-spoonfuls of sugar, three eggs, vanilla flavor. Put the gelatine in the milk, and let it stand for half an hour. Beat the yolks well with sugar, and stir into the milk. Set the kettle in a pan of hot water and stir until the mixture begins to thicken like soft custard. Have ready the whites of the eggs, beaten to a stiff froth; and the moment the kettle is taken from the fire, stir them in, quickly, and turn into the moulds. Set away in a cold place to harden.

When you cannot get cream, to make charlotte russe, this is a good filling, if you omit the whites of eggs, and fill the moulds when the cream is perfectly cold, but not hardened.

Lemon Sponge.

The juice of four lemons, four eggs, one cupful of sugar, half a package of gelatine, one generous pint of cold water. Soak the gelatine two hours in half a cupful of the water. Squeeze the lemons, and strain the juice on the sugar. Beat the yolks of the eggs and mix them with the remainder of the water. Add the sugar and lemon to this, and cook in the double boiler until it begins to thicken; then add the gelatine. Strain this mixture into a tin basin, which place in a pan of ice water. Beat with the whisk occasionally, until it has cooled, but not hardened. Now add the unbeaten whites of the eggs, and beat all the time until the

mixture begins to thicken. Let it thicken almost to the point where it cannot be poured, and then turn into a mould and set away to harden. Remember that the whites of the eggs must be added as soon as the mixture cools, which should be in about six or eight minutes, and that the mixture must be beaten until it begins to harden. The hardening is rapid after it once begins, so that it will be necessary to have the moulds all ready. The sponge will not be smooth and delicate if not poured into the moulds. If for any reason you should get the mixture too hard before pouring, place the basin in another of hot water, and let the sponge melt a little; then beat it up again. Serve with powdered sugar and cream.

Orange Sponge.

Make orange sponge the same as lemon, using a small pint of water and the juice of six large oranges.

Peach Sponge.

One pint of canned peaches, half a package of gelatine, the whites of five eggs, one scant cupful of sugar, one and a half cupfuls of water. Soak the gelatine for two hours in half a cupful of the water. Boil the cupful of water and the sugar fifteen minutes. Mash the peaches fine, rub through a sieve, and put in the syrup. Cook five minutes, stirring all the time. Place the saucepan in another of boiling water and add the gelatine. Stir for five or eight minutes, to dissolve the gelatine; then place the saucepan in a dish of ice water and beat the syrup until it begins to cool. Add the whites of the eggs, and beat until the mixture begins to harden. When it will just pour, turn it into the mould, and set away to harden. Serve with sugar and cream. Apricot and pear sponges can be made in the same manner.

Strawberry Sponge.

One quart of strawberries, half a package of gelatine, one cupful and a half of water, one cupful of sugar, the juice of a lemon, the whites of four eggs. Soak the gelatine two hours in half a cupful of the water. Mash the strawberries, and add half the sugar to them. Boil the remainder of the sugar and the cupful of water gently twenty minutes. Rub the strawberries through a sieve. Add the gelatine to the boiling syrup and take from the fire immediately; then add the strawberries. Place in a pan of ice water and beat five minutes. Add the whites of eggs and beat until the mixture begins to thicken. Pour into the moulds and set away to harden. Serve with sugar and cream. Raspberry and blackberry sponges are made in the same way.

Pineapple Sponge.

One small fresh pineapple, or a pint-and-a-half can of the fruit; one small cupful of sugar, half a package of gelatine, one cupful and a half of water, the whites of four eggs. Soak the gelatine two hours in half a cupful of the water. Chop the pineapple, and put it and the juice in a saucepan with the sugar and the remainder of the water. Simmer ten minutes. Add the gelatine, take from the fire immediately, and strain into a tin basin. When partially cooled, add the whites of the eggs, and beat until the mixture begins to thicken. Pour into a mould and set away to harden. Serve with soft custard flavored with wine.

Strawberry Bavarian Cream.

One quart of strawberries, one pint of cream, one large cupful of sugar, half a cupful of boiling water, half a cupful of cold water. Soak the gelatine two hours in the cold water. Mash the berries and sugar together, and let them stand one hour. Whip the cream to a froth. Strain the juice from the berries, pressing through as much as possible without the seeds. Pour the hot water on the gelatine, and when dissolved strain it into the strawberry juice. Place the basin (which should be tin) in a pan of ice water, and beat until the cream begins to thicken. When as thick as soft custard, stir in the whipped cream; and when this is well mixed, turn into the mould (it will make nearly two quarts), and set away to harden. Serve with whipped cream heaped around it, or, if the border mould is used, have the cream in the centre.

Raspberry and blackberry Bavarian creams are made the same as the strawberry.

Orange Bavarian Cream.

A pint and a half of cream, the juice of five oranges and grated rind of two, one large cupful of sugar, the yolks of six eggs, half a package of gelatine, half a cupful of cold water. Soak the gelatine two hours in the cold water. Whip the cream, and skim off until there is less than half a pint unwhipped. Grate the rind of the oranges on the gelatine. Squeeze and strain the orange juice, and add the sugar to it. Put the unwhipped cream in the double boiler. Beat the yolks of the eggs and add to the milk. Stir this mixture until it begins to thicken, and add the gelatine. As soon as the gelatine is dissolved, take off, and place in a pan of ice water. Stir until it begins to cool (about two minutes), and add the orange juice and sugar. Beat about as thick as soft custard, and add the whipped cream. Stir until well mixed, and pour into the moulds. Set away to harden. There will be about two quarts. Serve with whipped cream heaped around the orange cream.

Peach Bavarian Cream.

One quart of canned peaches, one large cupful of sugar, one pint of cream, half a box of gelatine, half a cupful of cold water. Mash the peaches and rub them and the juice through a sieve. Add the sugar. Soak the gelatine two hours in the cold water. Whip the cream to a froth. Put the peaches in a saucepan and let them simmer twenty minutes. Stir often. Add the gelatine to the hot peaches and remove from the fire immediately. Place the saucepan in a pan of ice water and beat until the mixture begins to thicken; then stir in the cream. Mix thoroughly, and pour into the mould. Set away to harden. Serve with whipped cream. Apricot and pear Bavarian creams are made in the same way.

Pineapple Bavarian Cream.

One pint of canned pineapple, one small teacupful of sugar, one pint of cream, half a package of gelatine, half a cupful of cold water. Soak the gelatine two hours in the cold water. Chop the pineapple fine and put it on with the sugar. Simmer twenty minutes. Add the gelatine, and strain immediately into a tin basin. Rub as much of the pineapple as possible through the sieve. Beat until it begins to thicken, and add the cream, which has been whipped to a froth. When well mixed, pour into the mould, and put away to harden. Serve with whipped cream.

Almond Bavarian Cream.

One pint and a half of cream, one pint of blanched sweet almonds, one fourth of a teaspoonful of essence of almond, half a package of gelatine, three eggs, one small cupful of sugar, half a cupful of milk. Soak the gelatine two hours in the milk. Whip the cream to a stiff froth, until about half a pint is left unwhipped. Pound the almonds to a paste in the mortar. Put the almonds and unwhipped cream in the double boiler. Beat the sugar and eggs together and stir in with the cream and almonds. Cook until the mixture begins to thicken; then stir in the gelatine, and remove from the fire. Strain this into a tin basin, and add the essence of almond. Beat until it begins to thicken, and add the whipped cream. Mix well, pour into the moulds, and set away. Serve with whipped cream. Pistachio Bavarian cream is made in the same way, using one pint of pistachio nuts instead of the almonds, and omitting the essence of almond.

Chocolate Bavarian Cream.

One pint of cream, one cupful of milk, half a cupful of sugar, half a box of gelatine, one square of Baker's chocolate (an ounce). Soak the gelatine in half a cupful of the milk. Whip the cream to a stiff froth. Scrape the chocolate, and add two table-spoonfuls of the sugar to it. Put in a small frying-pan with one table-spoonful of hot water. Stir over a hot fire until smooth and glossy. Have the remaining half-cupful of milk boiling. Stir the chocolate into it, and add the gelatine. Strain into a tin basin, and add the remainder of the sugar. Place the basin in a pan of ice water, and beat the mixture until it begins to thicken; then add the whipped cream; and when well mixed, turn into the mould. When hard, serve with whipped cream heaped around.

Coffee Bavarian Cream.

One cupful of strong coffee, one pint of cream, half a package of gelatine, one cupful of sugar, one third of a cupful of cold water. Soak the gelatine two hours in the cold water. Pour on this the coffee, boiling hot, and when the gelatine is dissolved, add the sugar. Strain into a tin basin, which put in a pan of ice water. Beat with a whisk until it begins to thicken; then add the cream, which has been whipped to a froth. When thoroughly mixed, turn into a mould and set away to harden. Serve with sugar and cream.

Directions for Freezing.

Pour the mixture that is to be frozen into the tin can, put the beater in this, and put on the cover. Place in the tub, being careful to have the point on the bottom fit into the socket in the tub. Put on the cross-piece, and turn the crank to see if everything is in the right place.

Next comes the packing. Ice should be broken in large pieces, and put in a canvas bag, and pounded fine with a mallet. Put a thick layer of it in the tub (about five inches deep), and then a thin layer of salt. Continue this until the tub is full, and pack down solid with a paddle or a common piece of wood. After turning the crank a few times add more salt and ice, and again pack down. Continue in this way until the tub is full. For a gallon can, three pints of salt and perhaps ten quarts of the ice will be required. Remember that if the freezer is packed solid at first, no more ice or salt is needed. The water must never be let off, as it is one of the strongest elements to help the freezing. If more salt than the quantity given is used, the cream will freeze sooner, but it will not be so smooth and rich as when less is used.

Turn the crank for twenty minutes, — not fast at first, but very rapidly the last ten minutes. It will be hard to turn when the mixture is frozen. Turn back the cross-piece, wipe the salt and ice from the cover, and take off the cover, not displacing the can itself. Remove the beater and scrape the cream from it. Work a large spoon up and down in the cream until it is light and the space left by taking out the beater is filled. Cover the can, cork up the hole from which the handle of the beater was taken, put on the cross-piece, and set the tub in a cool place until serving time. Then dip the can for a few seconds in water that is a trifle warm, wipe it, and turn on the dish. Rest it for a moment, and lift a little.

If the cream is to be served from a mould, remove it when you do the beater. Fill the mould and work the cream up and down with a spoon. This will press the cream into every part, and lighten it. Cover the top of the mould with thick white paper, put on the tin cover, and bury in fresh ice and salt.

There are a great many good freezers. The Packer is especially suited to family use. It turns so easily that any lady can make her own creams. For the first twelve minutes a child can work it. It is made of the best stock, and will last many years. The cogs on freezers should be oiled occasionally. When you have made cream, see that every part of the freezer is clean and perfectly dry before putting away.

Vanilla Ice Cream.

The foundation given in this rule is suitable for all kinds of ice cream. One generous pint of milk, one cupful of sugar, half a cupful of flour, scant; two eggs, one quart of cream, one table-spoonful of vanilla extract, and, when the cream is added, another teacupful of sugar. Let the milk come to a boil. Beat the first cupful of sugar, the flour and eggs together, and stir into the boiling milk. Cook twenty minutes, stirring often. Set away to cool, and when cool add the sugar, seasoning, and cream, and freeze.

Vanilla Ice Cream, No. 2.

One pint of sugar, one of water, three pints of cream — not too rich, the yolks of five eggs and one large table-spoonful of vanilla extract. Boil the sugar and water together for twenty-five minutes. Beat the yolks of the eggs with one fourth of a teaspoonful of salt. Place the basin of boiling syrup in another of boiling water. Stir the yolks of the eggs into the syrup, and beat rapidly for three minutes. Take the basin from the fire, place it in a pan of ice water, and beat until cold. Add the vanilla and cream, and freeze.

Lemon Ice Cream.

Make the same as vanilla cream, and flavor with one table-spoonful of lemon extract.

Lemon Ice Cream, No. 2.

Three teacupfuls of sugar, the juice of three lemons, three pints of cream, the yolks of eight eggs, one pint of water. Boil the water, sugar, and lemon juice together twenty minutes; then proceed as directed for vanilla ice cream, No. 2.

Orange Ice Cream.

Follow the second rule for lemon cream, but use the juice of six oranges instead of that of lemons.

Pineapple Ice Cream.

Make the same as vanilla, and flavor with a teaspoonful of extract of pineapple.

Pineapple Ice Cream, No. 2.

Pare a pineapple and cut it fine. Put it in a saucepan with one pint of water and a scant pint of sugar. Simmer gently for thirty minutes. Rub through a sieve, add the cream, gradually, and freeze.

Strawberry Ice Cream.

One quart of cream, one quart of strawberries, one pint of sugar. Mash the sugar and strawberries together, and let them stand one or two hours. Add the cream, rub through a strainer into the freezer, and freeze. Or, the cream can be made the same as the vanilla cream, and when half frozen the whole berries be stirred in.

Strawberry Ice Cream à la Surprise.

Put three pints of strawberries in a deep dish with one cupful of sugar. Season three pints of cream with a cupful and a half of sugar and two table-spoonfuls of wine. Freeze this. Take out the beater and draw the frozen cream to the sides of the freezer. Fill the space in the centre with the strawberries and sugar, which cover with the frozen cream. Put on the cover and set away for an hour or more. When the cream is turned out, garnish the base, if you please, with strawberries.

Raspberry Ice Cream.

Make raspberry ice cream the same as strawberry, using a little less sugar.

Apricot Ice Cream.

One quart of cream, one generous pint of canned apricot, one pint of sugar, the yolks of three eggs, one pint of water. Boil the sugar and water together twenty minutes. Rub the apricot through a sieve and add it to the boiling syrup; add also the beaten yolks of the eggs, and cook for six minutes, stirring all the while. Take from the fire and place in a pan of cold water. Beat the mixture ten minutes. If cold at the end of that time, add the cream, and freeze.

Peach Ice Cream.

Peach ice cream can be made like the apricot, having the pint of peaches a very generous one.

Banana Ice Cream.

Make this the same as the apricot, using, however, only one cupful and a half of sugar and six bananas. More bananas can be used if a strong flavor of the fruit is liked.

Chocolate Ice Cream.

Make a foundation with two eggs, one cupful of sugar, half a cupful of flour, and a pint of milk, the same as for vanilla ice cream. While this is cooking, scrape one square (an ounce) of Baker's chocolate, and add to it two table-spoonfuls of sugar and one of boiling water. Stir this over the fire until perfectly smooth and glossy, and add it to the boiling mixture. This quantity gives a very delicate flavor. If a stronger one is wished, use two squares of the chocolate. Put the mixture in cold water to cool. Stir occasionally. When cold, add one teacupful of sugar and one quart of milk. Freeze.

Brown Bread Ice Cream.

Dry the crust of brown bread in a warm oven. Roll fine and sift. Add one pint of the crumbs to the preparation for vanilla ice cream. The vanilla and two thirds of the second cupful of sugar must be omitted.

Macaroon Ice Cream.

Make a cream the same as for vanilla, except omit the second cupful of sugar and the vanilla flavor. Brown one dozen and a half macaroons in the oven. Let them cool, then roll them into fine crumbs. Add these and three table-spoonfuls of wine to the cream, and freeze.

Coffee Ice Cream.

Make the same as vanilla, with the addition of one cupful of strong coffee. This gives a strong flavor. Less can be used. The second cupful of sugar should be large.

Caramel Ice Cream.

Make the hot mixture, as for vanilla. Put the small cupful of sugar in a small frying-pan, and stir over the fire until the sugar turns liquid and begins to smoke. Turn into the boiling mixture, and put away to cool. When cold, add one quart of cream. Strain the mixture into the freezer, and freeze. The flavor of this cream can be varied by browning the sugar more or less.

Almond Ice Cream.

This is made the same as vanilla, except that one teaspoonful of extract of bitter almond is used for flavoring.

Almond Ice Cream, No. 2.

One pint of blanched almonds, the yolks of five eggs, one quart of cream, one and a half cupfuls of sugar, one pint of milk, one pint of water. Boil the water and sugar together for twenty-five minutes. Put the almonds in a frying-pan and stir over the fire until they are a rich brown. Remove from the fire, and pound to a paste in the mortar. Cook the milk and powdered almonds in the double boiler for twenty minutes. Beat the yolks of the eggs and stir them into the boiling syrup. Beat this for four minutes, having the basin in boiling water. Take from the fire, and gradually beat into it the almonds and milk. Strain the mixture through a sieve, and rub through as much as possible. Stir occasionally while cooling. When cold, add the cream and half a tea-spoonful of extract of almond. Freeze.

Pistachio Ice Cream.

One pint of pistachio nuts, half a cupful of blanched almonds, one quart of cream, one pint of water, one scant pint of sugar, the yolks of five eggs, one pint of milk, spinach green enough to give a delicate color (about a heaping teaspoonful, to be cooked with the nuts). Make the same as almond cream.

Walnut Ice Cream.

One pint of the meat of walnuts (the American are the best), pounded fine in a mortar, one pint of milk, one quart of cream, two small cupfuls of sugar, four eggs, one fourth of a teaspoonful of salt. Beat the eggs with one cupful of sugar. Put them and the milk in the double boiler, and stir constantly until the mixture begins to thicken; then add the salt, and put away to cool. When cold, add the cream and nut meat, and freeze.

Cocoanut Ice Cream.

One quart of cream, one pint of milk, three eggs, one cupful and a half of sugar, one cupful of prepared cocoanut, the rind and juice of a lemon. Beat together the eggs and the grated lemon rind, and put with the milk in the double boiler. Stir until the mixture begins to thicken. Add the cocoanut, and put away to cool. When cool, add the sugar, lemon juice, and cream. Freeze.

Fig Ice Cream.

One quart of milk, two table-spoonfuls of corn-starch, one of gelatine, one pint of cream, a cupful and a half of sugar, three eggs, two cupfuls of figs, cut fine; one table-spoonful of vanilla. Put the milk in the double boiler, reserving half a cupful. When it is boiling, stir in the corn-starch, which has been mixed with the cold milk. Cook ten minutes. Beat the eggs and sugar together. Pour the cooked mixture on this, stirring all the time. Return to the fire, add the gelatine, which has been soaking in four table-spoonfuls of cold water, and cook three minutes. Set away to

cool. When cold, add the cream and vanilla, and freeze. When the cream has been freezing ten minutes, take off the cover and stir in the figs. Cover again and freeze until hard. Take out the beater, and with a large spoon pack the cream smoothly. Set away until serving time.

Glacé Méringue.

One quart of cream, one large cupful of granulated sugar and six table-spoonfuls of powdered, one table-spoonful of vanilla extract, the whites of six eggs, one cupful of milk, one table-spoonful of gelatine soaked an hour in four of cold water. Let the milk come to a boil, and stir the gelatine into it. Strain into the cream. Add the vanilla and granulated sugar. Turn into the tin, and freeze. When the mixture is frozen (it will take about fifteen minutes), take out the beater and pack the cream smoothly, being careful to have the top perfectly level. Set away until serving time. It should stand half an hour at least. When ready to serve, beat the whites of the eggs to a stiff froth, and gradually beat into this the powdered sugar. Turn the cream out on an earthen dish and cover every part with the méringue. Brown in a hot oven, and serve immediately. If the dish is flat, put a board under it. This keeps the heat from the bottom. *Glacé méringue* is an elegant dish.

Bombe Glacée.

One quart of strawberry or raspberry sherbet, No. 2, one pint of sugar, one pint and a half of water, the yolks of eighteen eggs, one large table-spoonful of vanilla extract. Boil the sugar and water together twenty minutes. Beat the yolks of the eggs very light. Place the saucepan, with the syrup, in another of boiling water. Stir the beaten yolks of eggs into this syrup and beat with a whisk for ten minutes. Take from the fire, place the basin in a pan of cold water, and continue beating for twelve or fifteen minutes. Pack an ice-cream mould in salt and ice. Take the sherbet from the freezer and spread on the sides and bottom of the mould. When it is hard, put the cooked mixture in the centre, being careful not to disturb the sherbet. Cover the cream with a piece of thick white paper. Put on the cover, and cover the top of the mould with salt and ice. *Bombe glacée* can be made with any kind of (No. 2) sherbet, having the centre part flavored to correspond with the sherbet. The handsomest dishes are, of course, made with the brightest-colored sherbets.

Frozen Pudding.

One generous pint of milk, two cupfuls of granulated sugar, a scant half cupful of flour, two eggs, two table-spoonfuls of gelatine, one quart of cream, one pound of French candied fruit (half a pound will do), four table-spoonfuls of wine. Let the milk come to a boil. Beat the flour, one cupful of sugar, and the eggs together, and stir into the boiling milk. Cook twenty minutes, and add the gelatine, which has been soaking one or two hours in water enough to cover it. Set away to cool. When cool add the wine, sugar, and cream. Freeze ten minutes; then add the candied fruit, and finish freezing. Take out the beater, pack smoothly, and set away for an hour or two. When ready to serve, dip the tin in warm water, turn out the cream, and serve with whipped cream heaped around.

Nesselrode Pudding.

One pint of shelled almonds, one pint and a half of shelled chestnuts, one pint of cream, a pint can of pineapple, the yolks of ten eggs, half a pound of French candied fruit, one table-spoonful of vanilla extract, four of wine, one pint of water, one of sugar. Boil the chestnuts half an hour; then rub off the black skins, and pound in the mortar until a paste. Blanch the almonds, and pound in the same manner. Boil the sugar, water, and juice from the pineapple for twenty minutes in a saucepan. Beat the yolks of the eggs, and stir them into the syrup. Put the saucepan in another of boiling water, and beat the mixture with an egg beater until it thickens. Take off, place in a basin of cold water, and beat for ten minutes. Mix the almonds and chestnuts with the cream, and rub all through a sieve. Add the candied fruit and the pineapple, cut fine. Mix this with the cooked mixture. Add the flavor and half a teaspoonful of salt. Freeze the same as ice cream.

Lemon Sherbet.

The juice of five lemons, one pint of sugar, one quart of water, one table-spoonful of gelatine. Soak the gelatine in a little of the water. Boil one cupful of the water and dissolve the gelatine in it. Mix together the sugar, water, gelatine, and lemon juice. Turn into the can, and freeze. This is light and creamy.

Lemon Sherbet, No. 2.

One pint and a half of sugar, three pints of water, the juice of ten lemons. Boil the sugar and water together twenty-five minutes. Add the lemon juice, and strain and freeze. This makes a smooth, rich sherbet.

Orange Sherbet.

Make this the same as the lemon, using, however, ten oranges. In the spring, when oranges are not very acid, add the juice of a lemon.

Orange Sherbet, No. 2.

Make the same as lemon sherbet, No. 2, but use the juice of twenty oranges instead of ten lemons. Boil the syrup for this dish thirty minutes

WASHBURN CROSBY COMPANY'S
RECIPE FOR MAKING BREAD.

IN cold weather, warm the flour thoroughly before mixing. To one and one-half pounds of flour add one pint of water or milk (using compressed yeast). If liquid yeast is used, take one-quarter part yeast to three-quarter parts water or milk, making one pint of liquid to above amount of flour. Beat vigorously and continuously; the longer the better. Do not stir afterwards. Salt to taste. When shortening is used pure leaf lard is the best (one ounce to the above is sufficient). Set to rise about nine o'clock in the evening, if wanted the next morning. Great care should be used to always keep it warm (not hot, but warm). In making up in the morning before putting into pans, mould until quite smooth. Let it rise from one-half to one hour before baking. Much depends upon baking. Care is necessary to have the oven hot enough to bake as quickly as possible without burning. This recipe is for an ordinary family baking. For a larger quantity, use the same proportions of ingredients. Where compressed yeast is used, our experience leads us to believe it is better to set the flour to rise early in the morning rather than over night, as this yeast is much more rapid in its working than ordinary liquid yeast. This flour, being largely composed of the glutinous portion of the wheat, should be mixed much softer than other flour as it absorbs moisture more slowly than flour having a large percentage of starch. Thorough kneading improves the bread. (20 minutes is not too long.)

When ordering flour of your dealer, be sure to ask for

WASHBURN CROSBY COMPANY'S FLOUR,

and see that our name in full is on each package. We place a circular in every barrel of our Best Flour to enable the purchaser to prove its genuineness.

ASK YOUR GROCER FOR WASHBURN CROSBY CO.'S FLOUR.

GIFT BOOKS FOR ALL SEASONS.

THE LAST DAYS OF POMPEII. POMPEIIAN EDITION.

By BULWER (Lord Lytton.) This thrilling historical novel, the sublime creation of a genius, is produced in a superb manner befitting the brilliant conception of the author. It contains fifty photogravure illustrations from photographs of Pompeii as it now is, especially selected on the spot by a member of the firm, and also from celebrated restorations and Pompeiian frescoes.

The magnificent and distinctively Pompeiian binding far surpasses anything of the kind ever attempted in this or any other country.

2 vols., crown 8vo, embossed in full gold, ... $ 6.00
2 vols., crown 8vo, half levant morocco crushed, extra, gilt tops, ... 12.00

THE LAST DAYS OF POMPEII. PARCHMENT EDITION.

Limited to 250 copies, numbered and registered, and printed on fine laid paper with broad, ample margins. The illustrations are proof impressions on imperial Japanese paper.

2 vols., small quarto, genuine parchment covers embossed in full gold, gilt tops, ... $15.00

RIENZI. ROMANESQUE EDITION.

THE LAST OF THE ROMAN TRIBUNES. By BULWER (Lord Lytton).

A superb edition of this splendid historical romance, which stands without an equal, full of photogravure illustrations from Roman photographs, printed on supercalendered and plated paper. The paper is of excellent manufacture; the printing, the best; and the binding, magnificent.

2 vols., crown 8vo, embossed in gold, gilt tops, ... $ 6.00
2 vols., crown 8vo, half levant morocco crushed, extra, gilt tops, ... 12.00

RIENZI. PARCHMENT EDITION.

A limited edition of the above, printed on fine laid paper with broad, ample margins, with proof illustrations on imperial Japanese paper. Strictly limited to 250 numbered copies.

2 vols., small quarto, full parchment, embossed in gold, gilt tops, ... $15.00

ROMOLA. FLORENTINE EDITION.

By GEORGE ELIOT. This great historic story of Florentine life is produced in magnificent style with SIXTY FINE PHOTOGRAVURE illustrations from photographs selected by the publishers in Florence. The paper, presswork, and binding are of the highest artistic quality.

2 vols., crown 8vo, white vellum, red and gold, gilt tops, ... $ 6.00
2 vols., crown 8vo, half levant morocco crushed, extra, gilt tops, ... 12.00

THE LILY OF THE ARNO;

Or, FLORENCE, PAST AND PRESENT. By VIRGINIA W. JOHNSON.

In the beautiful Flower City of Italy, so attractive to Americans, there is an endless amount of historic folk-lore, an abundance of which the author has delicately interwoven with descriptions of the cathedrals, the campaniles and the Florentine people, making one of the most interesting, instructive, and thoroughly complete books of this class ever issued. Illustrated with twenty-five photogravures from photographs of points of interest in Florence.

1 vol., crown 8vo, vellum cloth, illuminated in gold and colors, ... $3.00

THE LADY OF THE LAKE. STIRLING EDITION.

By SIR WALTER SCOTT. A splendid edition of this celebrated romantic poem, with all of Scott's introductions and a complete appendix; printed on fine laid paper and containing numerous photogravures illustrating the Scottish scenery as so marvellously described by the author.

1 vol., imperial 8vo, vellum cloth, gold and silver, flat back, gilt tops, ... $4.00

NIGHT SONG. NEW EDITION.

By CHARLES REINICK, illustrated by Henry Sandham. This song, or poem, is unique from the fact that each and every line suggests a separate picture to the artist's mind These illustrations, 16 in number, are reproduced from paintings by Mr. Sandham, together with an equal number of fine pen and ink sketches accompanying the text of the song The whole makes one of the most distinguished holiday works ever issued.

1 vol., quarto, cloth, full gilt, REDUCED TO $5.00
1 vol., quarto, full seal morocco, ... 8.00

ORIANA.

And other poems. By TENNYSON. Illustrated with wood engravings by Andrew from paintings by Maud Humphrey, Garrett, Hamilton Gibson and others.

1 vol., small quarto, cloth, full gilt, ... $1.50

ESTES & LAURIAT, Publishers, Boston.

Pineapple Sherbet.

A pint-and-a-half can of pineapple, or, if fresh fruit is used, one large pineapple; a small pint of sugar, a pint of water, one table-spoonful of gelatine. Soak the gelatine one or two hours in cold water to cover. Cut the hearts and eyes from the fruit, chop it fine, and add to the sugar and the juice from the can. Have half of the water hot, and dissolve the gelatine in it. Stir this and the cold water into the pineapple. Freeze. This sherbet will be white and creamy.

Pineapple Sherbet, No. 2.

Two small cans of pineapple, one generous pint of sugar, one quart of water. Pour the juice of the pineapple into a bowl. Put the fruit in a saucepan with half the water, and simmer twenty minutes. Put the sugar and the remainder of the water on to boil. Cook fifteen minutes. Rub the cooked pineapple through a sieve, and add it to the boiling syrup. Cook fifteen minutes longer. Add the juice, and cool and freeze.

Strawberry Sherbet.

Two quarts of strawberries, one pint of sugar, one pint and a half of water, one table-spoonful of gelatine. Mash the berries and sugar together, and let them stand two hours. Soak the gelatine in cold water to cover. Add one pint of the water to the strawberries, and strain. Dissolve the gelatine in half a pint of boiling water, add this to the strained mixture, and freeze.

Strawberry Sherbet, No. 2.

One pint and a half of strawberry juice, one pint of sugar, one pint and a half of water, the juice of two lemons. Boil the water and sugar together for twenty minutes. Add the lemon and strawberry juice. Strain, and freeze.

Raspberry Sherbet.

This sherbet is made the same as the strawberry. When raspberries are not in season, use the preserved or canned fruit and a smaller quantity of sugar. The juice of a lemon or two is always an improvement, but is not necessary. The sherbet can also be made by following the second rule for strawberry sherbet.

Raspberry Sherbet, No. 2.

One bottle of German raspberries (holding a little more than a pint, and costing about $1.25), one cupful of sugar, one quart of water, the juice of two lemons. Mix all together, strain, and freeze.

Currant Sherbet.

One pint of currant juice, one pint and a half of water, the juice of one lemon, one pint of sugar, one table-spoonful of gelatine. Have the gelatine soaked in cold water, and dissolve it in half a pint of boiling water. Mix it with the pint of cold water, the sugar, lemon and currant juice, and freeze.

Currant Sherbet, No. 2.

One pint of sugar, one quart of water, one pint of currant juice, the juice of a lemon. Boil the water and sugar together half an hour. Add the currant and lemon juice to the syrup. Let this cool, and freeze.

Frozen Strawberries.

Two quarts of fresh strawberries, one pint of sugar, one quart of water. Boil the water and sugar together half an hour; then add the strawberries, and cook fifteen minutes longer. Let this cool, and freeze. When the beater is taken out, add one pint of whipped cream. Preserved fruit can be used instead of the fresh. In this case, to each quart of preserves add one quart of water, and freeze.

Frozen Raspberries.

Prepare raspberries the same as strawberries. When cold, add the juice of three lemons, and freeze. All kinds of canned and preserved fruits can be prepared and frozen in any of the three ways given.

Frozen Peaches.

One can of peaches, one heaping pint of granulated sugar, one quart of water, two cupfuls of whipped cream. Boil the sugar and water together twelve minutes; then add the peaches, and cook twenty minutes longer. Rub through a sieve; and when cool, freeze. When the beater is taken out, stir in the whipped cream with a large spoon. Cover, and set away until serving time. It should stand one hour at least.

Frozen Apricots.

One can of apricots, a generous pint of sugar, a quart of water, a pint of whipped cream, — measured after being whipped. Cut the apricots in small pieces, add the sugar and water, and freeze. When nearly frozen add the cream.

Biscuit Glacé.

Mix together in a deep bowl or pail one pint of *rich* cream, one third of a cupful of sugar, and one teaspoonful of vanilla extract. Put the mixture in a pan of ice water and whip to a stiff froth. Stir this down, and whip again. Skim the froth into a deep dish. When all the cream has been whipped to a froth, fill paper cases with it, and place these in a large tin box (or the freezer will do) that is nearly buried in ice and salt — two quarts of salt to six of ice — and is wholly covered after the cases are put in. Let these remain there two hours. Make a pint of strawberry sherbet. Put a thin layer of it on each case of cream, and return to the freezer. Let the cases stand half an hour longer, and serve. They should be arranged on a bright napkin, spread on a flat dish.

Biscuit Glacé, No. 2.

One pint of cream whipped to a froth, a dozen and a half macaroons, three eggs, half a cupful of water, two thirds of a cupful of sugar, a teaspoonful of vanilla extract. Boil the sugar and water together for half an hour. Beat the eggs well, and stir into the boiling syrup. Place the saucepan containing the mixture in another of boiling water, and beat for eight minutes. Take from the fire, place the saucepan in a pan of cold water, and beat the mixture until it is cold; then add the flavor and whipped cream. Stir well, and fill paper cases. Have the macaroons browned and rolled fine. Put a layer of the crumbs on the cream in the cases, and freeze as directed in the other recipe.

Chocolate Soufflé.

Two cupfuls of milk, one and a half squares of Baker's chocolate, three fourths of a cupful of powdered sugar, two table-spoonfuls of corn-starch, three eggs, one fourth of a teaspoonful of salt, half a teaspoonful of vanilla extract. Boil the milk in the double boiler, leaving out a third of a cupful to mix with the corn-starch. After mixing, stir into the boiling milk, and cook eight minutes. Dissolve the chocolate with half a cupful of the sugar and two table-spoonfuls of boiling water. Add to the other mixture. Beat the yolks, and add them and the salt. Cook two minutes. Set in cold water, and beat until cool; then add the flavor, and pour into a dish. Beat the whites of the eggs to a stiff froth, add the remaining sugar, and heap on the custard. Dredge with sugar. Brown with a salamander or hot shovel.

Orange Soufflé.

A pint of milk, five eggs, one fourth of a cupful of granulated sugar and three table-spoonfuls of powdered, five Florida oranges, and a speck of salt. Put the milk on to boil. Beat the yolks of five eggs and whites of two with the granulated sugar. Pour the milk, gradually, over this, stirring all the while. Return to the saucepan, place in a basin of boiling water, and stir until it begins to thicken like soft custard. This will be about two minutes. Add the salt, and set away to cool. Pare the oranges, remove the seeds, cut up fine, and put in a glass dish. Pour on the cold custard. Just before serving, beat the three remaining whites of eggs to a stiff froth, and beat in the powdered sugar. Heap this on the custard, and brown with a hot shovel or a salamander.

Surprise Soufflé.

One pint of the juice of any kind of fruit, one third of a package of gelatine, half a cupful of sugar (unless the fruit is very acid, in which case use a little more), one pint of soft custard, ten macaroons, half a cupful of water. Soak the gelatine two hours in a little of the water. Let the remainder of the water come to a boil, and pour it on the soaked gelatine. Place the basin in another of hot water and stir until all the gelatine is dissolved. Strain this into the fruit juice. Add the sugar. Place the basin in a pan of ice water, and as soon as the mixture begins to thicken, beat with a whisk until it hardens; then place in the ice chest for a few hours. Brown the macaroons in a cool oven. Let them cool and roll them fine. At serving time put the custard in a *soufflé* dish. Heap the jelly on this, and cover all with the macaroon crumbs.

Omelet Soufflé à la Crème.

Four eggs, two table-spoonfuls of sugar, a speck of salt, half a teaspoonful of vanilla extract, one cupful of whipped cream. Beat the whites of the eggs to a stiff froth, and gradually beat the sugar and the flavor into them. When well beaten, add the yolks, and lastly the whipped cream. Have a dish, holding about one quart, slightly buttered. Pour the mixture into this and bake *just twelve minutes*. Serve the moment it is taken from the oven.

Omelet Soufflé à la Poêle.

The whites of eight and yolks of four eggs, two table-spoonfuls of sugar, a speck of salt, two table-spoonfuls of butter, half a teaspoonful of any kind of flavor. Beat the yolks of the eggs, the sugar, salt, and flavor together. Beat the whites to a stiff froth. Stir this in with the beaten yolks. Have a large omelet-pan very hot. Put one table-spoonful of butter in this, and pour in half the mixture. Shake rapidly for a minute; then fold, and turn on a hot dish. Put the remainder of the butter and mixture in the pan, and proceed as before. Turn this omelet on the dish by the side of the other. Dredge lightly with sugar, and place in the oven for eight minutes. Serve the moment it comes from the oven.

Charlotte Russe.

Ten eggs, one cupful of sugar, four table-spoonfuls of wine, one of vanilla extract, a package of gelatine, one and a half cupfuls of milk, one pint of cream. Soak the gelatine in half a cupful of the milk. Beat the yolks of the eggs and the sugar together, and put in the double boiler with the remaining milk. Stir until the mixture begins to thicken; then

MISS PARLOA'S NEW COOK BOOK.

add the gelatine, and strain into a large tin basin. Place this in a pan of ice water, and when it begins to cool add the whites of the eggs, well beaten, the wine and flavor, and the whipped cream. Mix thoroughly, and pour into moulds that have been lined with sponge cake. Set away to harden. With the quantities given, two quart moulds can be filled. The lining may be one piece of sponge cake, or strips of it, or lady-fingers. The wine may be omitted.

Charlotte Russe, No. 2.

One pint of *rich* cream, one teaspoonful of vanilla flavor, one third of a cupful of sugar. Mix all together in a tin pail and place in a basin of ice water. Whip the cream to a stiff froth, and skim into a colander. When nearly whipped, return to the pail that which has drained through the colander, and whip it again. Have a quart mould lined with stale sponge cake. Fill it with whipped cream and set in the ice chest for an hour or two.

Apple Charlotte.

One scant pint of apples, steamed, and rubbed through a sieve; one third of a box of gelatine, soaked an hour in one third of a cupful of cold water; one cupful of sugar, the juice of a large lemon, the whites of three eggs. Pour half a cupful of boiling water upon the gelatine, stir until thoroughly dissolved, and pour upon the apple; then add the sugar and lemon juice. Place in a basin of ice water, and beat until it begins to thicken. Add the whites of the eggs, beaten to a stiff froth. Pour into a two-quart mould, which has been lined with sponge cake, and put on ice to harden. Make a soft custard of the yolks of the eggs, one pint of milk, and three table-spoonfuls of sugar. When the charlotte is turned out on a dish, pour this around.

Calf's Foot Jelly.

Four calf's feet, six quarts of water, the juice of two lemons and rind of one, two cloves, a two-inch piece of stick cinnamon, two cupfuls of sugar, a pint of wine, the whites and shells of two eggs. Wash the feet very carefully and put them on with the cold water. Boil gently until the water is reduced to two quarts; then strain through a napkin, and set away to harden. In the morning scrape off all the fat, and wipe the jelly with a clean towel. Break it up and put in a kettle with the other ingredients, having first beaten the whites of the eggs and the shells with half a cupful of cold water. Let the mixture come to a boil slowly, and set back for twenty minutes where it will keep at the boiling point. Strain through a napkin, mould, and set away to harden.

Wine Jelly.

One box of gelatine, half a pint of cold water, a pint and a half of boiling water, one pint of sherry, one of sugar, the juice of a lemon. Soak the gelatine two hours in the cold water. Pour the boiling water on it, and stir until dissolved. Add the lemon juice, sugar and wine. Strain through a napkin, turn into moulds, and, when cold, place in the ice chest for six or eight hours.

One good way to mould this jelly is to pour some of it into the mould, harden it a little, put in a layer of strawberries, pour in jelly to set them, and then enough to make another layer, then put in more berries, and a third layer of jelly, and so continue, until all the jelly has been used.

Cider Jelly.

A box of gelatine, one pint of sugar, a quart and half a pint of cider, half a pint of cold water. Soak the gelatine in the cold water for two hours. Let the cider come to a boil, and pour it on the gelatine. Add the sugar, strain through a napkin, and turn into moulds. When cold, place in the refrigerator for six or eight hours.

Lemon Jelly.

Two cupfuls of sugar, one of lemon juice, one quart of boiling water, one cupful of cold water, a box of gelatine. Soak the gelatine in the cold water for two hours. Pour the boiling water on it, add the sugar and lemon juice, strain through a napkin, mould, and harden.

Orange Jelly.

One box of gelatine, one pint of orange juice, the juice of a lemon, one pint of sugar, a pint and a half of boiling water, half a pint of cold water, the white and shell of an egg. Soak the gelatine as for the other jellies. Add the boiling water, sugar, the fruit juice, and the white and shell of the egg, beaten with two table-spoonfuls of cold water. Let the mixture come to a boil, and set back for twenty minutes where it will keep hot, but will not boil. Strain through a napkin. A pretty way to mould this jelly is to fill the mould to the depth of two inches with liquid jelly, and, when this is hardened, put on a layer of oranges, divided into eighths; to pour on a little more jelly, to set the fruit, and then fill up with jelly. Keep in the ice chest for six or eight hours.

Currant Jelly.

Make the same as wine jelly, using a pint of currant juice instead of wine.

Strawberry Jelly.

Three pints of ripe strawberries, a box of gelatine, a pint of sugar, one pint of boiling water, half a pint of cold water, the juice of a lemon.

Soak the gelatine for two hours in the cold water. Mash the berries with the sugar, and let them stand two hours. Pour the boiling water on the fruit and sugar. Press the juice from the strawberries and add it and the lemon juice to the dissolved gelatine. Strain through a napkin, pour into moulds, and harden. Raspberry jelly is made in the same way.

Pineapple Jelly.

A pint-and-a-half can of pineapple, a scant pint of sugar, the white and shell of an egg, a box of gelatine, the juice of a lemon, one quart of boiling water, half a pint of cold water. Cut the pineapple in fine pieces, put with the boiling water, and simmer gently twenty minutes. Soak the gelatine in the cold water for two hours. Add it, the sugar, lemon and pineapple juice, and the white and shell of the egg, to the boiling mixture. Let this boil up once, and set back for twenty minutes where it will keep hot, but will not boil. Strain through a napkin, turn into moulds, and set away to harden.

Coffee Jelly.

One pint of sugar, one of strong coffee, a pint and a half of boiling water, half a pint of cold water, a box of gelatine. Soak the gelatine two hours in the cold water. Pour the boiling water on it, and when it is dissolved, add the sugar and coffee. Strain, turn into moulds, and set away to harden. This is to be served with sugar and cream.

Soft Custard.

One quart of milk, one scant half-teacupful of sugar, half a teaspoonful of salt, the yolks of eight eggs and whites of two, one teaspoonful of lemon or vanilla flavor, or half as much of almond. Beat the sugar and eggs together, and add one cupful of milk. Let the remainder of the milk come to a boil, pour it on the beaten mixture, and put this on the fire in the double boiler. Stir until it begins to thicken, which will be in about five minutes, when add the salt, and set away to cool. When cold, add the flavor. Serve in custard glasses.

Soft Caramel Custard.

One quart of milk, half a cupful of sugar, six eggs, half a teaspoonful of salt. Put the milk on to boil, reserving a cupful. Beat the eggs, and add the cold milk to them. Stir the sugar in a small frying-pan until it becomes liquid and just begins to smoke. Stir it into the boiling milk; then add the beaten eggs and cold milk, and stir constantly until the mixture begins to thicken. Set away to cool. Serve in glasses.

Chocolate Whips.

One quart of milk, one (ounce) square of Baker's chocolate, one generous half-cupful of sugar, six eggs, a speck of salt. Scrape the chocolate fine and put it in a small frying-pan with two table-spoonfuls of the sugar and one of boiling water. When dissolved, add it to a pint and a half of the milk, which should be hot in the double boiler. Beat the eggs and the remainder of the sugar together, add the cold milk, and stir into the boiling milk. Stir constantly until it begins to thicken. Add the salt, and set away to cool. Season one pint of cream with two table-spoonfuls of sugar and half a teaspoonful of vanilla extract. Whip to a stiff froth. When the custard is cold, half fill glasses with it, and heap whipped cream upon it. Or, it can be served in one large dish, with the whipped cream on top.

Kisses.

Beat the whites of six eggs to a stiff froth. They should be beaten until so light and dry that they begin to fly off of the beater. Stir in a cupful of powdered sugar, gently and quickly. Spread paraffine paper over three boards, which measure about nine by twelve inches. Drop the mixture by spoonfuls on the boards, having perhaps a dozen on each one. Dry in a warm oven for about three quarters of an hour; then brown them slightly. Lift from the paper and stick them together at the base by twos. A dozen and a half can be made from the quantities given.

Cream Méringues.

These are made similar to kisses, but are put on the paper in oblong shape, and dried two hours. Take from the board, and with a spoon remove all the soft part. Season half a pint of rich cream with a table-spoonful of sugar and one of wine, or a speck of vanilla, and whip it to a stiff froth. Fill the shells with this, and join them. Or, they may be filled with ice cream. If the méringues are exposed to much heat they are spoiled.

Kiss Wafers.

Half a pint of blanched bitter almonds, one heaping cupful of powdered sugar, the whites of six eggs, one third of a cupful of flour, two table-spoonfuls of corn-starch. Blanch the almonds and pound them in a mortar. As soon as they are a little broken, add the white of an egg. Pound until very fine. When there is a smooth paste add the sugar, a little at a time, the whites of two eggs, one at a time, and the flour and corn-starch. When thoroughly mixed, add, by degrees, the three remaining whites. Butter the bottom of a flat baking-pan, and put the mixture on it in spoonfuls. Spread it *very thin*, especially in the centre, and bake in a quick oven. The moment the cakes are taken from the oven, roll into the shape of cornucopias. If allowed to cool, they cannot be rolled, and for this reason it is best to bake only half a dozen at a time. When all are shaped, fill with the kiss mixture, made by beating the whites of three eggs to a stiff froth, and stirring into them, lightly, four table-spoonfuls of powdered sugar. Place the wafers in a warm oven for twenty minutes or half an hour, to dry. With the quantities given two dozen can be made.

Brier Hill Dessert.

Stew one quart of blackberries with one quart of sugar and half a cupful of water. They should cook only fifteen minutes. When cold, serve with powdered cracker and sugar and cream. The cracker and berries should be in separate dishes.

Richmond Maids of Honor.

In the little town of Richmond, England, is a small pastry shop widely known for its cheese cakes. It is said that the original recipe for them was furnished by a maid of Queen Elizabeth, who had a palace at Richmond. In the neighboring city of London the cakes are in great demand, and the popular opinion there is that the only place to get them is the shop mentioned, where they are made somewhat as follows:

One cupful of sweet milk, one of sour, one of sugar, a lemon, the yolks of four eggs, a speck of salt. Put all the milk in the double boiler and cook until it curds; then strain. Rub the curd through a sieve. Beat the sugar and yolks of eggs together, and add the rind and juice of the lemon and the curd. Line little patty-pans with puff or chopped paste, rolled very thin. Put a large spoonful of the mixture in each one, and bake from fifteen to twenty minutes in a moderate oven. Do not remove from the pans until cold. These are nice for suppers or lunches, as well as for dessert.

Fanchonettes.

One cupful of sugar, half a cupful of water, one table-spoonful of corn-starch, one teaspoonful of butter, the yolks of four eggs, the juice and rind of two lemons. Mix the corn-starch with a little cold water, and stir in half a cupful of boiling water. Beat the sugar, eggs, and lemon together, and stir into the boiling corn-starch. Place the basin in another of boiling water, and stir (over the fire) until it thickens, perhaps from eight to ten minutes; then add the butter, and set away to cool. Line little patty-pans with puff paste, or any rich paste, rolled very thin. Put a spoonful of the mixture in each one, and bake in a slow oven from twelve to twenty minutes. When cool, slip out of the pans, and serve on a napkin. They are nice for lunch, tea or children's parties, only for parties make them small. The mixture for fanchonettes will keep a number of weeks in a cool place, so that if one makes a quantity at one time, portions can be used with the trimmings of pastry left from pies.

Fruit Glacé.

Boil together for half an hour one cupful of granulated sugar, one of water. Dip the point of a skewer in the syrup, after it has been boiling the given time, and then in water. If the thread formed breaks off brittle, the syrup is done. Have oranges pared, divided into eighths, and wiped free of moisture. Pour part of the hot syrup into a small cup, which keep in boiling water. Take the pieces of orange on the point of a large needle or skewer, and dip them in the syrup. Place them on a dish that has been buttered lightly. Grapes, cherries, walnuts, etc., can be prepared in the same way. Care must be taken not to stir the syrup, as that spoils it.

Gâteau Saint Honoré.

Make a paste the same as for *éclairs*. Butter three pie-plates. Roll puff or chopped paste very thin, and cover the plates with it. Cut off the paste about an inch from the edge all round the plates. Spread a thin layer of the cooked paste over the puff paste. Put a tube, measuring about half an inch in diameter, in a pastry bag. Turn the remainder of the paste into the bag, and press it through the tube on to the edges of the plates, where the puff paste has been cut off. Care must be taken to have the border of equal thickness all round the plates. With a fork, prick holes in the paste in the centre of the plate. Bake half an hour in a moderate oven. When the plates have been put in the oven, make what paste is left in the bag into balls about half the size of an American walnut. There will be enough for three dozen. Drop them into a pan that has been buttered lightly, and bake fifteen or twenty minutes. While they are baking, put half a cupful of water and half a cupful of granulated sugar in a small saucepan, and boil twenty-five minutes.

When the little balls and the paste in the plate are done, take the balls on the point of a skewer or large needle, dip them in the syrup, and place them on the border of paste (the syrup will hold them), about two inches apart. A word of caution just here: Do not stir the syrup, as that will make it grain, and of course spoil it. A good plan is to pour part of the syrup into a small cup, which place in hot water. That remaining in the saucepan should be kept hot, but it should not boil until needed. When all the balls have been used, dip four dozen French candied cherries in the syrup, and stick them between the balls. Reserve about fifteen cherries, with which to garnish the centre of the cake.

Whip one pint and a half of cream to a froth. Soak half a package of gelatine in half a cupful of milk for two hours. Pour on this half a cupful of boiling milk. Place the pan of whipped cream in another of ice water, and sprinkle over it two thirds of a cupful of sugar, and nearly a teaspoonful of vanilla flavor. Strain the gelatine on this, and stir gently from the bottom until it begins to thicken. When it will just pour, fill the three plates with it, and set them in the ice chest for half an hour. Garnish the top with the remaining cherries, and serve. This is an excellent dish for dessert on party suppers.

CAKE.

Rice Cake.

ONE cupful of butter, two of sugar, two and one fourth of rice flour, six eggs, the juice and rind of a lemon. Beat the butter to a cream; then gradually beat in the sugar, and add the lemon. Beat the yolks and whites separately, and add them to the beaten sugar and butter. Add also the rice flour. Pour into a shallow pan, to the depth of about two inches. Bake from thirty-five to forty-five minutes in a moderate oven.

Silver Cake.

One cupful of sugar, half a cupful of butter, the whites of three eggs, half a cupful of corn-starch dissolved in nearly half a cupful of milk, one and a fourth cupfuls of flour, half a teaspoonful of cream of tartar, one fourth of a teaspoonful of soda, and vanilla or almond flavor. Beat the butter to a cream, and gradually beat in the sugar. Add the flavor. Mix the flour, cream of tartar, and soda together, and sift. Beat the whites to a stiff froth. Add the corn-starch and milk to the beaten sugar and butter; then add the whites of the eggs and the flour. Mix quickly and thoroughly. Have the batter in sheets, and about two inches deep. Bake in a moderate oven for about half an hour. A chocolate frosting is nice with this cake. — [Mrs. L. C. A.

Gold Cake.

One cupful of sugar, half a cupful of butter, the yolks of three eggs and one whole egg, half a cupful of milk, one fourth of a teaspoonful each of soda and cream of tartar, one and three fourths cupfuls of flour. Mix the butter and sugar together, and add the eggs, milk, flavor, and flour, in the order named. Bake the same as the silver cake. A white frosting is good with this cake. — [Mrs. L. C. A.

Angel Cake.

The whites of eleven eggs, one and a half cupfuls of granulated sugar, one cupful of pastry flour, measured after being sifted four times; one teaspoonful of cream of tartar, one of vanilla extract. Sift the flour and cream of tartar together. Beat the whites to a stiff froth. Beat the sugar into the eggs, and add the seasoning and flour, stirring quickly and lightly. Beat until ready to put the mixture in the oven. Use a pan that has little legs at the top corners, so that when the pan is turned upside down on the table, after the baking, a current of air will pass under and over it. Bake for forty minutes in a moderate oven. Do not grease the pan.

Sunshine Cake.

This is made almost exactly like angel cake. Have the whites of eleven eggs and yolks of six, one and a half cupfuls of granulated sugar measured after one sifting, one cupful of flour measured after sifting, one teaspoonful of cream of tartar, and one of orange extract. Beat the whites to a stiff froth, and gradually beat in the sugar. Beat the yolks in a similar manner, and add to them the whites and sugar, and the flavor. Finally, stir in the flour. Mix quickly and well. Bake for fifty minutes in a slow oven, using a pan like that for angel cake.

Demon Cake.

One cupful of butter, one of sugar, one of molasses, two eggs, four and one fourth cupfuls of flour, one table-spoonful of ginger, one of cinnamon, four of brandy, half a grated nutmeg, one teaspoonful of soda dissolved in two table-spoonfuls of milk, one cupful of currants, and one of preserved ginger, cut in fine strips. Beat the butter to a cream; then beat in the sugar, molasses, brandy, and spice. Have the eggs well beaten, and add them. Stir in the soda and flour. Have two pans well buttered, or lined with paraffine paper. Pour the cake mixture, to the depth of about two inches, in each pan. Sprinkle a layer of fruit on it. Cover with a thin layer of the mixture, and add more fruit. Continue this until all the batter and fruit is used. Bake two hours in a moderate oven.

Ames Cake.

One generous cupful of butter, two of sugar, three cupfuls of pastry flour, one small cupful of milk, the yolks of five eggs and whites of three, one teaspoonful of cream of tartar, half a teaspoonful of soda, or one and a half teaspoonfuls of baking powder, one teaspoonful of lemon extract, or the juice of one fresh lemon. Beat the butter to a cream. Add the sugar, gradually, then the seasoning, the eggs, well beaten, next the milk, and then the flour, in which the soda and cream of tartar are mixed. Mix thoroughly, but quickly, and bake in two sheets in a moderate oven for twenty-five or thirty minutes. Cover with a frosting made by stirring two small cupfuls of powdered sugar into the whites of two eggs, and seasoning with lemon.

Black Cake.

Three cupfuls of butter, one quart of sugar, three pints of flour, half a pint of molasses, half a pint of brandy, half a pint of wine, one teaspoonful of saleratus, one ounce each of all kinds of spices, twelve eggs, three pounds of raisins, two of currants, half a pound of citron. Bake in deep pans, in a moderate oven, between three and four hours. This is one of the best of rich cakes.

White Fruit Cake.

One cupful of butter, two of sugar, three of flour, the whites of eight eggs, half a wine-glass of white wine, two teaspoonfuls of baking powder, one fourth of a pound of citron, cut fine ; half a pound of chopped almonds, one teacupful of desiccated cocoanut. Beat the butter to a cream, and gradually beat in the sugar, and then the wine. Beat the eggs to a stiff froth, and stir into the butter and sugar. Add the flour, which is thoroughly mixed with the baking powder, and lastly the fruit. Bake, in two loaves, forty minutes in a moderate oven.

Wedding Cake.

Nine cupfuls of butter, five pints of sugar, four quarts of flour, five dozen of eggs, seven pounds of currants, three and a half of citron, four of shelled almonds, seven of raisins, one and a half pints of brandy, two ounces of mace. Bake in a moderate oven for two hours or more. This will make eight loaves, which will keep for years.

Lady's Cake.

Three fourths of a cupful of butter, two cupfuls of sugar, half a cupful of milk, three cupfuls of pastry flour, the whites of six eggs, one teaspoonful of baking powder, one teaspoonful of essence of almond. Beat the butter to a cream. Add the sugar, gradually, then the essence, milk, the whites of eggs beaten to a stiff froth, and the flour, in which the baking powder has been mixed. Bake in one large pan or two small ones, and frost, or not, as you please. If baked in sheets about two inches deep, it will take about twenty-five minutes in a moderate oven.

Queen's Cake.

One cupful of butter, a pint of sugar, a quart of flour, four eggs, half a gill of wine, of brandy, and of thin cream, one pound of fruit, spice to taste. Warm the liquids together, and stir quickly into the beaten sugar, butter, and egg ; add the flour ; finally add the fruit. Bake in deep pans in a moderate oven.

Composition Cake.

One and one half quarts of flour, half a pint of sour milk, one pint of butter, three fourths of a quart of sugar, eight eggs, one wine-glass of wine and one of brandy, one scant teaspoonful of soda, one cupful of raisins stoned and chopped, two pounds of currants, half a pound of citron, a nutmeg, two teaspoonfuls of cinnamon, one of allspice, one of mace, half a teaspoonful of clove. Beat the butter to a cream, and add the sugar, gradually, the well-beaten eggs, the spice, wine, and brandy. Dissolve the soda in a table-spoonful of hot water ; stir into the sour milk, and add to the other ingredients. Then add the flour, and lastly the fruit. Bake two hours in well-buttered pans in a moderate oven. This will make three loaves.

Ribbon Cake.

Two cupfuls of sugar, one of butter, one of milk, four of flour (rather scant), four eggs, half a teaspoonful of soda, one of cream of tartar. Beat the butter to a cream. Add the sugar, gradually, beating all the while ; then the flavoring (lemon or nutmeg). Beat the eggs very light. Add them and the milk. Measure the flour after it has been sifted. Return it to the sieve, and mix the soda and cream of tartar with it. Sift this into the bowl of beaten ingredients. Beat quickly and vigorously, to thoroughly mix, and then stop. Take three sheet pans of the same size, and in each of two put one third of the mixture, and bake. To the other third add four teaspoonfuls of cinnamon, a cupful of currants, and about an eighth of a pound of citron, cut fine. Bake this in the remaining pan. When done, take out of the pans. Spread the light cake with a thin layer of jelly, while warm. Place on this the dark cake, and spread with jelly. Place the other sheet of light cake on this. Lay a paper over all, and then a thin sheet, on which put two irons. The cake will press in about two hours.

Regatta Cake.

Two pounds of raised dough, one pint of sugar, one cupful of butter, four eggs, a nutmeg, a glass of wine, a teaspoonful of saleratus, one pound of raisins. Mix thoroughly, put in deep pans that have been thoroughly greased, and let it rise half an hour, if in very warm weather, or fifteen minutes longer, if in cold weather. Bake in a moderate oven.

Nut Cake.

One cupful of sugar, half a cupful of butter, half a cupful of milk, two cupfuls of pastry flour, two eggs, one coffee-cupful of chopped raisins, one of chopped English walnuts, one teaspoonful of cream of tartar, half a teaspoonful of soda. Beat the butter to a cream. Add the sugar, gradually, and, when light, the eggs well beaten, then the milk and the flour, in which the soda and cream of tartar have been thoroughly mixed. Mix quickly, and add the raisins and nuts. Bake in rather deep sheets, in a moderate oven, for thirty-five minutes. Frost, if you please. The quantities given are for one large or two small sheets. If you use baking powder, instead of cream of tartar and soda, take a teaspoonful and a half.

Snow-Flake Cake.

Half a cupful of butter, one and a half of sugar, two of pastry flour, one fourth of a cupful of milk, the whites of five eggs, one teaspoonful of

cream of tartar, half a teaspoonful of soda, or a teaspoonful and a half of baking powder, the juice of half a lemon. Beat the butter to a cream. Gradually add the sugar, then the lemon, and, when very light, the milk, and whites of the eggs, beaten to a stiff froth ; then the flour, in which the soda and cream of tartar are well mixed. Bake in sheets in a moderate oven. When nearly cool, frost.

Frosting : The whites of three eggs, two large cupfuls of powdered sugar, half a grated cocoanut, the juice of half a lemon. Beat the whites to a stiff froth. Add the sugar, gradually, and the lemon and cocoanut. Put a layer of frosting on one sheet of the cake. Place the other sheet on this, and cover with frosting. Or, simply frost the top of each sheet, as you would any ordinary cake. Set in a cool place to harden.

Federal Cake.

One pint of sugar, one and a half cupfuls of butter, three pints of flour, four eggs, two wine-glasses of milk, two of wine, two of brandy, one teaspoonful of cream of tartar, half a teaspoonful of saleratus, fruit and spice to taste. Bake in deep pans, the time depending on the quantity of fruit used.

Sponge Rusks.

Two cupfuls of sugar, one of butter, two of milk, one of yeast, three eggs. Rub the butter, sugar, and eggs together. Add the milk and yeast, and flour enough to make a thick batter. Let this stand in a warm place until light, and then add flour enough to make as thick as for biscuit. Shape, and put in a pan in which they are to be baked, and let them stand two or three hours (three hours unless the weather is very warm). Bake about forty minutes in a moderate oven. It is always best to set the sponge at night, for it will then be ready to bake the following forenoon. If the rusks are wanted warm for tea, the sponge must, of course, be set early in the morning.

Taylor Cake.

Half a cupful of butter, two and a half of sugar, one of milk, three and a half of pastry flour, three eggs, one teaspoonful of cream of tartar, half a teaspoonful of soda, flavor to taste. Beat the butter to a cream, then beat in the sugar, next the eggs, well beaten ; the seasoning, the milk, and lastly the flour, in which the soda and cream of tartar have been thoroughly mixed. Bake in a moderate oven, either in loaves or sheets. If in sheets, twenty-five minutes ; if in loaves, forty-five. The quantities given are for two loaves or sheets. This cake is nice for Washington or chocolate pies, and is good baked in sheets and frosted.

Loaf Cake.

Two quarts of sugar, seven cupfuls of butter, six quarts of sifted flour, six pounds of fruit, one pint of wine, one pint of yeast, eight nutmegs, mace, twelve eggs, one quart of milk. It should be made at such an hour (being governed by the weather) as will give it time to get perfectly light by evening. It should stand about six hours in summer and eight in winter.

Put in half the butter and eggs, and the milk, flavor, and yeast, and beat thoroughly. In the evening add the remainder of the butter, rubbing it with the sugar, the rest of the eggs, and the spice. Let the cake rise again, until morning ; then add the fruit. Put in deep pans, and let rise about half an hour. Bake from two to three hours in a slow oven.

Chocolate Cake.

One and a half cupfuls of sugar, half a cupful of butter, half a cupful of milk, one and three fourths cupfuls of flour, a quarter of a pound of Baker's chocolate, three eggs, one teaspoonful of cream of tartar, half a teaspoonful of soda. Scrape the chocolate fine, and add five table-spoonfuls of sugar to it (this in addition to the cupful and a half). Beat the butter to a cream. Gradually add the sugar, beating all the while. Add three table-spoonfuls of boiling water to the chocolate and sugar. Stir over the fire until smooth and glossy ; then stir into the beaten sugar and butter. Add to this mixture the eggs, well beaten, then the milk and the flour, in which the soda and cream of tartar have been thoroughly mixed. Bake twenty minutes in a moderate oven. This will make two sheets. Frost it, if you like.

Chocolate Cake, No 2.

One cupful of butter, two of sugar, three and a half of flour, one of milk, five eggs (the whites of two being left out), one teaspoonful of cream of tartar and half a teaspoonful of soda, or one and a half of baking powder. Beat the butter to a cream. Add the sugar, gradually, then the eggs, well beaten, the milk, next the flour, in which the soda and cream of tartar have been well mixed. Bake in two sheets for thirty minutes in a moderate oven, and ice.

Icing : The whites of two eggs, one and a half cupfuls of powdered sugar, six table-spoonfuls of grated chocolate, one teaspoonful of vanilla. Put the chocolate and six table-spoonfuls of the sugar in a saucepan with two spoonfuls of hot water. Stir over a hot fire until smooth and glossy. Beat the whites to a froth, and add the sugar and chocolate.

Orange Cake.

Two cupfuls of sugar, a small half-cupful of butter, two cupfuls of flour, half a cupful of water, the yolks of five eggs and whites of four, half a teaspoonful of soda, a teaspoonful of cream of tartar, the rind of one orange and the juice of one and a half. Beat the butter to a cream.

Add the sugar, gradually, then the orange, the eggs well beaten, the water, and the flour, in which the soda and cream of tartar have been well mixed. Bake in sheets for twenty-five minutes, in a moderate oven, and, when cool, frost.

Frosting: The white of an egg, the juice of one and a half oranges and the grated rind of one, one cupful and a half of powdered sugar, unless the egg and oranges are very large, in which case use two cupfuls.

Railroad Cake.

Two cupfuls of sugar, two of flour, six table-spoonfuls of butter, two of milk, six eggs, one teaspoonful of saleratus, two of cream of tartar, lemon peel. Bake in shallow pans in a quick oven.

Hot Water Sponge Cake.

Six eggs, two cupfuls of sugar, two of pastry flour, half a cupful of *boiling* water, the grated rind of half a lemon, and one teaspoonful of the juice. Beat the yolks and sugar to a froth; also beat the whites to a stiff froth. Add the lemon to the yolks and sugar, then add the boiling water, next the whites, and, last of all, the flour. Mix quickly, and bake in two sheets for half an hour, in a moderate oven.

Sponge Cake.

Ten eggs, two and a half cupfuls of sugar, two and a half of pastry flour, the juice and grated rind of one lemon. Beat the yolks and sugar together until very light. Add the lemon. Beat the whites to a stiff froth. Stir the flour and this froth alternately into the beaten yolks and sugar. Have the batter about three inches deep in the pan. Sprinkle with sugar, and bake three quarters of an hour in a moderate oven. If the batter is not so deep in the pan it will not take so long to bake.

Sponge Cake, No. 2.

The yolks of a dozen eggs and whites of eight, one and three fourths cupfuls of sugar, the same quantity of flour, the rind of one lemon and juice of two. Beat the yolks and sugar together. Add the lemon rind and juice, and beat a little longer. Beat the whites to a stiff froth, and add them to the mixture. Gradually stir in the flour. Pour the mixture into a baking-pan to the depth of about two inches. Bake from thirty-five to forty minutes in a slow oven.

Viennois Cakes.

Cut any kind of plain cake into small squares. Cut a small piece from the centre of each square, and fill the cavity with some kind of marmalade or jelly. Replace the crust part that was removed, and cover with icing. These cakes are nice for dessert.

Dominos.

Have any kind of sponge cake baked in a rather thin sheet. Cut this into small oblong pieces, the shape of a domino. Frost the top and sides of them. When the frosting is hard, draw the black lines and make the dots with a small brush that has been dipped in melted chocolate. These are particularly good for children's parties.

Lady-Fingers.

Four eggs, three fourths of a cupful of pastry flour, half a cupful of *powdered* sugar. Have the bottom of three large baking-pans covered with paraffine paper or sheets of buttered note-paper. Beat the yolks of the eggs and the sugar to a froth. Beat the whites to a stiff, dry froth, and add to the yolks and sugar. Add the flour, and stir quickly and gently. Pour the mixture into the pastry bag, and press it through on to the paper in the shape and of the size you wish. When all the mixture has been used, sprinkle powdered sugar on the cakes, and bake from twelve to sixteen minutes in a *very* slow oven.

Caution. The mixture must be stirred, after the flour is added, only enough to mix the flour lightly with the sugar and eggs. Much stirring turns the mixture liquid. If the oven is hot the fingers will rise and fall, and if too cool they will spread. It should be about half as hot as for bread.

You will not succeed in using the pastry bag the first time, but a little practice will make it easy to get the forms wished. There are pans especially for baking lady-fingers. They are quite expensive.

Sponge Drops.

Make the batter the same as for lady-fingers, and drop on the paper in teaspoonfuls. Sprinkle with sugar. Bake in a slow oven from twelve to sixteen minutes.

Sponge Drops, No 2.

Three eggs, one and a half cupfuls of sugar, two of flour, half a cupful of cold water, one teaspoonful of cream of tartar, half a teaspoonful of saleratus. Beat the sugar and eggs together. Add the water when they are light, and then the flour, in which mix the saleratus and cream of tartar. Flavor with lemon. Have muffin-cups very lightly buttered, and drop a teaspoonful of the mixture into each one. Bake in a quick oven. These drops are nice for dessert or tea.

Sponge Cake for Charlotte Russe.

Line the bottoms of two shallow baking-pans with paraffine paper or buttered paper, and spread the lady-finger mixture on it. Bake slowly eighteen minutes. Cut paper to fit the sides of the mould. When the cake is cold, lay this pattern on it and cut with a sharp knife.

Jelly Roll.

Make the sponge-cake mixture as for lady-fingers, and bake in one shallow pan twenty minutes. While it is yet warm, cut off the edges, and spread the cake with any kind of jelly. Roll up, and pin a towel around it. Put in a cool place until serving time. Cut in slices with a sharp knife.

Molasses Pound Cake.

One quart of molasses, one pint of water, six and a half pints of flour, one ounce of soda, half an ounce of alum, one heaping cupful of butter, six eggs, one ounce of cinnamon, one pound of raisins. Boil the alum in part of the pint of water, and let it cool before mixing with the other ingredients. Instead of alum, one ounce of cream of tartar may be used.

Soft Gingerbread.

Six cupfuls of flour, three of molasses, one of cream, one of lard or butter, two eggs, one teaspoonful of saleratus, and two of ginger. This is excellent.

Hard Gingerbread.

One cupful of sugar, one of butter, one third of a cupful of molasses, half a cupful of sour milk or cream, one teaspoonful of saleratus, one table-spoonful of ginger, flour enough to roll. Roll thin, cut in oblong pieces, and bake quickly. Care must be taken that too much flour is not mixed in with the dough. All kinds of cakes that are rolled should have no more flour than is absolutely necessary to work them.

Canada Gingerbread.

One cupful of butter, two of sugar, one of molasses, five of flour, three eggs, one nutmeg, one teaspoonful of ginger, one of soda, one teacupful of cream or rich milk, one table-spoonful of cinnamon, one pound of currants. Beat the butter to a cream. Add the sugar, molasses, and spice; next the eggs, well beaten; then the milk, in which the soda has been dissolved; next the flour; and lastly the currants. This will make three sheets, or two very thick ones. Bake in a moderately quick oven, if in three sheets, twenty-five minutes; if in two sheets, ten minutes longer.

Fairy Gingerbread.

One cupful of butter, two of sugar, one of milk, four of flour, three fourths of a teaspoonful of soda, one table-spoonful of ginger. Beat the butter to a cream. Add the sugar, gradually, and, when very light, the ginger, the milk in which the soda has been dissolved, and finally the flour. Turn baking-pans upside down and wipe the bottoms very clean. Butter them, and spread the cake mixture very thin on them. Bake in a moderate oven until brown. While still *hot*, cut into squares with a case-knife and slip from the pan. Keep in a tin box. This is delicious. With the quantities given a large dish of gingerbread can be made. It must be spread on the bottom of the pan as thin as a wafer, and cut the moment it comes from the oven.

Shrewsbury Cake.

Two cupfuls of butter, one pint of sugar, three pints of flour, four eggs, half a teaspoonful of mace. Roll thin, cut into small cakes, and bake in a quick oven. Not a particle more of flour than what is given above must be used. The cakes should be made in a rather cool room, and they cannot be made in very warm weather. They can be kept a long time, and are delicious.

Jumbles.

Three cupfuls of sugar, two of butter, five of flour, one egg, half a tea-spoonful of soda, flavor to taste. Roll thin, sprinkle with sugar, cut in round cakes, and cut a small piece from the centre of each. Bake in a quick oven.

Seed Cakes.

Three fourths of a pint of sugar, one cupful of butter, a quart and half a pint of flour, one teaspoonful of saleratus, two eggs, and seeds. Roll thin, cut in round cakes, and bake quickly.

Cookies.

One cupful of butter, two of sugar, five of flour, a teaspoonful of saleratus dissolved in four of milk, one egg, flavor to taste. Roll and bake like seed cakes.

Hermits.

Two cupfuls of sugar, one of butter, one of raisins (stoned and chopped), three eggs, half a teaspoonful of soda dissolved in three table-spoonfuls of milk, a nutmeg, one teaspoonful each of clove and cinnamon, and six cupfuls of flour. Roll about one fourth of an inch thick, and cut with a round cake-cutter. Bake in a rather quick oven. It will take about twelve minutes. — [Mrs. L. C. A.

Kneaded Plum Cake.

Two and a half cupfuls of sugar, half a cupful of butter, half a cupful of sour milk, two spoonfuls of cream, a teaspoonful of saleratus, half a spoonful of cinnamon and of nutmeg, a cupful of chopped raisins, and flour enough to knead (about six cupfuls). Roll an inch thick, and cut in oblong pieces. Bake on sheets in a quick oven.

Éclairs.

Put one cupful of boiling water and half a cupful of butter in a large saucepan, and when it boils up turn in one pint of flour. Beat well with the vegetable masher. When perfectly smooth, and velvety to the touch, remove from the fire. Break five eggs into a bowl. When the paste is nearly cold, beat the eggs into it with the hand. Only a small part of the eggs should be added at a time. When the mixture is thoroughly beaten (it will take about twenty minutes), spread on buttered sheets in oblong pieces about four inches long and one and a half wide. These must be about two inches apart. Bake in a rather quick oven for about twenty-five minutes. As soon as they are done, ice with either chocolate or vanilla frosting. When the icing is cold, cut the *éclairs* on one side and fill them.

Chocolate Éclairs.

Put one cupful and a half of milk in the double boiler. Beat together two thirds of a cupful of sugar, one fourth of a cupful of flour, two eggs, and one fourth of a teaspoonful of salt. Stir the mixture into the boiling milk. Cook fifteen minutes, stirring often. When cold, flavor with one teaspoonful of vanilla extract. Put two squares of scraped chocolate with five table-spoonfuls of powdered sugar and three of boiling water. Stir over the fire until smooth and glossy. Dip the tops of the *éclairs* in this as they come from the oven. When the chocolate icing is dry, cut open, and fill with the cream, which should be cold. If a chocolate flavor is liked with the cream, one table-spoonful of the dissolved chocolate may be added to it.

Vanilla Éclairs.

Make an icing with the whites of two eggs and a cupful and a half of powdered sugar. Flavor with one teaspoonful of vanilla extract. Frost the *éclairs ;* and when dry, open, and fill with a cream, the same as chocolate *éclairs.* They may be filled with cream sweetened, flavored with vanilla, and whipped to a stiff froth. Strawberry and raspberry preserves are sometimes used to fill *éclairs.* They are then named after the fruit with which they are filled.

Frosting.

The white of one egg, one teacupful of powdered sugar, one table-spoonful of lemon juice. Put the white of the egg in a bowl and add the sugar by degrees, beating with a spoon. When all has been added, stir in the lemon juice. If the white of the egg is large it will require a very full cup of sugar, and if small, a rather scant cupful. The egg must *not* be beaten until the sugar is added. This gives a smooth, tender frosting, which will cover one small sheet of cake. The same amount of material, prepared with the whites of the eggs unbeaten, will make one third less frosting than it will if the eggs are beaten to a stiff froth before adding the sugar ; but the icing will be enough smoother and softer to pay for the extra quantity. It may be flavored with half a teaspoonful of vanilla.

Chocolate Icing.

Two squares of Baker's chocolate, the whites of two eggs, two cupfuls of powdered sugar, four table-spoonfuls of boiling water. Beat one and two thirds cupfuls of the sugar into the unbeaten whites of the eggs. Scrape the chocolate, and put it and the remaining third of a cupful of sugar and the water in a small frying-pan. Stir over a hot fire until smooth and glossy, and then stir into the beaten whites and sugar. With the quantity given two sheets of cake can be iced.

Chocolate Icing, No. 2.

Soak a teaspoonful of gelatine one or two hours in three table-spoonfuls of water. Pour on it one fourth of a cupful of boiling water, and stir into it one and two thirds cupfuls of powdered sugar. Prepare two squares of chocolate as for the first icing, and stir them into this mixture. Use immediately.

Caramel Frosting.

One cupful of brown sugar, one square of Baker's chocolate, scraped fine ; one table-spoonful of water. Simmer gently twenty minutes, being careful not to let it burn. Spread on the cake while hot.

Golden Frosting.

Into the yolks of two eggs stir powdered sugar enough to thicken, and flavor strongly with lemon. This does not have so good a flavor as other kinds of frosting, but it makes a change.

Marking Cakes in Gold.

Bake round cakes for the children, and when the frosting on them is hard, dip a small brush into the yolk of an egg, and write a word or name upon the cake. It pleases the little ones very much.

PRESERVING.

In using self-sealing glass jars great care must be taken. If the work is properly done, the fruit can be kept for years. Have a kettle of hot water on the stove beside the preserving kettle, and also a small dipper of hot water. Plunge a jar into the hot water, having the water strike both inside and outside the jar at the same time. If you set it down instead of plunging it, it will break. Put the cover in the dipper. When the jar is hot, lift it up and pour the water from it into the kettle. Stand the jar in the hot water and fill it with hot fruit from the preserving kettle. Fill to the brim with the hot syrup. Take the cover from the dipper of hot water and screw it on very tightly. In using the jars a second time have the right cover and band for each one. A large-mouthed tunnel, such as grocers have, is almost indispensable in the work of preserving.

Jellies and jams should be put in tumblers or bowls. A paper should be cut to fit the top, and then wet in brandy, and another paper should be pasted over it. Jelly tumblers with glass covers are more convenient than the old-fashioned ones, and where they are used the second paper cover is not necessary. It is better not to cover until some weeks after the jelly is made. White crushed sugar is much the nicest for preserving. If jelly does not seem hard, as it should be the day after it is made, it can be set in the sun for several hours, which will help it greatly.

Strawberries.

To each pound of berries allow half a pound of sugar. Put the berries in a kettle, and mash them a little, so that there will be juice enough to cook them without using water. Stir them to prevent scorching. Cook fifteen minutes ; then add the sugar, and let them boil hard one minute. Put them in the jars as directed. More or less sugar may be used, as one prefers.

Raspberries.

To each pound of berries allow three fourths of a pound of sugar, and cook the same as the strawberries.

Cherries.

Cherries may be preserved either with or without stones. Many think the stones give a richer flavor. To each pound of cherries allow one third of a pound of sugar. Put the sugar in the kettle with half a pint of water to three pounds of sugar. Stir it until it is dissolved. When boiling, add the cherries, and cook three minutes ; then put in the jars.

Currants.

Currants should be prepared the same as raspberries.

Pineapple.

Pare the fruit, and be sure you take out all the eyes and discolored parts. Cut in slices, and cut the slices in small bits, taking out the core. Weigh the fruit, and put in a pan with half as many pounds of sugar as of fruit. Let it stand over night. In the morning put it over the fire and let it boil rapidly for a minute only, as cooking long discolors it. Put it in the jars as directed.

Grated Pineapple.

Pare the fruit clean ; then grate it on a coarse grater, rejecting the cores. Weigh it, and put to each pound of fruit a pound of sugar. Let it stand over night. In the morning boil for a minute, and it is done. Put it in jars as directed.

Blackberries.

Blackberries are prepared like strawberries. If they are quite ripe, not quite so much sugar is needed.

Whortleberries.

To each quart of berries allow one third of a pound of sugar, and half a pint of water to three pounds of sugar. Put the water and sugar over the fire, and when boiling hot add the berries. Cook three minutes. Put in the jars as directed.

Crab-Apples.

To each pound of fruit allow half a pound of sugar, and a pint of water to three pounds of sugar. When the syrup is boiling hot, drop in the apples. They will cook very quickly. When done, fill a jar with the fruit, and fill it up with syrup.

Pears.

Pare the fruit and cut in halves. Throw into cold water, or they will be discolored. Use one pound of sugar for three of fruit, and one quart of water for three pounds of sugar. When the syrup is boiling, take the pears from the water, and drop into the syrup. Cook until they can be pierced easily with a silver fork. Fill the jars with fruit, and fill up to the brim with syrup, using a small strainer in the tunnel, that the syrup may look clear. Bartlett pears are delicious, as are also Seckel ; but many other varieties are good.

Peaches.

Have ready a kettle of boiling water. Fill a wire basket with peaches and plunge them into the boiling water. In two minutes take them out, and the skins will come off easily. Drop the fruit into cold water, to keep the color. For three pounds of fruit use one pound of sugar, and one pint of water for three pounds of sugar. When the syrup is boiling hot, take the fruit from the water, and drop into it. Put but a few in at a time, as they cook very quickly. Take them from the syrup with a silver fork, fill the jar, and fill up with strained syrup. Peaches are much nicer preserved whole, as the stones give a rich flavor.

Brandied Peaches

The Morris white peaches are the best. Take off the skins with boiling water. To each pound of fruit allow one pound of sugar, and half a pint of water to three pounds of sugar. When the syrup is boiling hot, put in the peaches, and as fast as they cook take them out carefully and spread on platters. When cool, put them in jars, and fill up these with syrup, using one half syrup and one half pale brandy. First-proof alcohol, diluted with an equal quantity of water, can be used instead of brandy, but it is not, of course, so nice.

Plums.

The large white plums must be skinned by using boiling water, as for peaches, and then throwing them into cold water. For one pound of fruit allow half a pound of sugar, and half a pint of water for three pounds of sugar. Cook but few at a time, and take them out carefully. Fill up the jar with hot syrup.

Damsons.

Wash the fruit, and for one pound of it use half a pound of sugar, and half a pint of water for three pounds of sugar. When the syrup is boiling hot, put in the fruit, and cook three minutes. Dip the plums and syrup together into the jars.

Quinces.

Pare and quarter the fruit, and take out all the cores and the hard place around them. Boil the fruit in clear water until tender; then spread it on towels to dry. For one pound of fruit allow half a pound of sugar, and one pint of water for three pounds of sugar. When the syrup is boiling hot, put in the fruit, and let it cook very slowly; or, set it back on the stove so that it hardly cooks at all, and keep it on for an hour or more, if you can without its cooking to pieces,—as the longer it cooks the brighter red color it will be. Put it in jars, and strain the syrup over it, as with other fruits.

Sour Oranges.

Grate off the rind, cut the orange into two parts, and remove the pulp. Weigh the peel, place it in a large stone pot, and cover with brine made of three gallons of water and a quart of salt. Let it stand twenty-four hours, and drain off the brine. Again cover the peel with brine made of the same quantity of water and half as much salt as was first used, and let it stand another day. Drain, cover with clear cold water, and let it stand a third day. Drain again, and put in a boiler and cover with fresh cold water. Let it come to a boil, and boil fifteen minutes; then take out and drain. Make a syrup of three quarts of sugar and one of water, for every six pounds of peel. When the syrup is clear, drop in the peel and boil until it is clear and tender,— perhaps four hours of slow boiling. Great care must be taken that it is not scorched. It must be stirred every fifteen minutes. The sugar may be either white or brown. The orange used is not the common orange, but the wild, sour fruit, found in Florida. The pulp may be used for marmalade.

Grapes.

Squeeze the pulp of the grapes out of the skins. Cook the pulp (a few minutes) until you can press it all through a sieve. Reject the seeds. Add a little water to the skins, and cook until they are quite tender. Then put the skins and pulp together. Measure; and to each pint add a pound of sugar, and boil fifteen minutes.

Apple Ginger.

Four pounds each of apple and sugar. Make a syrup of the sugar, adding a pint of water. Chop the apple very fine,— with one ounce of green ginger; or, if you cannot get the green ginger, use white ginger root. Put in the syrup with the grated rind of four lemons, and boil slowly for two hours, or until it looks clear.

Raspberry or Strawberry Jam.

For each pound of fruit allow a pound of sugar. Mash the fruit in the kettle. Boil hard for fifteen minutes; then add the sugar, and boil five minutes.

Orange Marmalade.

Take equal weights of sour oranges and sugar. Grate the yellow rind from a fourth of the oranges. Cut all the fruit in halves at what might be called the "equator." Pick out the pulp, and free it of seeds. Drain off as much juice as you conveniently can, and put it on to boil with the sugar. Let it come to a boil. Skim, and simmer for about fifteen minutes; then put in the pulp and grated rind, and boil fifteen minutes longer. Put away in jelly tumblers.

Quince Marmalade.

Cut up quinces, skins, cores, and all, cover with water, and boil until tender. Rub through a sieve, and to every pint of pulp add one pint of sugar. Boil two hours, stirring often. Peach, crab-apple, and, in fact, all kinds of marmalade may be made in the same manner.

Currant Jelly.

Wash the currants clean. Put them in the preserving kettle and mash them, and boil twenty minutes or more, or until they are thoroughly cooked. Put them, a quart or more at a time, in a strainer cloth, and squeeze out all the juice. Measure this, and for each pint allow one pound of sugar. Put the juice over the fire, and let it boil rapidly for five minutes; then add the sugar, and let it boil rapidly one minute longer. Take off of the fire, skim clear, and put in tumblers.

Barberry Jelly.

The barberries need not be stripped from the stems. Put the fruit in a kettle with water enough to come just to the top of the fruit, and boil until thoroughly cooked. Put in a strainer cloth and get out all the juice. To each pint of it allow one pound of sugar. Boil the juice hard for fifteen minutes. Add the sugar, and boil rapidly five or ten minutes, or until it is thick.

Grape Jelly.

Mash the grapes in a kettle, put them over the fire, and cook until thoroughly done. Drain through a sieve, but do not press through. To each pint of the juice allow one pound of sugar. Boil rapidly for five minutes. Add the sugar, and boil rapidly three minutes more.

Cider Apple Jelly.

Cut good, ripe apples in quarters, put them in a kettle, and cover them with *sweet* cider, just from the press. (It should, if possible, be used the day it is made, or at any rate before it has worked at all.) Boil until well done, and drain through a sieve. Do not press it through. Measure the liquor, and to each pint add one pound of sugar. Boil from twenty minutes to half an hour.

Crab-Apple Jelly.

Wash the fruit clean, put in a kettle, cover with water, and boil until thoroughly cooked. Then pour it into a sieve, and let it drain. Do not press it through. For each pint of this liquor allow one pound of sugar. Boil from twenty minutes to half an hour.

Other Jellies.

Jellies can be made from quinces, peaches, and Porter apples by following the directions for crab-apple jelly.

PICKLES AND KETCHUP.

Pickled Blueberries.

NEARLY fill a jar with ripe berries, and fill up with good molasses. Cover, and set away. In a few weeks they will be ready to use.

Sweet Melons.

Use ripe citron melons. Pare them, cut them in slices and remove the seeds. To five pounds of melon allow two and one half pounds of sugar and one quart of vinegar. The vinegar and sugar must be heated to the boiling point and poured over the fruit six times, or once on each of six successive days. In the last boiling of the syrup add half an ounce of stick cinnamon, half an ounce of white ginger root, and a few cloves. When the syrup boils, put in the melon, and boil ten minutes; then put in jars. Skim the syrup clear and pour it over the melon.

Peaches, Pears, and Sweet Apples.

For six pounds of fruit use three of sugar, about five dozen cloves, and a pint of vinegar. Into each apple, pear, or peach stick two cloves. Have the syrup hot, and cook until tender.

Sweet Tomato Pickle.

One peck of green tomatoes and six large onions, sliced. Sprinkle with one cupful of salt, and let them stand over night. In the morning drain. Add to the tomatoes two quarts of water and one quart of vinegar. Boil fifteen minutes; then drain again, and throw this vinegar and water away. Add to the pickle two pounds of sugar, two quarts of vinegar, two table-spoonfuls of clove, two of allspice, two of ginger, two of mustard, two of cinnamon, and one teaspoonful of cayenne, and boil fifteen minutes.

Spiced Currants.

Make a syrup of three pounds of sugar, one pint of vinegar, two table-spoonfuls of cinnamon, two table-spoonfuls of clove, and half a teaspoonful of salt. Add six pounds of currants, and boil half an hour.

Spiced Plums.

Make a syrup, allowing one pound of sugar to one of plums, and to every three pounds of sugar a scant pint of vinegar. Allow one ounce each of ground cinnamon, cloves, mace, and allspice to a peck of plums. Prick the plums. Add the spices to the syrup, and pour, boiling, over the plums. Let these stand three days; then skim them out, and boil down the syrup until it is quite thick, and pour hot over the plums in the jar in which they are to be kept. Cover closely.

Pickled Cucumbers.

Six hundred small cucumbers, two quarts of peppers, two quarts of small onions. Make enough brine to cover the pickles, allowing one pint of salt to four quarts of water, and pour it, boiling, over the pickles. Let them stand until the next morning; then pour off the brine, throw it away, make a new one, and scald again. The third morning scald this same brine and pour it over again. The fourth morning rinse the pickles well in cold water, and cover them with boiling vinegar. Add a little piece of alum, and two table-spoonfuls each of whole cloves and allspice, tied in a bit of muslin, if you like the spice.

Pickled Cucumbers, No. 2.

Wash and wipe six hundred small cucumbers and two quarts of peppers. Put them in a tub with one and a half cupfuls of salt, and a piece of alum as large as an egg. Heat to the boiling point three gallons of cider vinegar and three pints of water. Add a quarter of a pound each of whole cloves, whole allspice, and stick cinnamon, and two ounces of white mustard seed, and pour over the pickles. Cover with cabbage leaves.

Stuffed Peppers.

Get large bell peppers. Cut around the stem, remove it, and take out all the seeds. For the stuffing use two quarts of chopped cabbage, a cupful of white mustard seed, three table-spoonfuls of celery seed, two table-spoonfuls of salt, half a cupful of grated horse-radish. Fill each pepper with part of this mixture, and into each one put a small onion and a little cucumber. Tie the stem on again, put the peppers in a jar, and cover with cold vinegar.

Mangoes.

Get small green musk-melons or cantelopes. Cut a small square from the side of each one, and, with a teaspoon, scrape out all the seeds. Make a brine of one pint of salt to a gallon of water. Cover the mangoes with it while it boils. Let them stand two days; then drain them, and stuff with the same mixture as is used for peppers. Pour boiling vinegar over them, using in it a bit of alum.

Chopped Pickle.

One peck of green tomatoes, two quarts of onions, and two of peppers. Chop all fine, separately, and mix, adding three cupfuls of salt. Let them stand over night, and in the morning drain well. Add half a pound of mustard seed, two table-spoonfuls of ground allspice, two of ground cloves, and one cupful of grated horse radish. Pour over it three quarts of boiling vinegar.

Pickled Tomato.

One peck of green tomatoes, a dozen onions, sliced thin; two cupfuls of salt, a small (quarter of a pound) box of mustard, one quarter of a pound of mustard seed, one ounce each of ground allspice, clove, and pepper. Cut the tomatoes in thin slices, sprinkle with the salt, and let them stand two days; then drain them. Mix the spices. Put layers of tomato, onion, and spice in the kettle, and cover with vinegar. Cook slowly until the tomato looks clear, — about half an hour.

Pickled Cauliflowers.

Two cauliflowers, cut up; one pint of small onions, three medium-sized red peppers. Dissolve half a pint of salt in water enough to cover the vegetables, and let these stand over night. In the morning drain them. Heat two quarts of vinegar with four table-spoonfuls of mustard, until it boils. Add the vegetables, and boil for about fifteen minutes, or until a fork can be thrust through the cauliflower.

Tomato Ketchup.

Twelve ripe tomatoes, peeled; two large onions, four green peppers, chopped fine; two table-spoonfuls of salt, two of brown sugar, two of ginger, one of cinnamon, one of mustard, a nutmeg, grated; four cupfuls of vinegar. Boil all together till thoroughly cooked (about three hours), stirring frequently. Bottle while hot.

Tomato Ketchup, No. 2.

Skin the tomatoes, and cook them well. Press them through a sieve, and to each five pints add three pints of good cider vinegar. Boil slowly a long while (about two hours), until it begins to thicken; then add one table-spoonful of ground clove, one of allspice, one of cinnamon, and one of pepper, and three grated nutmegs. Boil until very thick (between six and eight hours), and add two table-spoonfuls of fine salt. When thoroughly cold, bottle, cork, and seal it.

Barberry Ketchup.

Three quarts of barberries, stewed and strained; four quarts of cranberries, one cupful of raisins, a large quince, and four small onions, all stewed with a quart of water, and strained. Mix these ingredients with the barberries, and add half a cupful of vinegar, three fourths of a cupful of salt, two cupfuls of sugar, one dessert-spoonful of ground clove and one of ground allspice, two table-spoonfuls of black pepper, two of celery seed, and one of ground mustard, one teaspoonful of cayenne, one of cinnamon, and one of ginger, and a nutmeg. Let the whole boil one minute. If too thick, add vinegar or water. With the quantities given, about three quarts of ketchup can be made.

POTTING.

For potting, one should have small stone or earthen jars, a little larger at the top than at the bottom, so that the meat may be taken out whole, and then cut in thin slices. All kinds of cooked meats and fish

can be potted. The meat must, of course, be well cooked and tender, so that it can be readily pounded to a paste. Of the fish, salmon and halibut are the best for potting. When the potted meat or fish is to be served, scrape off all the butter, run a knife between the meat and the jar, and when the meat is loosened turn it out on a dish. Cut it in thin slices, and garnish with parsley; or, serve it whole, and slice it at the table. The butter that covered meats can be used for basting roasted meats, and that which covered fish can be used for basting baked fish.

Beef.

Three pounds of the upper part of the round of beef, half a cupful of butter, one table-spoonful of salt, one fourth of a teaspoonful of pepper, a speck of cayenne, one eighth of a teaspoonful of mace, the same quantity of clove, a bouquet of sweet herbs, three table-spoonfuls of water. Cut the meat in small pieces and put it in a jar with the water, herbs, and seasoning. Mix one cupful of flour with water enough to make a stiff paste. Cover the mouth of the jar with paper, and spread over this the paste. Place the jar in a pan of hot water and put in a moderate oven for five hours. Take up, and remove the cover and herbs. Pound the meat to a paste, add half of the butter to it, and when thoroughly mixed pack solidly in small jars. Melt the remainder of the butter and pour it over the meat. Paste paper over the jars, put on the covers, and set away in a cool, dry place. Veal may be potted in the same manner, omitting the clove.

Chicken.

One quart of cold roasted chicken, one cupful of cold boiled ham, four table-spoonfuls of butter, a speck of cayenne, a slight grating of nutmeg, and two teaspoonfuls of salt. Free the chicken of skin and bones. Cut it and the ham in fine pieces. Chop, and pound to a paste. Add the butter and seasoning, and pack solidly in small stone pots. Cover these, and place them in a pan of hot water, which put in a moderate oven for one hour. When the meat is cold, cover with melted butter, and put away in a cool, dry place.

Tongue.

Pound cold boiled tongue to a paste, and season with salt, pepper, and a speck of cayenne. To each pint of the paste add one table-spoonful of butter and one teaspoonful of mixed mustard. Pack closely in little stone jars. Place these in a moderate oven in a pan of hot water. Cook half an hour. When cool, cover the tongue with melted butter. Cover, and put away.

Ham.

Cut all the meat, fat and lean, from the remains of a boiled ham, being careful not to mix with it either the outside pieces or the gristle. Chop very fine, and pound to a paste with the vegetable masher. To each pint of the paste add one teaspoonful of mixed mustard and a speck of cayenne, and if there was not much fat on the meat one table-spoonful of butter. Pack this smoothly in small earthen jars. Paste paper over these, and put on the covers. Place the pots in a baking-pan, which, when in the oven, should be filled with hot water. Bake slowly two hours. Cool with the covers on. When cold, take off the covers and pour melted butter over the meat. Cover again, and set away in a cool place. The ham will keep for months. It is a nice relish for tea, and makes delicious sandwiches.

Marbled Veal.

Trim all the roots and tough parts from a boiled pickled tongue, which chop and pound to a paste. Have two quarts of cold roasted or boiled veal chopped and pounded to a paste. Mix two table-spoonfuls of butter and a speck of cayenne with the tongue, and with the veal mix four table-spoonfuls of butter, one of salt, one fourth of a teaspoonful of pepper, and a speck of mace. Butter a deep earthen dish. Put a layer of the veal in it and pack down solidly; then put spoonfuls of the tongue here and there on the veal, and fill in the spaces with veal. Continue this until all the meat has been used, and pack very solidly. Cover the dish, and place it in the oven in a pan of water. Cook one hour. When cold, pour melted butter over it. Cover, and set away.

Fish.

Take any kind of cooked fish and free it of skin and bones. To each quart of fish add one table-spoonful of essence of anchovy, three of butter, two teaspoonfuls of salt, a little white pepper, and a speck of cayenne. Pound the fish to a paste before adding the butter and anchovy. When all the ingredients are thoroughly mixed, pack the fish closely in little stone jars. Place these in a pan of water and put in a moderate oven. Cook forty-five minutes. When cold, pour melted butter over the fish. Paste paper over the top, and set away.

Lobster.

Prepare and pot lobster the same as fish. If there is "coral" in the lobster, pound it with the meat.

Mackerel.

Nine pounds of small mackerel (about twenty-five in number), one ounce of whole cloves, one of pepper-corns, one of whole allspice, six teaspoonfuls of salt, three pints of vinegar. Wash the mackerel and pack them in small, deep earthen or stone pots. Three will be needed for the quantities given. Divide the spice into six parts. Put each portion in a small piece of muslin, and tie. Sprinkle two teaspoonfuls of salt on the fish in each pot, and put two of the little bags of spice in each pot. Cover the fish with the vinegar; and if there should not be enough, use more. Cover the pots with old plates, and place in a moderate oven. Bake the fish four hours. Cool, and put away in the pots in which they were baked. They will keep five or six months. Where oil is liked, half a cupful can be added to each pot with the vinegar. Any kind of small fish can be potted in this manner.

Smelts.

Six dozen smelts, one pint of olive oil, three pints of vinegar, or enough to cover the smelts; three table-spoonfuls of salt. Spice the same as potted mackerel, and prepare and cook the same as mackerel. More or less oil can be used. Smelts are almost as nice as sardines.

BREAKFAST AND TEA.

Meat Hash.

CHOP rather fine any kind of cold meat; corned beef is, however, the best. To each pint add one pint and a half of cold boiled potatoes, chopped fine, one table-spoonful of butter, and one cupful of stock; or, if no stock is on hand, two thirds of a cupful of hot water. Season with salt and pepper to taste. Put the mixture in a frying-pan and stir over the fire for about eight minutes, being careful not to burn. Spread smoothly. Cover the pan and set back where the hash will brown slowly. It will take about half an hour. When done, fold it like an omelet and turn on to a hot dish. Garnish with points of toast and parsley. Serve hot. If there are no cold potatoes, the same quantity of hot mashed potatoes may be used.

Vegetable Hash.

Chop, not very fine, the vegetables left from a boiled dinner, and season them with salt and pepper. To each quart of the chopped vegetables add half a cupful of stock and one table-spoonful of butter. Heat slowly in the frying-pan. Turn into a hot dish when done, and serve immediately. If vinegar is liked, two or more table-spoonfuls of it can be stirred into the hash while it is heating.

Breaded Sausages.

Wipe the sausages dry. Dip them in beaten egg and bread crumbs. Put them in the frying-basket and plunge into boiling fat. Cook ten minutes. Serve with a garnish of toasted bread and parsley.

Meat Fritters.

Cut any kind of cold meat into dice. Season well with salt and pepper. Make a fritter batter. Take up some of it in a large spoon, put a small spoonful of the meat in the centre, cover with batter, and slide gently into boiling fat. Cook about one minute. Drain on brown paper, and serve on a hot dish.

Lyonnaise Tripe.

About one pound of cooked tripe, cut in small pieces; two table-spoonfuls of butter, one of chopped onion, one of vinegar, salt, pepper. Put the onion and butter in a frying-pan, and when the onion turns yellow put in the tripe. Cook five minutes. Season with the salt, pepper, and vinegar. Serve on slices of toast.

Meat and Potato Sandwiches.

Any kind of cold meat, cut in slices and seasoned with salt and pepper; four large potatoes, two eggs, salt, pepper, one fourth of a cupful of boiling milk, one table-spoonful of butter. Have the meat cut in thin slices and seasoned with salt and pepper. Pare, boil, and mash the potatoes. Add the milk, butter, salt, pepper, and one well-beaten egg. Cover the slices of meat on both sides with this preparation, and dip in well-beaten egg. Put in the frying-basket and fry till a light brown. Serve on a hot dish.

Minced Veal and Eggs.

One quart of cold veal, chopped rather coarse; one teaspoonful of lemon juice, one cupful of stock or water, two table-spoonfuls of butter, one teaspoonful of flour, salt, pepper. Melt the butter in a frying-pan. Add the flour to it. Stir until smooth, and add the stock and seasoning. When it boils up, add the chopped veal. Heat thoroughly, and dish on slices of toast. Put a dropped egg in the centre of each slice, and serve very hot.

Mutton Réchauffé.

Cut cold roasted or boiled mutton in slices about half an inch thick, and cover both sides with sauce made in this way: Put two table-spoonfuls of butter in the frying-pan, and when melted add one of flour. Stir until smooth. Add, gradually, one cupful of stock and two table-spoonfuls of glaze. Boil for one minute, and stir in the yolks of two eggs. Season with salt, pepper, and one table-spoonful of lemon juice, and remove from the fire at once. Season the mutton with salt and pepper, and as soon as the sauce begins to cool dip both sides of the slices in it, and roll them in fine bread crumbs. Beat one whole egg and the two

whites together. Dip the sauced mutton in this and again in the crumbs. Fry in boiling fat for two minutes. Drain on brown paper, and serve with either tomato, Tartare, or Hollandaise sauce. Any kind of cold meat can be served in this manner.

Chicken in Jelly.

A little cold chicken (about one pint), one cupful of water or stock, one fifth of a box of gelatine, half a teaspoonful of curry powder, salt, pepper. Cut the meat from the bones of a chicken left from dinner. Put the bones on with water to cover, and boil down to one cupful. Put the gelatine to soak in one fourth of a cupful of cold water. When the stock is reduced as much as is necessary, strain and season. Add the curry and chicken. Season, and simmer ten minutes; then add the gelatine, and stir on the table until it is dissolved. Turn all into a mould, and set away to harden. This makes a nice relish for tea or lunch. If you have mushrooms, omit the curry, and cut four of them into dice. Stir into the mixture while cooking. This dish can be varied by using the whites of hard-boiled eggs or bits of boiled ham. To serve: dip the mould in warm water, and turn out on the dish. Garnish with parsley.

Chicken Cutlets.

Season pieces of cold chicken or turkey with salt and pepper. Dip in melted butter; let this cool on the meat, and dip in beaten egg and in fine bread crumbs. Fry in butter till a delicate brown. Serve on slices of hot toast, with either a white or curry sauce poured around. Pieces of cold veal make a nice dish, if prepared in this manner.

Broiled Liver.

Cut in slices and dip in melted butter, and lightly in flour. Broil over a bright fire eight or ten minutes.

Liver Fried in Crumbs.

Season slices with salt and pepper. Dip in beaten egg and very fine cracker crumbs. Fry six minutes in boiling lard.

Liver and Bacon.

Cut in slices, season with salt and pepper, and cut again into small squares. Place on a skewer pieces of liver and bacon, alternating. Fry five minutes in boiling fat. Slip off of the skewer on to toasted bread, and serve immediately.

Liver Sauté.

Cut the liver in *thin* slices. Season with salt and pepper. Heat together in a small frying-pan two table-spoonfuls of butter and a large one of flour. Lay in the liver, and brown it on both sides. Add a teaspoonful of chopped parsley, two table-spoonfuls of water, and one of wine. Taste to see if salt enough. Boil up once, and serve.

Liver Sauté, with Piquant Sauce.

Cut the liver in slices about one third of an inch thick, and if beef liver let it stand in warm water ten minutes (calves' livers will not need this). Drain dry, and put in the frying-pan with enough beef or pork drippings to prevent its sticking, and cook very slowly for eight minutes, turning constantly. Take up on a hot dish and pour a piquant sauce over it. Serve immediately.

Curry of Liver.

Cut the liver in small, thin pieces, and for every pound have four table-spoonfuls of butter, two slices of onion, two table-spoonfuls of flour, a speck of cayenne, salt, pepper, one teaspoonful of curry powder. Let the butter get hot; then cook the liver in it slowly for four minutes. Add the flour and other ingredients. Cook two minutes, and add slowly one cupful of stock. Let this boil up. Dish, and serve.

Chicken Livers Sauté.

Wash and wipe six livers. Put two table-spoonfuls of butter in the frying-pan, and when hot add a large slice of onion, which cook slowly ten minutes, and then take out. Dredge the livers with salt, pepper, and flour, and fry for ten minutes in the butter; add one teaspoonful of flour, and cook a minute longer. Pour in half a cupful of stock, one teaspoonful of lemon juice, one of vinegar and one fourth of a spoonful of sugar, and boil up once. Serve with a garnish of toasted bread.

Chicken Livers and Bacon.

Cut the livers in pieces the size of a half-dollar, and have thin slices of bacon of the same size. Nearly fill a small wire skewer with these, alternating. Place in the frying-basket and plunge into boiling fat for about one minute. Serve on the skewers, or on toast, with thin slices of lemon for a garnish. Or, the skewers can be rested on the sides of a narrow baking-pan and placed in a hot oven for five minutes. Serve as before. The livers of all other kinds of poultry can be cooked the same as chicken.

Chicken Livers in Papillotes.

Wash the livers and drop them into boiling water for one minute. Take them up, and, when drained, split them. For eight livers put two table-spoonfuls of butter in the frying-pan, and when hot add one table-spoonful of flour. Stir until smooth; then gradually add half a cupful of cold water. Stir into this two spoonfuls of glaze, if you have it. Season with pepper and salt, and stir into the sauce half a cupful of finely chopped ham. Spread this mixture on the livers, place them in *papillotes* the same as cutlets, lay them in a pan, and put in a slow oven for fifteen minutes. Have little squares of toast or of fried brown bread. Heap these in the centre of a hot dish, and arrange the livers around them. Serve very hot.

Stewed Kidneys.

Cut the kidneys in thin round slices. Cover them with cold water and let them stand half an hour; then wash them clean, and put them in a stewpan with one quart of water or stock, a clove, two table-spoonfuls of onion juice, and salt and pepper. Simmer two hours. Put one table-spoonful of butter in the frying-pan, and when hot add one of flour. Stir until it is brown and smooth, and add to the kidneys. Put a small bouquet of sweet herbs in the stewpan, and simmer half an hour longer. Taste to see if seasoned enough; if not, add more salt and pepper, and, if you like, one table-spoonful of lemon juice. Take out the bouquet and serve. This dish can be prepared any time in the day, as it is quite as good warmed over as when first prepared.

Kidneys Sauté.

Skin, wash, and wipe the kidneys, cut in thin round slices, and season with salt and pepper. Put one table-spoonful of butter and half a table-spoonful of flour in the frying-pan, and when hot put in the kidneys. Stir two minutes, then add half a cupful of stock or water. When the dish boils up, add half a table-spoonful of lemon juice. Serve with a garnish of points of toast.

Broiled Kidneys.

Skin, wash, wipe, and split sheep's or lambs' kidneys. Run a small skewer through each, to keep it open. Season with salt and pepper, dip in melted butter and in flour, place in the double broiler and cook six minutes over a bright fire. Serve on a hot dish.

Kidneys à la Maître d'Hôtel.

Split and cut in two, lengthwise, lambs' or sheep's kidneys. Wash and wipe them. Season with salt and pepper, and dip in melted butter and fine bread crumbs. Run a small skewer through each, to keep it open. Put them in the double broiler and cook about six minutes over a bright fire. Serve on a hot dish with *maître d'hôtel* butter.

Ham and Eggs on Toast.

Chop fine the trimmings from cold boiled or roasted ham. Toast and butter slices of stale bread. Spread the ham on these, and place in the oven for about three minutes. Beat six eggs with half a cupful of milk, a little pepper, and one teaspoonful of salt. Put this mixture in a saucepan with two table-spoonfuls of butter, and stir over the fire until it begins to thicken. Take off, and beat for a moment; then spread on the ham and toast. Serve immediately.

Ham Croquettes.

One cupful of finely chopped cooked ham, one of bread crumbs, two of hot mashed potatoes, one large table-spoonful of butter, three eggs, a speck of cayenne. Beat the ham, cayenne, butter, and two of the eggs into the potato. Let the mixture cool slightly, and shape it like croquettes. Roll in the bread crumbs, dip in beaten egg and again in crumbs, put in the frying-basket, and plunge into boiling fat. Cook two minutes. Drain, and serve.

Canapees.

After cutting the crust from a loaf of stale bread, cut the loaf in very thin slices, and toast to a delicate brown. Butter lightly, and spread with any kind of potted meat or fish. Put two slices together, and, with a sharp knife, cut them in long strips. Arrange these tastefully on a plate and serve at tea or evening parties. Sardines may be pounded to a paste and mixed with the yolks of hard-boiled eggs, also pounded to a paste, and used instead of potted meats. In this case, the slices of bread may be fried in salad oil.

Welsh Rare-Bit.

Half a pound of cheese, two eggs, a speck of cayenne, a table-spoonful of butter, one teaspoonful of mustard, half a teaspoonful of salt, half a cupful of cream. Break the cheese in small pieces and put it and the other ingredients in a bright saucepan, which put over boiling water. Stir until the cheese melts; then spread the mixture on slices of crisp toast. Serve immediately. A cupful of ale or beer can be used instead of the cream.

Welsh Rare-Bit, No. 2.

Grate one pint of cheese. Sprinkle on it half a teaspoonful of mustard, one fourth of a teaspoonful of salt, and a speck of cayenne. Heap this on slices of buttered toast. Put in the hot oven for a few moments, and when the cheese begins to melt, serve at once.

Corn Pie.

Four ears of cold boiled corn, two eggs, one table-spoonful of butter, one of flour, half a cupful of milk, half a teaspoonful of salt, a little pep-

per. Cut the corn from the cobs. Mix the milk, gradually, with the flour. Beat the yolks and whites of the egg separately, and add them and the other ingredients to the flour and milk. The butter should be melted. Bake twenty minutes in two squash-pie plates. This is a dish for breakfast.

Hominy.

Wash a cupful of hominy in two waters; then stir it into one quart of boiling water, with a teaspoonful of salt, and boil from thirty to sixty minutes. The latter time is the better. Be careful that the hominy does not burn. It can be used more than oatmeal, as it is good with any kind of meat. It is appropriate for any meal, and is nice eaten warm or cold with milk.

Oatmeal.

Oatmeal, Indian meal, and hominy all require two things for perfection,—plenty of water when put on to boil, and a long time for boiling. Have about two quarts of boiling water in a large stewpan, and into it stir a cupful of oatmeal, which has been wet with cold water. Boil one hour, stirring often, and then add half a spoonful of salt, and boil an hour longer. If it should get too stiff, add more boiling water; or, if too thin, boil a little longer. You cannot boil too much. The only trouble in cooking oatmeal is that it takes a long time, but surely this should not stand in the way when it is so much better for having the extra time. If there is not an abundance of water at first, the oatmeal will not be very good, no matter how much may be added during the cooking. Cracked wheat is cooked in the same way.

Strawberry Short-Cake.

One pint of flour, measured before sifting; one teaspoonful of cream of tartar, half a teaspoonful of soda, one fourth of a teaspoonful of salt, two table-spoonfuls of sugar, four of butter, one teacupful of milk. Mix the other dry ingredients with the flour, and rub through a sieve. Rub the butter into the mixture, and add the milk. Butter two tin squash-pie plates. Spread the mixture in them, and bake in a quick oven from eighteen to twenty minutes. Mash one quart of strawberries with three fourths of a cupful of sugar. When the cakes are taken from the oven, split and butter them, and put half of the strawberries and sugar in each cake. Serve immediately.

Sweet Strawberry Short-Cake.

Three eggs, one cupful of sugar, two of flour, one table-spoonful of butter, one scant teaspoonful of cream of tartar, a small half-teaspoonful of soda. Beat the butter and sugar together. Add the eggs, well beaten. Mix the soda and cream of tartar with the flour, and rub through a sieve. Stir into the beaten egg and sugar. Bake in deep tin plates. Four can be filled with the quantities given. Have three pints of strawberries mixed with a cupful of sugar. Spread a layer of strawberries on one of the cakes, lay a second cake over this, and cover with berries. Or, a méringue, made with the white of an egg and a table-spoonful of powdered sugar, may be spread over the top layer of strawberries.

MUFFINS AND CAKES.

English Muffins.

ONE quart of flour, one teaspoonful of salt, one third of a cake of compressed yeast, or one third of a cupful of liquid yeast; one cupful and a half of water. Have the water blood warm. Dissolve the yeast in one third of a cupful of cold water. Add it and the salt to the warm water, and gradually stir into the flour. Beat the dough thoroughly; cover, and let it rise in a warm place until it is spongy (about five hours). Sprinkle the bread board with flour. Shape the dough into balls about twice the size of an egg, and drop them on the floured board. When all the dough has been shaped, roll the balls into cakes about one third of an inch thick. Lay these on a warm griddle, which has been lightly greased, and put the griddle on the back of the stove, where there is not much heat. When the cakes have risen a little, draw the griddle forward and cook them slowly, turning often, to keep the flat shape. It will take about twenty minutes for them to rise on the griddle, and fifteen to cook. Tear them apart, butter them, and serve.

Muffins, No. 1.

One quart of flour, two cupfuls of milk, half a cupful of sugar, two eggs, two teaspoonfuls of cream of tartar, one of soda, half a teaspoonful of salt, butter the size of an egg. Mix the other dry ingredients with the flour, and rub through a sieve. Melt the butter with four table-spoonfuls of boiling water. Beat the eggs light, and add the milk. Stir into the flour, and add the butter. Beat thoroughly. Bake in buttered muffin pans from twenty-five to thirty minutes, in a quick oven.

Muffins, No. 2.

One cupful of milk, one of flour, one teaspoonful of sugar, a scant half-teaspoonful of salt, two eggs. Beat the eggs light, and add the milk, salt, and sugar. Pour gradually on the flour. Beat till light and smooth. Pour into buttered muffin pans and bake in a *hot* oven for twenty minutes.

THE CUISINE

WILL BE

PERFECTION + ITSELF

—IF—

WASHBURN CROSBY CO.'S

FLOUR

IS USED.

BEAUTIFUL
- **Bread,**
- **Rolls,**
- **Biscuit,**
- **Puddings.**

EVERY GOOD GROCER SELLS

WASHBURN CROSBY COMPANY'S FLOUR

Raised Muffins.

One pint of warm milk, half a cake of compressed yeast or half a cupful of liquid yeast, one quart of flour, one table-spoonful of butter. Beat two eggs well, and add them and the salt, butter, and yeast to the milk. Stir gradually into the flour. Beat until the batter is light and smooth. Let it rise four hours in a warm place. Fill buttered muffin pans two thirds to the top with the batter, and let them stand until the batter has risen to the brim. Bake half an hour.

Graham Muffins.

Into a bowl put one and a half pints of Graham, half a cupful of sugar, and a teaspoonful of salt. Into a sieve put half a pint of flour, a teaspoonful of saleratus, and two of cream of tartar. Mix thoroughly with the flour, and sift on to the material in the bowl. Mix all thoroughly while dry, and add two well-beaten eggs and a pint of milk. Fill muffin cups about two thirds to the top, and bake in a quick oven.

Raised Graham Muffins.

These are made the same as Graham bread. Fill tin muffin pans two thirds to the brim and let the mixture rise to the top. This will take an hour. Bake in a rather quick oven for twenty minutes.

Corn Muffins.

One pint of flour, one of Indian meal, one third of a cupful of sugar, one teaspoonful of soda, two of cream of tartar, two eggs, a pint of milk, one table-spoonful of melted butter. Mix the dry ingredients together, and sift them. Beat the eggs light, add the milk to them, and stir into the dry ingredients. Bake twenty minutes in buttered muffin pans. Two dozen muffins can be made with the quantities given.

Fried Indian Muffins.

One pint of Indian meal, one pint of *boiling* water, two eggs, one teaspoonful of salt, one table-spoonful of sugar, one heaping table-spoonful of flour. Pour the boiling water gradually on the meal, salt, and sugar. Beat thoroughly, and set away in a cool place. In the morning add the eggs, well beaten, and the flour. Dip a table-spoon in cold milk, fill it with batter, and drop this into boiling fat. Cook ten minutes.

Corn Cake.

One quart of milk, one pint of Indian meal, two eggs, one teaspoonful of salt, butter the size of an English walnut. Let the milk come to a boil, and gradually pour it on the meal. Add the butter and salt, and beat well, and set away in a cool place. Do this at night. In the morning beat thoroughly. Beat the eggs well, and add them. Pour the mixture into buttered deep earthen plates. Bake from twenty to thirty minutes. Success depends upon a good beating of the cake in the morning.

Corn Cake, No. 2.

Two teacupfuls of corn meal, one of flour, three of sour milk, two eggs, one table-spoonful of sugar, or of molasses if you prefer, one teaspoonful of soda, one of salt. Mix together the sugar, salt, meal, and flour. Beat the eggs light. Dissolve the soda in two table-spoonfuls of boiling water, and pour into the sour milk. Stir well, and add to the other mixed ingredients. Add the eggs, and mix thoroughly. Pour into buttered tins to the depth of about an inch and a half. Bake twenty-five minutes in a quick oven.

Raised Corn Cake.

One pint of Indian meal, one pint and a half of boiling milk or water, one table-spoonful of sugar, two of butter, an egg, one teaspoonful of salt, one fourth of a cake of compressed yeast, or one fourth of a cupful of liquid yeast. Pour the boiling milk, gradually, on the meal; then add the salt, sugar, and butter, and beat well. Set away to cool. When blood warm, add the compressed yeast, dissolved in two table-spoonfuls of cold water, or the liquid yeast, and the egg, well beaten. Let the batter rise five hours. Turn into buttered pans to the depth of about two inches. Let it stand in a warm place for half an hour, and then bake it from thirty-five to forty-five minutes.

Thin Corn Cake.

One cupful of Indian meal, one fourth of a teaspoonful of salt, butter the size of an egg, one cupful and a half of *boiling* water, one teaspoonful of sugar. Pour the boiling water on the meal, sugar, and salt. Beat thoroughly. Add the butter, and, when well mixed, spread *very* thin on buttered tin sheets. Bake slowly for about twenty minutes.

Rye Muffins.

One pint of rye meal, not flour; one pint of wheat flour, one pint of milk, half a cupful of sugar, one teaspoonful of salt, one of soda, two of cream of tartar, and two eggs. Put the meal in a mixing bowl. Put the flour and other ingredients in a sieve, and mix thoroughly, and sift. Beat the eggs light. Add the milk to them and pour on the dry ingredients. Beat well. Butter the muffin tins and bake twenty minutes in a quick oven. The quantities given will make twenty-four muffins. To make a less quantity, divide the dry mixture after it is prepared (it can be used whenever it may be wanted if it is kept dry); then halve the other ingredients.

Fried Rye Muffins.

One cupful and a half of rye meal, one cupful and a half of flour, one cupful of milk, two eggs, one teaspoonful of soda, two of cream of tartar, two generous table-spoonfuls of sugar, half a teaspoonful of salt. Put the meal in a large bowl. Put the flour, cream of tartar, soda, sugar, and salt in the sieve, and rub through on to the meal. Beat the eggs well, add the milk to them, and stir into the dry ingredients. Fry the same as Indian muffins.

Rice Muffins.

One pint of milk, one quart of flour, one pint of boiled rice, three eggs, two table-spoonfuls of sugar, one teaspoonful of salt, one of soda, two of cream of tartar. Mix the sugar, salt, soda, and cream of tartar with the flour, and rub through a sieve. Beat the eggs and add to the milk. Stir gradually into the flour. When a smooth, light paste, add the rice. Beat thoroughly. Bake thirty-five minutes in buttered pans. Three dozen muffins can be made from the quantities given.

Raised Rice Muffins.

One pint of warm milk, two cupfuls of warm boiled rice, one quart of bread flour, one teaspoonful of salt, two tablespoonfuls of butter, one third of a cake of compressed yeast. Mix the butter, rice, and milk together. Pour the mixture on the flour, and beat till a light batter is formed. Mix the yeast with four table-spoonfuls of cold water, and add it and the salt to the batter, which let rise over night in a cool place. In the morning fill buttered muffin pans two thirds to the top, and set them in a warm place till the batter has so risen as to fill the tins. Bake thirty-five minutes. One third of a cupful of liquid yeast may be substituted for the compressed yeast.

Hominy Muffins.

A pint of milk, a quart of Haxall flour, one teaspoonful of salt, two table-spoonfuls of butter, one third of a cake of compressed yeast, or one third of a cupful of liquid yeast; half a cupful of hominy, measured before cooking. Wash the hominy, and add a pint of boiling water. Boil one hour, stirring often. Then add the milk, salt, yeast, and butter. Pour this, gradually, on the flour, beating well. Let it rise over night. In the morning put in buttered muffin pans and let rise from half to three quarters of an hour. Bake thirty-five minutes. The muffins may be put to rise in the morning for tea.

Gems.

One pint of flour, one of milk, an egg, half a teaspoonful of salt. Beat the egg until light, add the milk and salt to it, and beat, gradually, into the flour. Bake twenty minutes in hot gem pans. · A dozen cakes can be made with the quantities given.

Hominy Drop-Cakes.

One pint of fresh boiled hominy (or cold hominy may be used — if the latter, break into grains as lightly as possible with a fork, and heat in a farina kettle without adding water), one table-spoonful of water, two eggs, whites and yolks beaten separately. Stir the yolks into the hominy first, then the whites, and a teaspoonful of salt, if the hominy has not been salted in cooking; or, if it has, use half a teaspoonful. Drop, in table-spoonfuls, on well-buttered tin sheets, and bake to a good brown in a quick oven.

Squash Biscuit.

One cupful and a half of sifted squash, half a cupful of sugar, half a cake of compressed yeast, or half a cupful of liquid yeast; one cupful of milk, half a teaspoonful of salt, four table-spoonfuls of butter, five cupfuls of flour. Dissolve the yeast in a scant half-cupful of cold water. Mix it and the milk, butter, sugar, salt, and squash together, and stir into the flour. Knead well, and let it rise over night. In the morning shape into biscuit. Let these rise an hour and a half, and bake them half an hour.

Sally Lunn.

One quart of flour, one generous pint of milk, two table-spoonfuls of sugar, two eggs, three table-spoonfuls of butter, one teaspoonful of salt, half a cake of compressed yeast. Have the milk blood warm, and add the butter, melted; the eggs, well beaten; and the yeast, dissolved in three table-spoonfuls of cold water. Pour, gradually, on the flour, and beat into a smooth batter; then add the salt and sugar. Butter baking-pans, and pour in the batter to the depth of about two inches. Let it rise two hours in a warm place. Bake half an hour.

Snow Pancakes.

Half a pint of milk, an egg, an apple, pared, quartered, and chopped very fine, a cupful and a half of flour, one fourth of a teaspoonful of salt, a bowl of snow. Beat the egg light, and add the milk to it. Pour gradually on the flour, and beat until smooth and light. Add the apple and salt, and at the last moment the snow. Drop by spoonfuls into boiling fat, and cook until a rich brown.

Waffles.

One pint of sifted flour, milk enough to make a thin batter (about two thirds of a pint), two eggs beaten very light, a table-spoonful of melted butter, and a little salt. Gradually mix the milk with the flour until there is a smooth paste; then add the salt and butter, and lastly the eggs. Have waffle irons about as hot as a griddle for cakes, and butter them well, or grease with pork as you would a griddle. Pour in enough of the batter to cover an iron, and put the other side gently down upon it. Keep over the fire about half a minute; then turn over, and let the other side remain to the fire the same time. Remove, and place the waffles where they will keep warm until enough are cooked to serve.

Many people butter the waffles as they place them on the dish, and others add sugar. This is very well if known to be to the taste of the family, but it is always safe to let each suit himself at the table.

Waffles, No. 2.

One pint of milk, two eggs, two table-spoonfuls of butter, one tea-spoonful of cream of tartar, half a teaspoonful of soda, one scant pint and a half of flour. Mix the other dry ingredients with the flour, and rub through a sieve. Beat the eggs very light. Add the milk and the butter, which should be melted with two table-spoonfuls of boiling water. Stir into the flour.

Raised Waffles.

One pint of milk, one pint and a half of flour, an egg, a teaspoonful of salt, one fourth of a yeast cake, or one fourth of a cupful of liquid yeast. Dissolve the yeast in two table-spoonfuls of cold water. Have the milk blood warm, and add to it the yeast, salt, and the egg, well beaten. Stir gradually into the flour. Cover, and let it rise four hours. Cook as usual.

Indian Waffles.

Half a cupful of Indian meal, two cupfuls of boiling milk, two eggs, one generous cupful of flour, one table-spoonful of butter, half a tea-spoonful of baking powder, half a teaspoonful of salt. Pour the boiling milk on the meal and butter. Beat well, and set away to cool. Mix the other dry ingredients with the flour, and sift. Beat the eggs, and add them and the flour to the cold mixture.

Rice Waffles.

Stir two cupfuls of boiled rice into the mixture for waffles, No. 2. Hominy waffles can be made in the same way.

Flannel Cakes.

One cupful of Indian meal, two of flour, three of boiling milk, one fourth of a yeast cake, or one fourth of a cupful of liquid yeast; one tea-spoonful of salt, one table-spoonful of sugar, two of butter. Have the milk boiling, and pour it on the meal and butter. When cool, add the flour, salt, sugar, and the yeast, which has been dissolved in four table-spoonfuls of cold water. Let the mixture rise over night. Fry like griddle cakes.

Graham Griddle Cakes.

Two cupfuls of Graham, one of flour, two and a half of milk, one table-spoonful of sugar, one teaspoonful of salt, one of cream of tartar, half a teaspoonful of soda, two eggs. Let half the milk come to a boil. Pour it on the Graham, and stir until perfectly smooth; then add the cold milk, and set away to cool. Mix the other dry ingredients with the flour, and rub through a sieve. Add, with the eggs well beaten, to the Graham and milk. Rye griddle cakes are made the same way.

Squash Griddle Cakes.

One pint of flour, nearly a pint of milk, two eggs, one teaspoonful of cream of tartar, half as much soda, four table-spoonfuls of sugar, one teaspoonful of salt, two cupfuls of sifted squash. Mix the flour with the other dry ingredients, and rub through a sieve. Beat the eggs well, add them and the milk to the squash, and pour on the flour. Beat till smooth and light. This gives a thin batter. If the cakes are liked thick, a little more flour may be used. Fry as usual.

Indian Griddle Cakes.

One cupful of Indian meal, one of flour, three of boiling milk, two eggs, one teaspoonful of salt, one of cream of tartar, half a teaspoonful of soda, two table-spoonfuls of sugar. Have the milk boiling, and grad-ually pour it on the meal. Put the other dry ingredients with the flour, and rub through a sieve. When the scalded meal is cool, add to it the flour and the eggs, well beaten.

Hominy Griddle Cakes.

To a pint of warm boiled hominy add a pint of milk or water and a pint of flour. Beat two or three eggs and stir into the batter with a little salt. Fry as any other griddle cakes. They are delicious.

EGGS.

Omelets.

THERE is no better form in which to serve eggs than as an omelet, but so few people make a good omelet that that is one of the last things the inexperienced housekeeper or cook will attempt. Yet the making is a simple operation, the cause of failure usually being that the pan for cook-ing is not hot enough, and too much egg is put in at one time. When there is too much egg in the pan, one part will be cooked hard before the other is heated through. A pan measuring eight inches in diameter will cook an omelet made with four eggs; if more eggs are used, a larger pan is necessary.

Plain Omelet.

Four eggs, one teaspoonful of salt, two table-spoonfuls of milk, one table-spoonful of butter. Beat the eggs with a Dover, or any other good egg beater, and add the salt and milk. Have the pan *very hot*. Put in the spoonful of butter and pour in the beaten egg. Shake vigorously on the hottest part of the stove until the egg begins to thicken; then let it stand a few seconds to brown. Run the knife between the sides of the omelet and the pan, fold, and turn on a *hot* dish. Serve without delay.

Quaker Omelet.

A Quaker omelet is a handsome and sure dish when care is taken in the preparation. Three eggs, half a cupful of milk, one and a half table-spoonfuls of corn-starch, one teaspoonful of salt, one table-spoonful of butter. Put the omelet pan, and a cover that will fit closely, on to heat. Beat well together the yolks of the eggs, the corn-starch, and the salt. Beat the whites to a stiff froth. Add to the well-beaten yolks and corn-starch. Stir all together very thoroughly, and add the milk. Put the butter in the hot pan. When melted, pour in the mixture. Cover, and place on the stove where it will brown, but not burn. Cook about seven minutes. Fold, turn on a hot dish, and serve with cream sauce poured around it. If the yolks and corn-starch are thoroughly beaten, and if, when the stiff whites are added, they are well mixed, and the pan and cover are very hot, there can hardly be failure.

Cheese Omelet.

Make the same as plain omelet, and as soon as it begins to thicken sprinkle in three table-spoonfuls of grated cheese.

Ham Omelet.

The same as plain omelet, and add three table-spoonfuls of cooked ham, chopped rather fine, as soon as it begins to thicken.

Chicken Omelet.

The same as plain omelet, and, just before folding, add one cupful of cooked chicken, cut rather fine, and warmed in cream sauce.

Jelly Omelet.

A jelly omelet is made like the others, and, just before folding, spread with any kind of jelly (currant or grape is the best, however). Fold quickly, and serve.

Savory Omelet.

This is made like a plain omelet, with the addition of salt and one table-spoonful of chopped parsley. A little grated onion may be used also, if you like it.

Fish Omelet.

Boil a shad roe twenty minutes in salt and water. Chop it fine, and add to it a cupful of any kind of cold fish, broken fine. Season with salt and pepper, and warm in a cupful of cream sauce. Make a plain omelet with six eggs. When ready to fold, spread the prepared fish on it. Roll up, dish, and serve immediately.

Corn Omelet.

One pint of cold boiled corn, four eggs, half a cupful of milk, one tea-spoonful and a half of salt, a little pepper, three table-spoonfuls of butter. Beat the eggs, and add to them the salt, pepper, milk, and corn. Fry like a plain omelet.

Baked Omelet.

One pint and a half of milk, four eggs, one table-spoonful of flour, one of butter, one teaspoonful of salt. Let the milk come to a boil. Mix the butter and flour together. Pour the boiling milk on the mixture, which then cook five minutes, stirring all the while. Put away to cool. When cooled, add the salt and the eggs, the yolks and whites having been beaten separately. Pour into a buttered dish, and bake twenty minutes in a quick oven. Serve at once. The dish should hold a little more than a quart.

Dropped Eggs.

Have one quart of boiling water and one table-spoonful of salt in a frying-pan. Break the eggs, one by one, into a saucer, and slide carefully into the salted water. Cook until the white is firm, and lift out with a griddle-cake turner and place on toasted bread. Serve immediately.

Scrambled Eggs.

Four eggs, one table-spoonful of butter, half a teaspoonful of salt. Beat the eggs, and add the salt to them. Melt the butter in a saucepan. Turn in the beaten eggs, stir quickly over a hot fire for one minute, and serve.

Poached Eggs.

Two eggs, two table-spoonfuls of milk, half a teaspoonful of salt, half a teaspoonful of butter. Beat the eggs, and add the salt and milk. Put the butter in a small saucepan, and when it melts add the eggs. Stir over the fire until the mixture thickens, being careful not to let it cook hard. About two minutes will cook it. The eggs, when done, should be soft and creamy. Serve immediately.

Soft-boiled Eggs.

Place the eggs in a warm saucepan, and cover with *boiling* water. Let them stand where they will keep hot, but *not* boil, for ten minutes. This method will cook both whites and yolks.

Soft-boiled Eggs, No. 2.

Put the eggs in boiling water, and boil three minutes and a half. By this method the white of the egg is hardened so quickly that the heat does not penetrate to the yolk until the last minute, and consequently the white is hard and the yolk hardly cooked enough. The first method is, therefore, the more healthful.

Hard-boiled Eggs.

Put the eggs in hot water to cover, and boil twenty minutes. Ten minutes will boil them hard, but they are not so digestible as when boiled twenty. Ten minutes makes the yolks hard and soggy; twenty makes them light and mealy.

Spanish Eggs.

Cook one cupful of rice thirty minutes in two quarts of boiling water, to which has been added one table-spoonful of salt. Drain through a colander, and add one table-spoonful of butter. Spread very lightly on a hot platter. On the rice place six dropped eggs, and serve.

Eggs Sur le Plat.

Little stone china dishes come expressly for this mode of serving eggs. Heat and butter the dish, and break into it two eggs, being careful not to break the yolks. Sprinkle lightly with salt and pepper, and drop on them half a teaspoonful of butter, broken in small pieces. Place in a moderately hot oven until the white is set, which will be in about five minutes. There should be a dish for each person. The flavor can be changed by sprinkling a little finely chopped ham or parsley on the plate before putting in the eggs.

Creamed Eggs.

Boil six eggs twenty minutes. Make one pint of cream sauce. Have six slices of toast on a hot dish. Put a layer of sauce on each one, and then part of the whites of the eggs, cut in thin strips, and rub part of the yolks through a sieve on to the toast. Repeat this, and finish with a third layer of sauce. Place in the oven for about three minutes. Garnish with parsley, and serve.

Stuffed Eggs.

Cut six hard-boiled eggs in two. Take out the yolks and mash them fine. Add two teaspoonfuls of butter, one of cream, two or three drops of onion juice, and salt and pepper to taste. Mix all thoroughly. Fill the eggs from the mixture, and put them together. There will be a little filling left, to which add a well-beaten egg. Cover the other eggs with this last preparation, and roll in cracker crumbs. Fry in *boiling* lard till a light brown.

Scotch Eggs.

One cupful of cooked lean ham, chopped very fine; one third of a cupful of stale bread crumbs, one third of a cupful of milk, half a teaspoonful of mixed mustard, cayenne enough to cover a silver five-cent piece, one raw egg, and six hard-boiled. Cook the bread and milk together until a smooth paste. Add to the ham, and add the seasoning and raw egg. Mix thoroughly. Break the shells from the hard-boiled eggs, and cover with this mixture. Put in a frying-basket, and plunge into boiling fat for two minutes. These are nice for lunch, tea, or picnics.

Eggs Brouillé.

Six eggs, half a cupful of milk, or, better still, of cream; two mushrooms, one teaspoonful of salt, a little pepper, three table-spoonfuls of butter, a slight grating of nutmeg. Cut the mushrooms into dice, and fry them for one minute in one table-spoonful of the butter. Beat the eggs, salt, pepper, and cream together, and put them in a saucepan. Add the butter and mushrooms to these ingredients. Stir over a moderate heat until the mixture begins to thicken. Take from the fire and beat rapidly until the eggs become quite thick and creamy. Have slices of toast on a hot dish. Heap the mixture on these, and garnish with points of toast. Serve immediately.

ECONOMICAL DISHES.

Calf's Liver Braised.

WASH and wipe a calf's liver. Lard one side of it. Cover the bottom of the braising-pan with slices of salt pork, using about a quarter of a pound. Cut an onion and half a carrot in small pieces, and spread over the pork. Lay the liver on this, and dredge thickly with salt, pepper, and flour. Cover the pan, and place where it will cook slowly for half an hour. Add a bouquet of sweet herbs and three pints of stock or water. Put the pan in a moderate oven and cook for two hours. Baste frequently with the gravy in the pan, and salt, pepper, and flour. About twenty minutes before the liver is done, add one teaspoonful of vinegar and one of lemon-juice. Strain the gravy over the liver when it is dished.

Beef Stew.

Take the bones and hard, tough parts left from a roast of beef. Remove all the meat from the bones, and cut it in small pieces. Cut about a quarter of a pound of the fat of the meat in very small pieces. Put it in the stewpan to fry. When it begins to brown, put in half a carrot, one small turnip, and two onions, cut fine. Stir over the fire for ten minutes. Take out the fat and vegetables, and put the bones in the bottom of the kettle. Add the meat and the cooked vegetables, but not the fat. Dredge well with salt, pepper, and flour, shaking in at least half a cupful of flour. Add three pints of water, and simmer gently one hour; then put in six potatoes, pared and cut in slices. Simmer one hour longer. Taste to see if seasoned enough. Draw forward where it will boil more rapidly. Stir the stew, and put in the dumplings. Cook just ten minutes. The cover of the stewpan must fit tightly. There should be about two pounds of meat for this stew, not counting the bones.

Cold Meat with Purée of Potato.

Six good-sized potatoes, one table-spoonful of butter, one cupful of boiling milk, salt and pepper to taste. Pare and boil the potatoes, and mash light and fine. Add the butter, seasoning, and boiling milk. Beat up light, and spread on a hot platter. Lay on this handsome slices of any kind of cold meat, and on each slice put a table-spoonful of hot gravy. Put a little gravy around the dish, and set in the oven for five minutes. Garnish with parsley, and serve. If there is no gravy left from the dinner of the day before, make a pint in the following manner: Put a quart of water with some of the hard pieces and bones of the meat, and boil down to one pint. Put one table-spoonful of butter in a frying-pan, and, when hot, add one table-spoonful of flour. Stir until dark brown, and strain the broth on this. Season with salt, pepper, and, if you please, one spoonful of Halford sauce.

Shepherds' Pie.

One quart of any kind of cold meat, eight large potatoes, one small onion, one cupful of boiling milk, salt, pepper, and nearly a pint of gravy or stock, thickened with one table-spoonful of flour. Season the meat and put in a deep earthen dish. Grate the onion into the gravy, and pour over the meat. Pare, boil, and mash the potatoes. Add the salt, pepper, and milk, and one table-spoonful of butter. Cover the pie with this, and bake gently half an hour.

Shepherds' Pie, No. 2.

Cut into dice one quart of any kind of cold meat. Mince very fine two table-spoonfuls of salt pork, and add to the meat. Pare and cut into dice four large uncooked potatoes; grate or chop fine one onion; chop fine one table-spoonful of parsley. Mix, and season well with salt and pepper, and add a large cupful of water. Put in a deep earthen dish. Make a paste with four potatoes, two table-spoonfuls of butter, a large cupful of boiling milk, and a pint of flour. Pare, boil, and mash the potatoes; then add butter, salt, and milk. When all is very light, beat in the flour, gradually. Sprinkle the board with flour, and roll the paste a little larger than the dish. Make a hole in the centre, to let out the air. Cover the dish with the paste, being careful to have the edge come inside the dish. Bake gently one hour.

Escaloped Meat.

Chop the meat rather coarse. Season with salt and pepper. For one pint of meat use half a cupful of gravy and a heaping cupful of bread crumbs. Put a layer of the meat in an escalop dish, then gravy, then a thin layer of crumbs; and continue this until the dish is full. The last layer should be a thick one of crumbs. Cook in a hot oven from fifteen to twenty minutes. All kinds of cold meat can be escaloped, but beef is so dry that it is not so good as mutton, veal, etc.

Curry of Cold Meat.

Three table-spoonfuls of butter, three teaspoonfuls of flour, one onion, one teaspoonful of curry powder, salt, pepper, one generous pint of stock or water, about two pounds of any kind of cold meat, cut in thin slices. Put the butter in the frying-pan, and, when hot, add the onion. When the onion turns yellow, add the flour and curry powder. Stir two minutes, add the stock or water, simmer five minutes, and strain on the meat. Simmer all together for ten minutes. Serve with a border of rice or mashed potatoes.

Barley Stew.

About a quarter of a pound of cold roasted or broiled meat, two onions, four potatoes, a quarter of a cupful of barley, one table-spoonful of flour, one quart of water, and salt and pepper to taste. Cut the meat into dice; wash the barley; cut the onions *very fine*. Put all in a stewpan, and dredge with the flour, half a table-spoonful of salt, and one eighth of a teaspoonful of pepper. Add the water, and simmer two hours. Pare and slice the potatoes. Add them to the stew, and simmer one hour longer. Taste to see if there is enough salt and pepper, and if there is not, add more.

Dumplings.

One pint of flour, measured before sifting; half a teaspoonful of soda, a teaspoonful of cream of tartar, one of sugar, half a teaspoonful of salt. Mix all thoroughly and run through the sieve. Wet with a small cupful of milk. Sprinkle a little flour on the board. Turn the dough (which should have been stirred into a smooth ball with a spoon) on it, roll to the thickness of half an inch, cut into small cakes, and cook ten minutes.

By remembering that the soup should be boiling rapidly when the dumplings are put in; that they should not sink too deep in it; that they should boil *just ten minutes*; that the cover should fit tightly, so that the steam shall not escape; and that the pot boils all the time, so that the steam is kept up; and by following the other directions, success is insured.

BREAD.

WHEN you put the bread on the board, pat it lightly. Do not *press down*, but let all motions be as elastic as possible. Knead with the *palm* until the dough is a flat cake, and then fold. Keep doing this until the dough is light and smooth, and will not stick to the board or hands. Use as little flour as possible in kneading. Do not stop until you have fully finished, for bread that has "rested" is not good. Milk can be used instead of water in mixing. It should always be first scalded, and then allowed to cool to blood heat. One table-spoonful of lard or butter makes the bread tenderer when water is used.

In cold weather some kitchens grow cold very quickly after the fire is out. In this case the bread should be made earlier in the evening, and set in a warmer place (about eighty or ninety degrees); because, if it begins to rise within the first two hours, it will continue to rise, unless the temperature falls to the freezing point. The reason for letting the rolls rise longer than the loaves is, that the former, being smaller, are penetrated by heat much more quickly than the loaves are, and, of course, fermentation is stopped sooner; therefore, the rolls do not rise as much in the oven as the loaves.

Rolls should be made into smooth little balls, and should be placed in even rows in a shallow pan. Breakfast rolls are first made into little balls, and then rolled between the hands until three inches long. They are placed close together in even rows in the pan. Dinner and French rolls, after being made into little balls, are put on a well-floured board, and a little well-floured rolling-pin, two and a half inches in diameter, is pressed nearly through their centre. The rolls are to be so placed in pans as not to touch each other. Being so small, and baking so quickly, they have a sweet taste of the wheat.

The best-sized pan for loaves is made of block tin, is eight and a half inches long, four and a half wide, and three deep. Those for wheat bread should be greased very slightly with either butter or lard. For rye, Indian, or Graham, they must be greased thoroughly, as the dough clings more to the tins. There are many kinds of bread that can be made readily and safely after once learning to make good common bread. It is difficult to give exact rules for flour, as it varies, some kinds requiring much more water than others. The "new process" flour has so much more starch, and packs so much more closely than the "old process," that one eighth less is required, or one eighth more of liquid; but if the flour is weighed, the same amount of water is taken for a pound of flour made by either process. The best flour is always the cheapest for bread. As there is no one article of food of so great importance for the health and happiness of the family as bread, make it as nearly perfect as possible.

Yeast.

Put two quarts of water and two table-spoonfuls of hops on to boil. Pare and grate six large potatoes. When the hops and water *boil*, strain the water on the grated potatoes, and stir well. Place on the stove and boil up once. Add half a cupful of sugar and one fourth of a cupful of salt. Let the mixture get blood warm; then add one cupful of yeast, or one cake of compressed yeast, and let it rise in a warm place five or six hours. When well risen, turn into a stone jug. Cork this tightly, and set in a cool place.

As poor yeast is the chief cause of poor bread, pains should be taken to make yeast properly and to keep it well. It must never be allowed to stand in a warm room after it has risen, and the jug in which it is kept should be carefully washed and *scalded* each time the yeast is renewed. As much care must be taken with the stopper as with the jug.

When it is convenient to get fresh cakes of Fleischmann's compressed yeast, it will be much better and cheaper to use them than to make your own. This yeast is wholly free of any injurious substance, and with it good bread can always be made, provided the flour is good and the rules are followed.

Yeast Bread, No. 1.

With these materials two loaves can be made: Two quarts of flour, half a cupful of yeast, nearly a pint and a half of water, half a table-spoonful each of lard, sugar, and salt. Sift the flour into a bread-pan, and, after taking out a cupful for use in kneading, add the salt, sugar, yeast, and the water, which must be about blood warm (or, say one hun-

dred degrees if in cold weather, and about eighty in the hot season). Beat well with a strong spoon. When well mixed, sprinkle a little flour on the board, turn out the dough on this, and knead from twenty to thirty minutes. Put back in the pan. Hold the lard in the hand long enough to have it very soft. Rub it over the dough. Cover closely, that neither dust nor air can get in, and set in a warm place. It will rise in eight or nine hours. In the morning shape into loaves or rolls. If into loaves, let these rise an hour where the temperature is between ninety and one hundred degrees; if into rolls, let these rise an hour and a half. Bake in an oven that will brown a teaspoonful of flour in five minutes. (The flour used for this test should be put on a bit of crockery, as it will have a more even heat.) The loaves will need from forty-five to sixty minutes to bake, but the rolls will be done in half an hour if placed close together in the pan; and if French rolls are made, they will bake in fifteen minutes. As soon as baked, the bread should be taken out of the pans and placed on a table where it can rest against something until cool. It should then be put in a stone pot or tin box, which has been thoroughly washed, scalded, and dried, and be set away in a cool, dry place.

Yeast Bread, No. 2.

One cupful of Indian meal, two quarts of flour, one pint and a half of boiling water, one table-spoonful of sugar, one teaspoonful of salt, half a cake of compressed yeast. Pour the boiling water on the Indian meal. Stir well, and set away to cool. When blood warm, add the yeast, salt, and sugar to it. Stir this mixture into the flour, and proceed as for yeast bread, No. 1.

Bread made with Dried Yeast.

Two quarts of flour, one yeast cake, one generous pint of water, blood warm; one table-spoonful of sugar, one of butter, one teaspoonful of salt. Dissolve the yeast in the water, and stir gradually into one pint of the flour. Set in a warm place for two hours. It will then be risen to a sponge. Stir it into the remainder of the flour. Knead well, and put in a warm place to rise. It will rise in about five hours if the heat is about seventy-five or eighty degrees. Or, it will rise during the night in a heat of sixty degrees. In the morning treat like yeast bread, No. 1.

Sticks.

Four cupfuls of flour, one table-spoonful of sugar, one fourth of a cupful of butter, one cupful of boiled milk, the white of an egg, one fourth of a cake of compressed yeast, one scant teaspoonful of salt. Dissolve the butter in the milk, which have blood warm. Beat the white of the egg to a stiff froth. Dissolve the yeast in three table-spoonfuls of cold water. Add all the other ingredients to the flour, and knead well. Let the dough rise over night, and in the morning make into balls about the size of a large English walnut. Roll each of these balls into a stick about a foot long. Use the moulding-board. Place the sticks about two inches apart in long pans. Let them rise half an hour in a cool place, and bake twenty-five minutes in a very moderate oven. Sticks should be quite dry and crisp. They cannot be if baked rapidly.

Graham Bread.

With this material two loaves or two dozen muffins can be made: One pint of water or milk, one of flour, one *large* pint of Graham, half a cupful of yeast, half a cupful of sugar, one teaspoonful of salt. Have the milk or water blood warm, and add the yeast. Sift the flour into a deep dish. Add the milk and yeast, gradually, and beat until wholly smooth. Set in a rather cool place (about sixty degrees) to rise over night. In the morning add the salt and sugar and then the Graham, a little at a time, beating vigorously all the while. When thoroughly beaten, turn into pans, and let it rise an hour in a temperature of from ninety to one hundred degrees. Bake an hour.

Togus Bread.

Three cupfuls of sweet milk and one of sour, three cupfuls of Indian meal and one of flour, half a cupful of molasses, one teaspoonful of saleratus, one of salt. Steam three hours.

Brown Bread.

One cupful of rye meal, one of Indian meal, one of molasses, two of flour, one pint and a half of sour milk, a teaspoonful of soda, an egg, one teaspoonful of salt. Mix the dry ingredients together. Dissolve the soda in two table-spoonfuls of boiling water. Add it and the milk to the molasses. Stir well, and pour on the other mixed ingredients. Beat the egg and add it. Mix thoroughly, and pour into a well-buttered tin pan that holds two quarts. Steam four hours, and then put in the oven for half an hour.

DRINKS.

Cocoa.

COCOA is rich in nutritive elements. Like milk, it has all the substances necessary for the growth and sustenance of the body. It is the fruit of a small tree that grows in Mexico, Central America, the West Indies, and other islands. The fruit is in shape like a large, thick cucumber, and contains from six to thirty beans. There are a number of forms in which it is sold in the market, the most convenient and nutritious being chocolate. Next comes cocoa, then cocoa nibs, and lastly cocoa shells. The beans of the cocoa are roasted in the same manner as coffee. The husks or shells are taken off, and the beans then ground between hot rollers. Sometimes the husks are not removed, but ground with the bean. The ground bean is called cocoa; and mixed with sugar, after being ground very fine, is termed chocolate. Vanilla is often added as a flavor. Sometimes the cocoa is mixed with starch. When the bean is broken in small pieces, these are called nibs.

To make Cocoa.

Put a gill of the broken cocoa in a pot with two quarts of water, and boil gently three hours. There should be a quart of liquid in the pot when done. If the boiling has been so rapid that there is not this quantity, add more water, and let it boil once again. Many people prefer half broken cocoa and half shells. If the stomach is delicate, this is better than all cocoa. Sugar and milk are used, as with coffee.

Shells.

Use twice the quantity of shells that you would of broken cocoa, and boil twice as long.

Chocolate.

Scrape fine an ounce (one of the small squares) of Baker's or any other plain chocolate. Add two table-spoonfuls of sugar, and put in a small saucepan with a table-spoonful of hot water. Stir over a hot fire for a minute or two, until it is perfectly smooth and glossy, and then stir it all into a quart of boiling milk, or half milk and half water. Mix thoroughly, and serve at once. If the chocolate is wanted richer, take twice as much chocolate, sugar, and water. Made in this way, chocolate is perfectly smooth, and free of oily particles. If it is allowed to boil after the chocolate is added to the milk, it becomes oily and loses its fine flavor.

Coffee.

There are a variety of coffees; but, unlike the teas, they do not owe their difference of flavor or color to the curing, but to the soil and climate in which they grow. Coffee grows on small trees. The fruit is something like the cherry, but there are two seeds in it. The beans are separated by being bruised with a heavy roller, and are then washed and dried. The longer the raw berry is kept, the riper and better flavored it becomes. In countries where coffee is grown, the leaves are used as much as the berry. Like tea, coffee must be roasted, that the fine flavor shall be developed. There are large establishments for roasting and grinding coffee. The work is done by machinery; and nearly always the grains are evenly roasted, and just enough to give the right flavor. If the coffee, after roasting, is put in close tin cans, it will retain its best qualities for a long time. It can be ground when needed for use. Many persons think that heating the dry coffee just before making improves the flavor. There are many modes of making coffee, each having its advantages and disadvantages. Some people think that by first wetting the coffee with cold water, and letting it come to a boil, and by then adding the boiling water, more of the strength of the coffee is extracted. When there is not cream for coffee the milk should be boiled, as it makes the coffee richer. As soon as the milk boils up it should be taken off of the stove, since it grows strong and oily by much boiling. To many people it is injurious to drink coffee; but physicians say that, taken without milk, it is harmless. Some element of the coffee combines with the milk to form a leathery coating on the stomach, which impairs digestion. A great many substances are mixed with coffee, when sold, to cheapen it, — chiccory, beans, peas, rye, and wheat being the commonest. To obtain it pure, the safest way is to buy it unground, unless you purchase of a strictly honest dealer. Coffee drinkers, as a rule, eat less than other people, though coffee, and also tea, have little direct food value; but they retard the waste of the tissues, and so take the place of food. The sugar and milk used with them give some nutriment.

Boiled Coffee.

The old method of boiling coffee is still practised by at least one half the housekeepers in this country. The coffee is sometimes boiled with an egg, which makes it perfectly clear, and also enriches it. When an egg is not used, a small piece of salt-fish skin is boiled with the coffee to clear it.

Directions for making: A small cupful of roasted and ground coffee, one third Mocha and two thirds Java; a small egg, shell and all, broken into the pot with the dry coffee. Stir well with a spoon, and then pour on three pints of boiling water. Let it boil from five to ten minutes, counting from the time it begins to boil. As soon as it has boiled enough, pour in a cupful of cold water, and turn a little of the coffee into a cup, to see that the nozzle of the pot is not filled with grounds. Turn this back, and let the coffee stand a few moments to settle, taking care that it does not boil again. The advantages of boiled coffee are that when the egg is used the yolk gives a very rich flavor, and when the milk or cream is added the coffee has a rich, yellow look, which is pleasing. It has also a peculiar flavor, which many people prefer to the flavor gained by any other process. The disadvantages are that the egg coats the dry coffee, and when the hot water is added the coating becomes hard, and a great deal of the best of the coffee remains in the grounds after boiling. Also, in boiling, much of the fine flavor is lost in the steam that escapes from the pot.

Filtered Coffee.

Another — and really the most economical and the easiest — way of making coffee is by filtering. The French coffee biggin is valuable for this. It consists of two cylindrical tin vessels, one fitting into another, and the bottom of the upper being a fine strainer. Another coarser strainer, with a rod running from the centre, is placed upon this. Then the coffee, which must be finely ground, is put in, and another strainer is placed at the top of the rod. The boiling water is poured on, and the pot set where it will keep hot, but not boil, until the water has gone through. This will make a clear, strong coffee, with a rich, smooth flavor. The advantage of the two extra strainers is that the one coming next to the fine strainer prevents the grounds from filling up the fine holes, and so the coffee is clear, and made more easily. The upper strainer causes the boiling water to fall on the coffee like rain. In this way it is more evenly distributed, and the fine coffee is not carried through the fine strainer, as it would be if the water were poured directly on the dry coffee. When milk or cream is added to filtered coffee it does not turn a rich yellow, as in the case of that boiled with an egg. A few spoonfuls of this coffee, without sugar or milk, taken after dinner, is said to help digestion.

Vienna Coffee.

A quarter of a cupful of boiled milk. Add three table-spoonfuls of whipped cream, and fill up with filtered coffee.

Café au Lait.

This is simply one pint of filtered coffee added to one pint of milk that has come just to the boiling point.

Steamed Coffee.

Another mode of preparing coffee is to steam it. The coffee is put in a pot, and boiling water poured on it. This pot, which is made to fit into a tea-kettle, is placed in the kettle, and the coffee is cooked from ten to twenty minutes, the water in the kettle boiling all the time. This will make a clear and delicious drink.

Tea.

There are three varieties of the tea plant; both black and green tea can be prepared from them all. Green tea is made from leaves which are dried quickly, and black from leaves which have first been allowed to stand twelve hours or more before roasting. The leaves wilt and grow moist in that time, and that is what gives the dark and peculiar appearance to this tea. In making tea the pot should be earthen, rinsed with boiling water, and left to stand a few moments on the stove to dry. Put in the tea leaves, and let the pot stand a few minutes longer. Pour on boiling water, leaving the pot standing where it will be at the boiling point, yet will not boil, for from three to five minutes. For moderate strength use one teaspoonful of tea to half a pint of water. If the water is soft it should be used as soon as it boils, for boiling causes all the gases which flavor the water to escape; but if the water is hard it is best to boil from twenty to thirty minutes. The gases escape from hard water also, but boiling causes the mineral matter which hardens the water to settle on the bottom of the kettle, and the water becomes softer.

Lemonade.

Good lemonade can be made with half a pint of lemon juice (extracted with a squeezer, and strained), three pints of water, and a generous pint of sugar. Have the drink cold. Hot lemonade is highly recommended for a cold. A glass can be made with the juice of a lemon, one large table-spoonful of sugar, and a cupful of boiling water. Drink it hot.

HOW—

To Blanch Almonds.

Shell the nuts, and pour boiling water over them. Let them stand in the water a minute, and then throw them into cold water. Rub between the hands.

To Corn Beef.

For fifty pounds of beef make a pickle with two gallons of water, four pounds of salt, one and a half pounds of brown sugar, one and a half ounces of saltpetre, half an ounce of saleratus. Put these ingredients on to boil, and when they boil, skim, and put away to cool. When cold, put the beef in it. Put weights on the meat, to keep it under the brine.

To Scrape Chocolate.

If only one square of chocolate is needed, draw a line across the two squares at the end, dividing them in halves. With a sharp knife shave off the chocolate until you come to the line. By this method there is no waste of time or material. If you want two or more squares, all that is necessary is, of course, to shave off until you come to the dividing line already there. The pound packages of Baker's chocolate consist of two cakes, each of which has eight squares; so one of these squares is an ounce.

To Use the Salamander.

The salamander is a circular iron plate, to which is attached a long handle. It is made red-hot in the fire, and held over the article to be browned, being careful not to have it touch. If you have not a salamander, the fire shovel can be heated and used in the same way; but the shovel is not improved by the operation.

To Clean English Currants.

Pick all the stones, bits of dirt, and long stems from the currants. Add one pint of flour to two quarts of currants, and rub well between the hands. This starts the stems and dirt from the fruit. Put about a pint of currants in the flour sieve and rub them until all the flour has passed through; then put them in the colander and shake until the stems have passed through. When all the fruit has been treated in this manner, put it in a large pan of cold water. Wash thoroughly, and drain in the colander. Repeat this operation three times. When the fruit is well drained, spread it on boards or flat dishes and dry in a warm place. Put away in jars.

To Remove Jellies and Creams from Moulds.

Have in a pan water enough (a little more than blood warm) to come to the top of the mould. If the mould is tin, set it in this for about half a minute; if earthen, keep it in long enough to have the heat pass through the mould. Wipe the mould, place over it the dish into which the jelly is to be turned, and turn both dish and mould simultaneously. Let the mould rest a moment before lifting it gently from the jelly.

To Whip Cream.

Very rich or *very* poor cream will not whip well. When too rich it turns to butter, and when too poor the froth becomes liquid almost as soon as it has been skimmed. Thick cream, that will hardly pour, should have an equal quantity of milk added to it before whipping. Such cream as one gets from the milkman will rarely be found *too* rich for whipping. It is more likely to be the other way; and one is often disappointed in finding it too poor to froth. The cream should be ice cold.

Have a large bowl or tin pail, rather narrow at the bottom. Place this in a pan of ice water. Have a bright tin pan in another of ice water. Put the cream in the bowl, and put the whip churn in this. Hold the churn with the left hand, tipping it slightly, that the cream may flow out at the bottom. With the right hand draw the dasher lightly about half way up the cylinder; then press down hard. It must not be forgotten that the *up* stroke is *light*, and the *down* stroke is *hard*. When the bowl is full, skim the froth into a tin pan. Continue this until nearly all the cream has been whipped. Draw the froth in the pan to one side, and turn the liquid cream at the bottom of the pan back into the bowl. Whip it again. A little of the cream will always become liquid again.

When the cream is for whips, or for a garnish for frozen pudding or Bavarian creams, sweeten it, and flavor with anything you please, before whipping. If the cream is very rich a Dover beater will whip it; but there is nothing that will do it so quickly and so well as the whip churn, consisting of a tin cylinder, perforated on the bottom and sides, in which a dasher of tin, also perforated, can be easily moved up and down.

To Boil Sugar.

The degrees of boiling sugar are variously divided by different cooks. Some give six, and others as high as eight. The French boil sugar for nearly all their desserts. For all practical purposes a cook need understand only three stages. Put one cupful of granulated or loaf sugar and half a cupful of water on to boil. When the mixture has boiled fifteen minutes, dip the forefinger and thumb in cold water and take up a little of the syrup between them. If, upon drawing them apart, the syrup forms a thread, it is at the second degree. This is the best stage for frozen fruits, sherbets, and preserves.

If, a little later, when some syrup is taken up with a spoon and blown hard, it flies off in tiny bubbles, it is at the fourth degree, called the *soufflé.* It takes about twenty minutes' boiling for this. The syrup is then used for *biscuit glacé* and various kinds of creams. At this stage it also gives sherbets and fruits a much richer flavor than when used at the second degree.

If, when a little syrup is taken up on the point of a stick or skewer and dipped in cold water, it breaks off brittle, the sixth degree has been reached. This is the stage where it is used for icing fruit and cake, the dish being called *fruit glacé* or *gâteau glacé.* The syrup must *never* be stirred, as this will cause it to grain. Great care must be taken that it does not boil after coming to the sixth degree, as it burns quickly after that point is reached.

To make and use a Pastry Bag.

Fold a piece of strong cotton cloth (perhaps a foot square) from two opposite corners, so as to give it a triangular shape. On one side sew together the two edges, thus making a bag shaped like a "dunce's cap." Cut the cloth at the apex just enough to permit a short tin tube, somewhat like a tailor's thimble, to be pushed through. The tube for *éclairs* measures about three fourths of an inch at the smallest opening; that for lady-fingers is three eighths of an inch, and that for meringues and kisses half an inch. The tubes for decorating with frosting are very small.

Fill the bag with the mixture to be forced through, and gather the cloth together at the top with the left hand. Hold the point of the tube close to the pan on which the mixture is to be spread. Press the mixture out with the right hand. If the cakes are to be large, use a good deal of

pressure; but if to be small, very little will do. At first, it will be hard to get the shapes, but with a little practice it will seem comparatively easy.

To make Paper Cases.

This is not difficult, if one will carefully study for a moment the diagram below and the directions following.

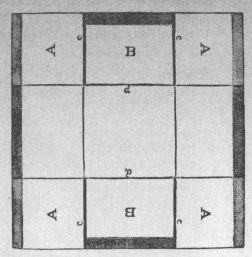

Cut the paper on the dark lines, — there are *eight*.

Crease on every dotted line.

At each end turn the parts lettered A over that lettered B, so that the lines *c* rest on the line *d*, and one A overlaps the other.

Fold the parts B up against the backs of the parts A.

Fold inward those parts of the edges which are lightly shaded, and fold outward those which are heavily shaded.

Stick the parts of the box together with the white of an egg mixed with a little flour.

Remember that it is a box that is to be made, and after the first two steps it may be easy to guess how to complete the work. By tracing a copy of the diagram, one obtains a good model one quarter of the size the case should be; that is, the square should be five inches on a side instead of two and one half. After experimenting with this, the shape may be varied to suit the taste. Stiff white paper should be used. Cases can be bought of restaurateurs. They are used for *biscuit glacé, biscuit soufflé,* and other dainties.

To Lard.

Larding is a simple operation. The pork should be firm and young (salt, of course). Cut thin, even slices parallel with the rind, and cut these in long, narrow strips that will fit into the needle. For beef, veal, turkey, or chicken the strips should be about as large round as a lead pencil, and about three and a half inches long; and for birds, chops, and sweetbreads they should be about as large round as a match. Three slices are all that can be cut from one piece of pork, because when you get more than an inch away from the rind, the pork is so tender that it will break when in the needle.

Put the strips in a bowl of broken ice, to harden. Have the meat, if beef or veal, free of skin and gristle. Put a strip (also called a lardoon) into the needle as far as it will go. With a skewer or knife draw a line on both sides of the meat and along the upper part. Thrust the needle into the meat at one of the side lines; and when it is about half-way through to the top of the piece, press the steel slightly with the thumb and forefinger, to hold the lardoon in place until it has entered the meat. Now push the needle through to the top, and gently draw it out, leaving about three quarters of an inch of the strip exposed at both the side and upper part of the meat. That part of the pork which is hidden should be half an inch under the surface. The needle's course is as if it started under the eaves of a gable roof and came out at the ridge-pole. Continue until all the rows are filled with lardoons. Two rows are enough for a fillet of beef. If the strips are too large for the needle they will be pressed out as soon as the lower part of the needle enters the meat.

To Stew.

The meat and vegetables for stews should, when it is possible, be browned in a little fat, and hot water should then be added. As soon as the stew comes to the boiling point, skim it, and set back where it will just simmer, not boil, the given time. The pieces of meat in a stew should come to the table whole and tender and juicy, and they will be in this condition only with *slow* cooking.

To Braise.

Braising is one of the best modes of preparing meat. There are pans expressly for braising; but any deep tin, sheet-iron, or granite-ware pan, with a cover, will answer quite well. The meat to be cooked must always be browned in some kind of fat, the vegetables fried in the same fat, and enough stock (if possible) or water be added to half cover the meat. The pan should then be covered and placed in the oven. The meat must cook *slowly* and thoroughly, and be basted frequently. No matter how tough, if properly braised it will become tender and juicy. If, however, the cooking is hurried, the dish will be spoiled.

To Fry.

There are two modes of frying. One is to have just enough fat to prevent the article from burning or sticking; and the other is to have enough not only to cover the food, but to float it. The latter is by far the better way, as all the surface of the article is instantly hardened, and therefore will not absorb fat. It is also the cheaper way, because the fat can be used so many times. If the drippings saved from meats, soups, and gravies should not be enough for frying purposes, buy pure lard to use with it. Many recommend buying beef suet for this same purpose; but food fried in suet is more liable to absorb fat than that fried in lard. The reason of this is that lard can be heated to a higher temperature without burning than can beef or any of the other fats. Butter is also often recommended for frying. If used, it should be free of salt. But aside from being so expensive, it is not so nice for frying purposes as fats, for it burns at a much lower temperature than either beef fat or lard. The Scotch kettle is the *best* utensil for frying. It rests on a rim, which lifts the bottom from the stove, and the inside surface is polished very smooth; therefore, the fat is less liable to burn than if the surface were rough and the bottom rested on the hot stove. The fat should heat gradually; and when the food is plunged into it a slight smoke should rise from the *centre*. It will smoke at the sides some time before it has become hot enough for frying. After the food has been put in, let the kettle stand on the hottest part of the stove until it regains its former temperature, and then set it back where it is not quite so hot. In frying fish-balls, doughnuts, etc., put only a few at a time in the boiling fat; then wait a few moments for the fat to regain its former temperature, and put in a few more. Fish-balls are often spoiled by the putting of a great many in the kettle at once. The temperature of the fat is instantly reduced, and the balls absorb the fat. When an article of food is fried, drain the fat from it, and lay it on a sheet of brown paper in a warm pan. The paper will absorb any fat that may remain on the food. As soon as you are through frying, take the fat from the fire, and, when cooled a little, strain it. If the directions given are followed, there will be no difficulty in having food fried without its being saturated with grease.

To Serve.

The dishes on which meats, fish, jellies, and creams are placed should be large enough to leave a margin of an inch or so between the food and the lower edge of the border of the dish.

It is well to pour the sauce for cold puddings around the pudding, especially if there will be a contrast in color.

It is a great improvement to have the sauce poured around the article instead of over it, and to have the border of the dish garnished with bits of parsley, celery tops, or carrot leaves.

When sauce is poured around meat or fish the dish must be quite hot, or the sauce will cool quickly.

Small rolls or sticks of bread are served with soup. Potatoes and bread are usually served with fish, but many people prefer to serve only bread. Butter is not served at the more elegant dinners. Two vegetables will be sufficient in any course. Cold dishes should be very cold, and hot dishes *hot*.

It is a good idea to have a dish of sliced lemons for any kind of fish, and especially for those broiled or fried.

Melons, cantelopes, cucumbers, radishes, and tomatoes, when served in slices, should all be chilled in the ice chest.

Be particular not to overdo the work of decorating. Even a simple garnish adds much to the appearance of a dish, but too much decoration only injures it. Garnishes should be so arranged as not to interfere with serving.

Potato-balls and thin fried potatoes make a nice garnish for all kinds of fried and broiled meats and fish.

Cold boiled beets, carrots, and turnips, and the whites of hard-boiled eggs, stamped out with a fancy vegetable cutter, make a pretty garnish for cold or hot meats.

Thin slices of toast, cut into triangles, make a good garnish for many dishes.

Whipped cream is a delicate garnish for all Bavarian creams, blanc-manges, frozen puddings, and ice creams.

Arrange around jellies or creams a border of any kind of delicate green, like smilax or parsley, or of rose leaves, and dot it with bright colors,—pinks, geraniums, verbenas, or roses. Remember that the green should be dark, and the flowers small and bright. A bunch of artificial rose leaves, for decorating dishes of fruit at evening parties, lasts for years. Natural leaves are preferable when they can be obtained.

Wild roses, buttercups, and nasturtiums, if not used too freely, are suitable for garnishing a salad.

HOUSEHOLD NECESSITIES.

SOCIAL CUSTOMS.

New edition, REDUCED IN PRICE. Complete Manual of American etiquette. By FLORENCE HOWE HALL, daughter of Mrs. Julia Ward Howe. Handsomely printed and neatly bound in extra cloth, gilt top; uncut Small 8vo, ... $1.75

DO YOU ALWAYS KNOW JUST WHAT TO DO? Do you know how to encourage Mrs. D. Lightful, accept and return her courtesies, as they deserve; and politely but firmly avoid and defeat Mrs. Bore in her inroads on your privacy and more agreeable engagements? If you do not, let us recommend for EVERY SOCIAL QUESTION the above entertaining and instructive book, or its new baby relative, "THE CORRECT THING," mentioned below, for with these two books, one can make no mistake in life, as every possible question may be answered from their combined wisdom. They are *comprehensive, practical, reliable and authoritative.*

THE CORRECT THING.

By FLORENCE HOWE HALL, author of "Social Customs." 18mo. Very neatly bound in extra cloth, gilt top, ... $0.75

SAME. Bound in full flexible morocco, gilt edges (in a box), . . , ... 1.25

This new manual is neatly printed in a size not too large to be slipped into the pocket, and is arranged so that one page reminds the reader that "IT IS THE CORRECT THING" to do this, while *per contra* the opposite page tells him that "IT IS NOT THE CORRECT THING" to do that. Its consiseness recommends it to many who would not take the time to master any more comprehensive manual.

"It is indeed, a treasure of good counsel, and like most advice, it has the merit of not being expensive." —*Montreal Gazette.*

ESTES & LAURIAT, Publishers, Boston, Mass.

Celebrated War Stories.

THE BOYS OF '61;

OR, FOUR YEARS OF FIGHTING. A record of personal observation with the Army and Navy from the battle of Bull Run to the fall of Richmond. By CHARLES CARLETON COFFIN, author of "The Boys of '76," "Our New Way 'Round the World," "The Story of Liberty," "Winning His Way," "Old Times in the Colonies," etc. With numerous illustrations.

1 vol., 8vo, chromo-lithographed board covers and linings, ... $1.75

1 vol., 8vo, cloth, gilt, ... 2.50

THE SAILOR BOYS OF '61.

By Prof. J. RUSSELL SOLEY, author of the "Boys of 1812," etc. This volume contains an accurate and vivid account of the naval engagements of the great Civil War, and the deeds of its heroes. Elaborately and beautifully illustrated from original drawings.

1 vol., 8vo, chromo-lithographed board covers, ... $1.75

1 vol., 8vo, cloth, gilt, ... 2.50

THE BOYS OF 1812.

By Prof. J. RUSSELL SOLEY, author of "Blockaders and Cruisers," "The Sailor Boys of '61," etc., etc. This "most successful war book for the young, issued last year," is now made boards with an illustrated cover designed by Barnes.

1 vol., 8vo, chromo-lithographed board covers, ... $1.75

1 vol., 8vo, cloth, gilt, ... 2.50

"Prof SOLEY'S books should be read by every American boy, who cares for the honor of his country." — *Boston Beacon.*

"He must be a dull boy who can read such records of heroism without a quickening of the pulses." — *San Francisco Chronicle.*

"We are in no danger of cultivating too much patriotism, and such a book as this is an excellent educator along an excellent line of thought." — *Chicago Daily Inter-Ocean.*

MY DAYS AND NIGHTS ON THE BATTLEFIELD.

By CHARLES CARLETON COFFIN. With eighteen full-page plates. Small quarto. Bound in illuminated board covers, ... $1.25

FOLLOWING THE FLAG.

By CHARLES CARLETON COFFIN. With eighteen full-page plates. Small quarto. Bound in illuminated board covers, ... $1.25

WINNING HIS WAY.

By CHARLES CARLETON COFFIN. With twenty-one full-page plates. Small quarto. Bound in illuminated board covers, ... $1.25

THE CARLETON SERIES OF JUVENIIES.

CONSISTING OF

WINNING HIS WAY.   FOLLOWING THE FLAG.

MY DAYS AND NIGHTS ON THE BATTLEFIELD.

3 vols., 16mo, cloth, in a box, ... $3.75

Any volume sold separately, ... 1.25

ESTES & LAURIAT, Publishers, Boston, Mass.